THE RHETORIC OF

ECONOMICS

RHETORIC OF THE HUMAN SCIENCES

The Rhetoric of Economics
Donald N. McCloskey

Lying Down Together: Law, Metaphor, and Theology
Milner S. Ball

Heracles' Bow: Essays on the Rhetoric
and Poetics of Law
James Boyd White

The Rhetoric of Economics

BY DONALD N. McCLOSKEY

THE UNIVERSITY OF WISCONSIN PRESS

Published in 1985 in the United States of America by
The University of Wisconsin Press
114 North Murray Street
Madison, Wisconsin 53715

Published in Great Britain by
Wheatsheaf Books Ltd
A Member of the Harvester Press Publishing Group
16 Ship Street, Brighton, Sussex

First printing

Printed in the United States of America

Library of Congress Cataloging in Publication Data
McCloskey, Donald N.
  The rhetoric of economics.   HB
  (Rhetoric of the human sciences)   71
  Bibliography: pp. 189–202.   M38
  Includes index.   1985
  1. Economics. 2. Rhetoric. I. Title.
II. Series.
HB71.M38 1985   330   85-40373
ISBN 0-299-10380-3

Ad universitatem Iowae,
montuosam, humanam, urbanam,
quamvis in fustibus positam.

CONTENTS

Acknowledgments xi
Exordium xvii

1   THE POVERTY OF ECONOMIC MODERNISM 3

The Official Methodology of Economics Is
  Modernist 5
Modernism Is a Poor Method 11
  It Is Obsolete in Philosophy 11
  Falsification Is Not Cogent 13
  Prediction Is Not Possible in Economics 15
  Modernism Itself Is Impossible, and Not
    Adhered To 16

2   FROM METHODOLOGY TO RHETORIC 20

Any Rule-Bound Methodology Is Objectionable 20
Methodology Is Bourgeois 24
Good Science Is Good Conversation 27
Rhetoric Is a Better Way to Understand Science 28
The Jokes of Economists Tell 30
Other Sciences Have Rhetorics 32

3   ANTI-ANTI-RHETORIC 36

The Alternative to Modernism Is Not
  Irrationalism 36
The Political Arguments for Methodology Are
  Weak 39
We Wish to Make Plausible Statements, Whether
  "Scientific" or Not 42
The Philosophical Objections to Rhetoric Are Not
  Persuasive 46
Anti-Modernism Is Nice 50
Rhetoric Is Good for You 51

Contents

4   THE LITERARY CHARACTER OF ECONOMIC SCIENCE 54

Science Uses Literary Methods 54
Proofs of the Law of Demand Are Mostly Literary 57
Linguistics Is an Appropriate Model for Economic
    Science 62
Literary Thinking May Improve Applied Economics
    65

5   FIGURES OF ECONOMIC SPEECH 69

Even a Modernist Uses, and Must Use, Literary
    Devices: The Case of Paul Samuelson 69
Most of the Devices Are Only Dimly Recognized 72
Models Are Nonornamental Metaphors: The Case of
    Gary Becker 74
Both Mathematical and Nonmathematical Reasoning
    in Economics Rely on Metaphor 79
The Master Tropes Rule Economics: The Case of
    Robert Solow 83

6   THE RHETORIC OF SCIENTISM: HOW JOHN MUTH
           PERSUADES 87

Muth's Article Was Ill-Written But Important 87
Muth's Main Points Can Be Expressed in English 91
Muth's Article Engages in the Usual Appeals to
    Scientific Method 96
Muth's Appeal Is in Fact to the Community of
    Scholars 99
The Explicit Arguments Are Rhetorically Complex
    102
Muth's Rhetoric Is Indistinguishable from That in
    Other Fields 105

Contents

7   THE PROBLEM OF AUDIENCE IN HISTORICAL ECONOMICS:
ROBERT FOGEL AS RHETOR 113

The Text Was Important 113
Fogel's Book Poses a Rhetorical Puzzle 116
Fogel's Book Is Self-Consciously Rhetorical 118
The Rhetorical Density Explains Its Successes and Its
     Failures 120
Fogel's Book Uses Intensively the Common Topics
     126
The Book Also Uses the Special Topics of Economics
     130
The Text Invented an Audience 133

8   THE UNEXAMINED RHETORIC OF ECONOMIC
QUANTIFICATION 138

Rhetorical Standards Are Necessary to Measure the
     Integration of Markets 141
In Like Fashion, Rhetorical Standards Are Necessary
     in Linguistics to Measure the Similarity of
     Languages 147
That Is, the Speech Acts of Scholars Are Social
     Actions 150

9   THE RHETORIC OF SIGNIFICANCE TESTS 154

The Discussion of Purchasing Power Parity Is
     Rhetorically Muddled 154
The Test of Statistical Significance Is a Poor Rhetoric
     of Economic Argument 159
The Rhetorical History of Statistics Is the Source of
     the Difficulty 164
The Unexamined Rhetoric Damages the Practice of
     Economists 169

10   THE GOOD OF RHETORIC IN ECONOMICS 174

Rhetoric Can Improve Economic Prose 175
Rhetoric Can Improve Teaching 178
Rhetoric Can Improve Relations with Other
    Disciplines 179
Rhetoric Can Improve Economic Argument 181
And Improve the Temper of Economists 183

Works Cited 189
Index 203

ACKNOWLEDGMENTS

The question arises why an economist wished to learn a little about philosophy, linguistics, literary criticism, the history of science, and other pieces of the nonmathematical culture, and then felt he had to tell other economists that their culture was in part nonmathematical, too. Often the best way to see someone's point is autobiography. This is why academic seminars so often begin with "how I came to this problem," and why some scientists complain about the strictly nonautobiographical conventions of scientific prose.

Even while marching in the positivist armies that revolutionized economic history during the 1960s and 1970s I was becoming less persuaded by the official positivism of economics. The rough-and-tumble of graduate seminars in economic history, econometrics, and transportation economics at Harvard in the middle 1960s was the first of many experiences of seeing economists argue in nonpositivist ways while preaching positivism. At the University of Chicago for a dozen years from 1968 to 1980 it seemed to me that the brilliance of the talk in seminar and lunchroom by my fellow Chicago economists contrasted strangely too with the dull-normal science recommended in their methodology.

The experience of being a Chicago economist, as I have been more or less since the second year of graduate school at Harvard, was another education in rhetoric. The unreasonable dogmatism of both sides of any debate involving Chicago—I participated to varying degrees in a half dozen of the major ones from monetarism through American slavery down to rational expectations, and have wounds inflicted by outraged enemies of dogma to prove it—suggested to me that all was not well in the way economists ran their arguments.

An economic historian must in any case take seriously the arguments and the doubts of others, especially historians. I was first educated in these during the late 1960s by other students of British economic history, trained in another tradition (and in another country), and then during the late 1970s by colleagues at Chicago in the Department of History. The experience exhibited a model of scholarship alternative to the official method of economics. It was more cause to doubt the positivist ceremonial.

The germ of the book was presented as a talk to the Program in xii

Acknowledgments

Economics, Politics, Rhetoric, and Law at the University of Chicago in 1980. The prospect of a public hanging in the presence of Wayne Booth, Ira Katznelson, Edward Levi, Philip Kurland, and the like wonderfully concentrated the intellect (the hanging proceeded as planned). I had read Paul Feyerabend's *Against Method* a little earlier, picking it up by accident in a bookstore, and found it congenial. Booth's *Modern Dogma and the Rhetoric of Assent* and, on Booth's recommendation, Michael Polanyi's *Personal Knowledge* prepared me for the Chicago talk, and shortly after it I read the book of another Chicago colleague, Stephen Toulmin's *The Uses of Argument*, picked up again by chance in a bookstore. Glory be to bookstores.

In the first year at Iowa I discussed these matters with my new colleagues in economics and history, beginning, with Alan Nagel, an "Iowa Faculty Colloquium on Rhetoric," meeting every two weeks winter and summer to discuss pieces of argument and the art of argument. It was there that I received from Nagel, and from Gerald Bruns, Evan Fales, Bruce Gronbeck, Paul Hernadi, John Lyne, Michael McGee, Allan Megill, Jay Semel, and above all John Nelson, the elements of an education in literary theory, philosophy, and speech communication. The colloquium gradually expanded in ambition, though keeping its focus on what we came to call the "rhetoric of inquiry." This we viewed as a way of understanding and perhaps improving the conversations of scholarship. In 1984 the colloquium led to a conference financed by the National Endowment for the Humanities, the Iowa Humanities Board, and the University of Iowa. Out of this came a book (Nelson, Megill, and McCloskey, forthcoming).

I had spent the summer of 1982 at the Institute for Advanced Studies at Australian National University working on these matters. Amidst the intense intellectuality of the groups at ANU in economic history, economics, philosophy, and history of ideas I was especially fortunate to overlap for a month with Richard Rorty. Talking to him, and reading his book *Philosophy and the Mirror of Nature*, made many things clear. He directed me, as he is directing many, towards pragmatism: this too fit with my inclinations. The institute was the ideal place to rework the little paper from Chicago.

I have dined out on the work for years. During 1982 seminars in the antipodes heard the paper at ANU itself, at Adelaide, Melbourne, Monash, New South Wales, and Western Australia; and at Auckland and Victoria University of Wellington. Although everywhere I was startled at the warmth of the reception economists gave to a paper critical of their way of talking, the reception at the University of Tasmania was especially inspiring. In the United States one or another chapter was given to the Speech Communication Association's Third Conference on Argumentation at Alta, Utah, in 1983; to the Conference on Codes at the Humanities Center of Brooklyn College, CUNY, in 1983; to the Rhetoric of Economics conference at Middlebury College in 1984; to the Temple University/Speech Communication Association Conference on Kenneth Burke at Philadelphia in 1984; and to the American Economic Association convention at Dallas in 1984.

Seminars at the World Bank, the National Science Foundation, the Washington Area Economic History Workshop, the Columbia Economic History Seminar, and Miami University of Ohio heard pieces, as did groups at the universities of British Columbia, California at Davis, Chicago, Connecticut, Nebraska, the Pacific, Pennsylvania, Toronto, Virginia; Baruch (CUNY), Grinnell, Queens (CUNY), Union, and Williams colleges; and Ball State, Emory, Indiana, Iowa State, McMaster, North Carolina State, Princeton, Rutgers, Simon Fraser, Wesleyan, and Yale universities. I learned from this procession of free lunches more than which fork to pick up first. Each audience raised points that had escaped me. Like oratory, argument depends for its virtues on the virtues of its audience.

Fred Carstensen, A. W. Coats, Stanley Engerman, Arjo Klamer, Robert Higgs, Thomas Mayer, and Robert Solow wrote comments on the work early and often, as the Chicago expression goes. Such performances impart special force to the metaphor of scholarship as a conversation. Many other economists and economic historians have commented in writing on drafts of the chapters or on published papers, many at length and repeatedly. The commentary—favorable or unfavorable—has been inspiriting and enlightening. I am uneasily aware that the list misses some, but it includes Irma Adelman, Moses Abramovitz, J. D. Alexander, Edward Ames, Peter Bauer, M. Cristina Bicchieri, Mark Blaug, Richard Boltuck, Thomas Borcherding, William Breit, Martin Bronfenbrenner, James Buchanan, Phillip Cagan, Bruce Caldwell, Rondo Cameron, Filippo Cesarano, Gregory Clark, Robert Clower, Ronald Coase, John Cochrane, Gordon Crovitz, Stephen De Canio, Arthur Diamond, J. E. Easley, Jr., Billy Eatherly, David Felix, Alex Field, Robert Fogel, Milton Friedman, Walter Galenson, Allan Gibbard, Robert Goodin, Robert Gordon, Frank Hahn, Gary Hawke, Robert Heilbroner, Willie Hendersen, Abraham Hirsch, Albert Hirschman, A. B. Holmes, J.R.T. Hughes, Eric Jones, Charles Kindleberger, Claudia Goldin, John Latham, Edward Leamer, Harvey Leibenstein, David Landes, Timothy Lane, Richard Langlois, Nathaniel Leff, Axel Leijonhufvud, Wassily Leontief, David Levy, H. G. Lewis, Peter Lindert, Rodney Maddock, Pedro Carvalho de Mello, Neil de Marchi, Terry Marsh, John Martin, Charles

Nelson, Thomas McCaleb, Michael McPherson, Philip Mirowski, David Mitch, Richard Nathan, Richard Nelson, D. P. O'Brien, Avner Offer, Ian Parker, William Parker, Mark Perlman, Boris Pesek, Sidney Ratner, Joseph D. Reid, Jr., Robert Renshaw, Vernon Ruttan, T. W. Schultz, Amartya Sen, Frank Spooner, Paul Streeten, John Thorkelson, Thomas Ulen, Larry Westphal, Oliver Williamson, Gordon Winston, Gavin Wright, and Leland Yeager.

The implied reader of the book is an economist, but I have tried to make the argument intelligible and persuasive to noneconomists as well. On this score and others the detailed remarks by Wayne Booth and Richard Rorty on various versions, especially on the next-to-last draft, were immensely useful. Without their advice the book would have been even more offensive to the sensibilities of literary critics and philosophers.

The other noneconomists who have written to me about the book in one form or another include (here I suspect even more that I am overlooking some) Keith Baker, Charles Bazerman, Howard Becker, Robert Boynton, Bernard Cohn, Harry Collins, John Comaroff, Colin Day, Mary Douglas, Otis Dudley Duncan, Stanley Fish, James O. Freedman, Elizabeth Fricker, Clifford Geertz, Gerald Geison, Nelson Goodman, Allen Graubard, Stephen Graubard, Joseph Gusfield, Daniel Hausman, Martin Hollis, Martin Kessler, J. Morgan Kousser, William Kruskal, Laurence Lafore, John Laffey, Donald Levine, Leonard Liggio, Michael Mahoney, Donald Marshall, William McNeill, Laura McCloskey, Franklin Mendels, Denton Morrison, Peter Novick, Samuel Patterson, Amelie Oksenberg Rorty, Renato Rosaldo, Martin Rudwick, John Schuster, Herbert Simons, Donald Sutherland, Stephen Toulmin, and David Warsh. Humanists are less startled than are economists by the message that technical economics involves literary, ethical, and rhetorical issues. I thank them for their indulgence towards the messenger.

I owe financial debts to the John Simon Guggenheim Foundation, the Institute for Advanced Study, the National Endowment for the Humanities (for its program in Humanities, Science, and Technology, and especially David E. Wright), and the University of Iowa. The time away from other duties during 1983-84 brought the book substantially to its present form.

Jackie Askin of the College of Business Administration at the University of Iowa shepherded my financial sheep, keeping heart when some were eaten by positivist wolves. Leanne Swenson was very helpful as a research assistant, and Marguerite Knoedel typed the drafts with Iowan intelligence and energy.

My editor at Wisconsin, Gordon Lester-Massman, has been encouraging well beyond the call of profit. He is to be credited with initiating this series in the rhetoric of inquiry. Ginalie Swaim and Carolyn Moser exercised extraordinary care and intelligence on the manuscript, and improved it.

I thank the editors and publishers of the following journals and collections of essays for permission to publish here revised versions of material that appeared first in their pages:

"The Rhetoric of Economics," *Journal of Economic Literature* 31 (June 1983): 434–61.
"The Character of Argument in Modern Economics: How Muth Persuades," in *Argument in Transition: Proceedings of the Third Summer Conference on Argumentation* (Annandale, Va.: Speech Communication Association, 1983)
"The Literary Character of Economics," *Daedalus*, Summer 1984, pp. 97–119.
"The Problem of Audience in Historical Economics: Rhetorical Thoughts on a Text by Robert Fogel," *History and Theory* 24 (1985): 1–22.
"The Loss Function Has Been Mislaid: The Rhetoric of Significance Tests," *American Economic Review* 75 (May 1985): 201–5.
"The Dismal Science and Mr. Burke: Economics as Critical Theory," in Herbert Simons and Trevor Melia, eds., *The Legacy of Kenneth Burke* (forthcoming).

Looking again at the writings most important to my thinking has destroyed any illusion of originality. Ideas and even forms of words that I had come to imagine were my own turn out to have been pillaged from Paul Feyerabend, Wayne Booth, Michael Polanyi, Stephen Toulmin, Richard Rorty, Thomas Kuhn, and Kenneth Burke (in order of the major pillagings, from 1980 to 1984). The only comfort is another phrase from Rorty, which he in turn borrowed from Michael Oakeshott, of intellectual life as a conversation, now in parts some 3,000 years old. We should, after all, be influenced by our interlocutors, and we should take over as our own their forms of words.

EXORDIUM

If translated into English, most of the ways economists talk among themselves would sound plausible enough to poets, journalists, businesspeople, and other thoughtful though noneconomical folk. Like serious talk anywhere—among boat designers and baseball fans, say—the talk is hard to follow when one has not made a habit of listening to it for a while. The culture of the conversation makes the words arcane. But the people in the unfamiliar conversation are not Martians. Underneath it all (the economist's favorite phrase) conversational habits are similar. Economics uses mathematical models and statistical tests and market arguments, all of which look alien to the literary eye. But looked at closely they are not so alien. They may be seen as figures of speech—metaphors, analogies, and appeals to authority.

Figures of speech are not mere frills. They think for us. Someone who thinks of a market as an "invisible hand" and the organization of work as a "production function" and his coefficients as being "significant," as an economist does, is giving the language a lot of responsibility. It seems a good idea to look hard at his language.

If the economic conversation were found to depend a lot on its verbal forms, this would not mean that economics would be not a science, or just a matter of opinion, or some sort of confidence game. Good poets, though not scientists, are serious thinkers about symbols; good historians, though not scientists, are serious thinkers about data. Good scientists also use language. What is more (though it remains to be shown) they use the cunning of language, without particularly meaning to. The language used is a social object, and using language is a social act. It requires cunning (or, if you prefer, consideration), attention to the other minds present when one speaks.

The paying of attention to one's audience is called "rhetoric," a word that I later exercise hard. One uses rhetoric, of course, to warn of a fire in a theatre or to arouse the xenophobia of the electorate. This sort of yelling is the vulgar meaning of the word, like the president's "heated rhetoric" in a press conference, or the "mere rhetoric" to which our enemies stoop. Since the Greek flame was lit, though, the word has been used also in a broader and more amiable sense, to mean the study of all the ways of accomplishing things with language: inciting a mob to lynch the accused, to be sure, but also persuading readers of a novel that its characters breathe, or bringing scholars to accept the better argument and reject the worse.

The question is whether the scholar—who usually fancies himself an announcer of "results" or a stater of "conclusions" free of rhetoric—speaks rhetorically. Does he try to persuade? It would seem so. Language, I just said, is not a solitary accomplishment. The scholar doesn't speak into the void, or to himself. He speaks to a community of voices. He desires to be heeded, praised, published, imitated, honored, en-Nobeled. These are the desire. The devices of language are the means.

Rhetoric is the proportioning of means to desires in speech. Rhetoric is an economics of language, the study of how scarce means are allocated to the insatiable desires of people to be heard. It seems on the face of it a reasonable hypothesis that economists are like other people in being talkers, who desire listeners when they go to the library or the laboratory as much as when they go to the office or the polls. The purpose here is to see if this is true, and to see if it is useful: to study the rhetoric of economic scholarship.

The subject is scholarship. It is not the economy, or the adequacy of economic theory as a description of the economy, or even mainly the economist's role in the economy. The subject is the conversation economists have among themselves, for purposes of persuading each other that the interest elasticity of demand for investment is zero or that the money supply is controlled by the Federal Reserve.

Unfortunately, though, the conclusions are of more than academic interest. The conversations of classicists or of astronomers rarely affect the lives of other people. Those of economists do so on a large scale. A well-known joke describes a May Day parade through Red Square, with the usual mass of soldiers, guided missiles, rocket launchers. At last come rank upon rank of people in gray business suits. A bystander asks, "Who are those?" "Aha!" comes the reply, "those are *economists:* you have no idea what damage they can do!" Their conversations do it.

It is not merely the economists in Moscow or Washington who do damage. Even out of range of congressmen and bureaucrats the way economists converse with each other has effects. J. M. Keynes made the point in another remark trite among them: "The ideas of economists and political philosophers, both when they are right and when they are wrong, are more powerful than is commonly understood. Indeed, the world is ruled by little else. . . . Madmen in authority, who hear voices in the air, are distilling their frenzy from some academic scribbler a few years back."

The purpose of thinking about how economists converse with each other is to help the field mature, not to attack it. For all the jokes, from Shaw to L. J. Peter ("If all economists were laid end to end, they would not reach a conclusion"; "An economist is an expert who will know tomorrow why the things he predicted yesterday didn't happen today"), economics is successful. It is unsuccessful as social weather forecasting, a role forced on it by the rhetoric of politics and journalism. But it is successful as social history. Economics, like geology or evolutionary biology or history itself, is a historical rather than a predictive science. Not widely regarded as an imposing creation of the human mind, it nonetheless is. It is social self-understanding (a critical theory, indeed, like Marxism or psychoanalysis), more remarkable even than anthropology or history.

In the flight of rockets the layman can see the marvel of physics, and in the applause of audiences the marvel of music. No one understands the marvel of economics well who has not studied it with care. This leaves its reputation in the hands of politicians and journalists, who have other things on their minds. The result is much mistaken criticism of economics as being too mathematical or as not being "realistic" enough or as not saving the world from its folly. The misinformation is a pity, really, and worth trying to offset. Yet these outside observers of economics cannot be blamed for misunderstanding it. Economics does not very well understand itself. If it understood its own way of conversing—its rhetoric—maybe some of its neurotic behavior would stop, such as its compulsive handwashing in statistical procedures.

The service that literature can do for economics is to offer literary criticism as a model for self-understanding. Literary criticism does not merely pass judgments of good or bad; in its more recent forms the question seems hardly to arise. Chiefly it is concerned with making readers see how poets and novelists accomplish their results. An economic criticism of the sort exercised below is not a way of passing judgment on economics. It is a way of showing how it accomplishes its results. It applies the devices of literary criticism to the literature of economics.

Not many economists think this way. A larger though small proportion of other social scientists do: such thinking is not unheard of in anthropology or sociology. What the French call the "human sciences" generally—the disciplines, from English to paleoanthropology, that study humankind—can assemble nowadays quite a few people who think critically in this particular sense. And, as will become clear, many scholars in mathematics, physics, computer science, biology, paleontology, communication, political science, law, sociology, anthropology, history,

history of science, philosophy, theology, comparative literature, and English have seen particular merit in rhetorical criticism.

What follows, then, will explore a rhetoric of inquiry in economics. It uses an ancient rhetorical device, the figure *a fortiori*, "from the stronger": if even the study of hog farmers and railroads is literary as well as mathematical, if even the science of human maximization under constraints is part of the humanities as much as it is part of the sciences, then all the stronger is the hope for the rest.

THE RHETORIC OF

ECONOMICS

1 THE POVERTY OF

ECONOMIC MODERNISM

Economists agree on more than is commonly under-
stood. Their disagreements about prediction and politics give them an
unhappy reputation, yet they agree on many things: the index number
problem, the law of demand, the logic of entry. They agree above all
on how to talk like economists. Whether descended from Marx or
Menger or Marshall among the grandsons of Adam Smith, they participate together in a conversation begun two centuries ago, a conversation
sharply divided in its style of talk from neighboring ones in history,
sociology, or ethics.

The economic conversation has heard much eloquent talk, but its
most eloquent passages have been mathematical. Especially since the
1930s economists of all schools have become enchanted by the new and
scientific way of talking. Most journals of economics nowadays look
like journals of applied mathematics or theoretical statistics.

The *American Economic Review* of the early 1930s, by contrast, contained hardly an equation; assumptions were not formalized; the graphs
were plots of series, and not common; the fitting of a line to a scatter
of points was rare. The consequence of the primitive machinery for
conversation was an inability to speak clearly. Economists could not
keep clear, for instance, the difference between a movement of an entire
curve and a movement along a curve. Being mathematically innocent,
they were unable to talk in curvy metaphors. They might think of the
Labor Problem, as Harry A. Millis did in his presidential address to the
American Economic Association in December of 1934, as having something to do with marginal productivity (pp. 4-5). After reading J. R.
Hicks' book of 1932, *The Theory of Wages*, as Millis had, they might
recognize that marginal productivity did affect wages. But the economists before the reception of mathematics fell headlong, as Millis did,
into confusions that a little mathematics would have cleared up: confusions about working conditions (which they did not see as merely
another item with income in the utility function) or about bargaining
strength (which they did not see as determined by aggregated marginal
productivities and supply curves of labor). Mathematical metaphors
were not then available to most economists.

The Poverty of Economic Modernism

Now they are available in bulk, especially to the bourgeois, English-speaking economists who dominate the profession (and of whom I am an example). Of the 159 full-length papers published in the *American Economic Review* during 1981, 1982, and 1983, only 6 used words alone and only 4 added to their words tabular statistics alone, the one formal device common in 1931-33. The techniques of mathematics, statistics, diagrams, and explicit simulation, which economists viewed once as useless and arcane, had become routine.

Fully two-thirds of the papers used mathematics explicitly, and most of the others were speaking in a mathematics-saturated environment in which the words "production function" and "demand curve" would call up the mathematics anyway. Nearly half of the papers used diagrams in the fashion economists have come to use them, puzzling other students of society by talking definitely about curves that do not have definite shapes. Nearly a third of the papers used regression analysis, often in quite elaborate ways. Over a tenth used explicit simulation that only academic engineers and physical scientists could have followed fifty years ago. Mathematical analysis illustrated by diagrams (and without facts, in keeping with the abstract character of economic conversation) was used in 60 of the 159. Any one of these techniques would have dazzled and dismayed an audience of economists in 1934.

Yet this gain, like most gains, was achieved at a cost. Books on technical economics are no longer even superficially accessible to laypeople; and young economists overvalue a narrow, and occasionally silly, ingenuity of technique. But the main cost is not so often noticed. It is that during their conversion to a mathematical way of talking the economists adopted a crusading faith, a set of philosophical doctrines, that makes them prone now to fanaticism and intolerance. The faith consists of scientism, behaviorism, operationalism, positive economics, and other quantifying enthusiasms of the 1930s. In the way of crusading faiths, these doctrines have hardened into ceremony, and now support many nuns, bishops, and cathedrals.

A faith of some sort was needed during the struggle for Jerusalem. No young economist in 1950 would have risked his professional life for the values merely of tolerance and methodological balance. The gray haired, who admire such sober virtues, do not have the energy to storm citadels. Many of the mathematically unskilled in economics around 1950 were ignorantly obdurate: they would have none of that, and had often the institutional means to prevent it. The times warranted citadel storming.

But now, so long after the victory, one might ask whether the faith which supported it still serves a social function. One might ask whether the strident talk of Science in economics, which served well in bringing clarity and rigor to the field, has outlived its usefulness.

The Official Methodology of Economics Is Modernist

Economists have two attitudes towards discourse, the official and unofficial, the explicit and the implicit. Most of what I will have to say has to do with the unofficial attitudes, exhibited in how economists actually argue. But economists put great store by their official attitudes, which they believe to be derived from the best thinking in the history and philosophy of science. The official attitude obstructs their view of how they actually argue. They cannot see how they actually argue because the scene is veiled by certain philosophies. Before getting to the main business of looking at what economists actually do, then, I must spend time—quite a lot of time, I am afraid—on how they describe officially what they do.

Their official rules of speaking well, to which economists pay homage in methodological ruminations and in teachings to the young, declare them to be Scientists in the modern mode. The credo of scientific methodology, known to its critics as the Received View, is, roughly speaking, "positivism." It argues that knowledge is to be modeled on the early twentieth century's understanding of certain pieces of nineteenth-century and especially seventeenth-century physics.

To emphasize its pervasiveness in modern thinking well beyond science, however, it is best called "modernism." Modernism gleams diamond-hard from many facets, and the word can be fully defined only in use. But in a preliminary way it can be said to be, as the literary critic Wayne Booth has put it, the notion that we know only what we cannot doubt and cannot really know what we can merely assent to. It is the attitude that the only real knowledge is, in common parlance, "scientific," that is, knowledge tested by certain kinds of rigorous scepticism. Philosophically speaking, modernism is the program of Descartes, regnant in philosophy since the seventeenth century, to build knowledge on a foundation of radical doubt.

Modernism coheres, one part with the other. There are modernist philosophers, modernist architects, modernist musicians, modernist politicians, and modernist economists. That is the reason for using so many-sided a word: the thing itself is many-sided. One can detect modernism as much in Symphony Hall and the Museum of Modern Art as in the temples to social engineering in Washington or London. The

The Poverty of Economic Modernism

modernism espoused by the economist is reinforced in him from all sides.

As religious faith retreated among the intelligentsia in the nineteenth and twentieth centuries, a modernist faith flowed in. Its full tide shows in the way we talk. One hears on the street: "That's just your opinion"; "My biases are such and such"; "I came to this conclusion on the basis of facts"; "You're not being objective"; "That's a very subjective view"; "That's just theology"; "That's just an aesthetic judgment"; "If you can't measure it, I don't think it's objective"; "You tell me the facts, I'll decide on the values"; "You are not being scientific: why should I listen?" Sophomores talk like this. In more literate form their professors talk like it, too: only falsifiable hypotheses are meaningful; the evidence is consistent with the hypothesis; *de gustibus non est disputandum*, of tastes one ought not, of course, to quarrel.

Modernism views science as axiomatic and mathematical and takes the realm of science to be separate from the realm of form, value, beauty, goodness, and all unmeasurable quantity. Being functionalist and given to social engineering and utilitarianism, the modernist is antihistorical, uninterested in cultural or intellectual traditions, at least while in church. The faith can be seen in some scientists and in many who wish especially to be scientific. At its best it produces a disinterested and efficient investigator; at its worst a Dr. Strangelove.

The modernist comes, it should be noted, in another, irrationalist form: at the best an artist or preacher, at the worst a surfer strung out on the latest mysticism. The rationalist and the irrationalist pray to the same god. An irrationalist believes himself different from the rationalist, and in the way he cuts his hair he sometimes is. But in his theory of knowledge he is not. He is merely a protestant, irritated by the rituals of the church of science and scornful of its selling of indulgences, but sharing with it a belief in a trinity of fact, definition, and holy value. Each part of the trinity, on this view, can have its separate devotees: the scientist, the mathematician, and the litterateur. In the modernist view, whether rationalist or irrationalist, these various worshippers need not get in one another's way. Each can specialize in one kind of argument. Arguments do not cross: this year's GNP is one thing; an axiom of social choice is another; sympathy for the poor still another.

The reaction to the modernist theory of knowledge is by now broad. Its leading figures range from professional philosophers (Willard Quine, Nelson Goodman, Stephen Toulmin, Paul Feyerabend, Richard Rorty) to a miscellany of practitioners-turned-philosophers in chemistry (Michael Polanyi), law (Chaim Perelman), and literary criticism (Wayne Booth). The reach of the idea that fact is more than experiment and that argument is more than syllogism is by now long: as, for example, in the lucid treatment of it in Glenn Webster, Ada Jacox, and Beverly Baldwin in "Nursing Theory and the Ghost of the Received View" (1981, pp. 25-35).

The reach, however, has not extended far into economics, and not into neoclassical economics at all. Austrian, institutionalist, and Marxist economists, to be sure, have for a century been attacking certain parts of positivism as the basis for economic knowledge. But they have seized on other parts with redoubled fervor and have expressed their remaining doubts obscurely. In their own way they have been as narrow as thoroughgoing positivists: the rejection of econometrics by Austrian economists, for instance, would be reasonable only if the more naive claims of econometrics were to be taken seriously. For the rest, economists have let philosophical scribblers of a few years back supply their official thinking about good argument.

The mark of modernism is plain in Anglo-American economics since the 1930s. Notwithstanding its gleams of steely brilliance, it has produced by now many crippled economists. Many are bored by history, disdainful of other social scientists, ignorant of their civilization, thoughtless in ethics, and unreflective in method. Even the wise and good among the congregation, who are numerous, find it hard to reconcile their faiths with the ceremonies required of them on Sunday.

Only religion can be like this—at once both noble and corrupting. The Ten Commandments and Golden Rule of modernism in economic and other sciences are

1. Prediction and control is the point of science.
2. Only the observable implications (or predictions) of a theory matter to its truth.
3. Observability entails objective, reproducible experiments; mere questionnaires interrogating human subjects are useless, because humans might lie.
4. If and only if an experimental implication of a theory proves false is the theory proved false.
5. Objectivity is to be treasured; subjective "observation" (introspection) is not scientific knowledge, because the objective and the subjective cannot be linked.
6. Kelvin's Dictum: "When you cannot express it in numbers, your knowledge is of a meagre and unsatisfactory kind."[1]

---

1. Kelvin 1883, 1:73, quoted in Kuhn 1977, pp. 178n, 183n. An approximation to this version is inscribed on the front of the Social Science Research Building at the University of Chicago. Jacob Viner, the famous University of Chicago economist, is said to have

7. Introspection, metaphysical belief, aesthetics, and the like may well figure in the discovery of an hypothesis but cannot figure in its justification; justifications are timeless, and the surrounding community of science irrelevant to their truth.
8. It is the business of methodology to demarcate scientific reasoning from nonscientific, positive from normative.
9. A scientific explanation of an event brings the event under a covering law.
10. Scientists—for instance, economic scientists—ought not to have anything to say as scientists about the oughts of value, whether of morality or art.

And: the Golden Rule (Hume's Golden Fork): "When we run over libraries persuaded of these principles, what havoc must we make? If we take in our hand any volume; of divinity or school metaphysics, for instance, let us ask, *Does it contain any abstract reasoning concerning quantity or number?* No. *Does it contain any experimental reasoning concerning matter of fact and existence?* No. Commit it then to the flames: for it can contain nothing but sophistry and illusion" (Hume 1748, last page).

It is at the level of applied, not theoretical, philosophy, among professional economists, not professional philosophers, that these commandments thrive. No more than a few philosophers now believe as many as half of the commandments. A substantial, respectable, and growing minority believes none of them. But all of them are believed by a majority of economists (and psychologists, sociologists, political scientists, medical scientists, and other nonphilosophers enchanted by modernism).

Certainly an earlier generation of economic methodologists believe them. Methodology and its search for certitude has infected each school of economics. In American economics, however, a methodology of modernism and scientism is particularly associated with the Chicago School. The main texts of economic modernism after Terence Hutchison's *The Significance and Basic Postulates of Economic Theory* (1938), such as Gary Becker and George Stigler's "De Gustibus Non Est Disputandum" (1977) or, above all, Milton Friedman's "The Methodology of Positive Economics (1953), bear a Chicago postmark; and the more extreme interpretations of the texts flourish among economists bearing a Chicago degree.

---

remarked on it one day: "Yes, and when you *can* express it in numbers your knowledge is of a meagre and unsatisfactory kind." Frank Knight, the famous University of Iowa economist, wrote, "Yes, and when you can't measure, measure anyway" (Knight 1940, p. 166n).

This is odd. It is odd that a group so annoying to other economists in most of its activities should have their assent in the matter of official method. Yet, a watered-down version of Friedman's essay of 1953 is part of the intellectual equipment of most American economists, and its arguments come readily to their lips.[2]

Premeditated writing on method is usually sweeter than methodological remarks in the course of nonmethodological business. In precept one can be sweetly vague, earning universal assent; in practice one must make enemies. To take a typical example of first-chapter methodology at the full tide of modernism, Kalman Cohen and Richard Cyert in their otherwise admirable book present an outline of modernism, asserting that it is the method "used in all scientific analyses" (1975, p. 17). The "method" they then outline, with a bibliography weighted towards logical positivism and its allies, is not much more than an appeal to be honest and thoughtful. Only when such a phrase as "at least in principle testable by experiment and observation" (p. 23) is given content by practice does it become clear what is at stake.

Sweetly vague precepts, of course, are not without their uses. To take again the leading example, when in 1953 Friedman published his essay, the practice of economics was riven into theory without fact and fact without theory. His modernist chanting, supported by hooded choruses of philosophers, was at the time probably good for the soul. But again one must ask whether it is not time to stop the chanting.

Friedman's essay is the central document of modernism in economics and deserves respectful review. Even though published early, before the tide of modernism had crested in the human sciences, it was more postmodernist than one might suppose from slight acquaintance with the text. Friedman did, for example, mention with approval the aesthetic criteria of simplicity and fruitfulness that an economist might use to select among a multiplicity of theories with the same predictions, though in the next sentence he attempted to reduce them to matters of prediction (p. 10).[3] He accepted that questionnaires, forbidden to the modern-

2. Nothing here is meant to give comfort to the enemies of Chicago. Having long been a victim of anti-Chicago dogmatism, it is hard for me to credit the assertion that Chicago economics is peculiarly dogmatic. Chicago looks merely like a candid version of a dogmatic impulse common to economics, expressing itself in methodological imperatives. Economists appear to believe that economics is too important to be left to the open-minded. Chicago looks no worse than the rest. *Immo, civis Chicagonus sum, subspecies TP* (cf. Reder 1982).

3. When economists or philosophers claim, as Friedman did, that one should first eliminate theories with inferior predictions and then eliminate theories of inferior beauty, they are claiming—in the cases I have seen, without further argument—that the choice among theories, unlike the choice among most other things, should be lexicographic, the

The Poverty of Economic Modernism

ist in economics, are useful for suggesting hypotheses, though in the next sentence he asserted that they are "almost entirely useless as a means of *testing* the validity of economic hypotheses" (p. 31n). He emphasized the role of the community to which the scientist speaks in producing conviction—whether made up of sociologists, say, or of economists—though in the next sentence he returned to an "objective" theory of testing.

In other words, Friedman, like Karl Popper, another transitional figure, appeared to be struggling to escape the grip of positivism and its intellectual traditions, though with only sporadic success. The *locus classicus* of economic modernism contains much antimodernism, suggesting that modernism cannot survive intelligent discussion even by its best advocates. Abraham Hirsch and Neil de Marchi (1985) have argued persuasively that the explanation for the cognitive dissonance in Friedman is that in his essay he was not in fact positivist at all, not even Popperian, but Deweyan. To follow John Dewey in this is to be pragmatist and American, more interested in the uses of knowledge than in its foundations. This is a satisfying reading, and Friedman likes it too. The problem is then to find a reason for the misunderstanding that long associated Friedman with the more European positivism of, say, Paul Samuelson. Perhaps it was that pragmatism, along with other American toys, had even by the early 1950s acquired a musty odor; the new governess from Europe had already banished it to the attic.

However Friedman is to be taken, the unpremeditated remark in the heat of economic argument usually has a crudely modernist content, often using Friedman's words.[4] An important article by Richard Roll and Stephen Ross on finance, for instance, asserts that "the theory should be tested by its conclusions, not by its assumptions" and that "similarly, one should not reject the conclusions derived from firm profit maximization on the basis of sample surveys in which managers claim that they trade off profit for social good" (1980, p. 1093 and n.). The same can be found elsewhere, in nearly identical terms, dating back

---

way one looks up "lexicographic" in the dictionary, first going to the *l*'s; then looking for the *le*'s, then for the *lex*'s, and so forth. Psychologists such as Maslow believe that first one satisfies physiological "needs," then safety needs, then social, then ego, then self-fulfillment. Economists are inclined to view such ranking as irrational. They point out that the chooser will be happier if he allows himself a bit of self-fulfillment while pursuing safety, fondly recalling Jack London's story, say, as he tries to build a fire. He, and the scientist allegedly pursuing predictive power, might even be safer.

4. Or Fritz Machlup's words (1955), which were widely interpreted as seconding Friedman's.

to Friedman's essay: William Sharpe (1970, p. 77), for instance, writing on the same matter as Roll and Ross, takes it as a rule of polite scientific behavior that "the realism of the assumptions matters little. If the implications are reasonably consistent with observed phenomena, the theory can be said to 'explain' reality." Intoned so often, in harmony with others, such phrases have become incantations. Economic modernism is a revealed faith, and a ritualistic one.

Most economists, at least most English-speaking economists, would thrill to the epithet of modernist Scientist. This is one piece of evidence, indeed, that economists are philosophical modernists. There is other evidence: the prevalence of methodological declarations such as those of Friedman, and especially of Friedman's followers; the feeling anyone fluent in economics has that modernism provides the grammar for discourse; and the reaction to antimodernist arguments, in which someone can be relied on to leap up and declare that "ultimately" the only "fundamental" proof of an economic assertion is "objective," quantitative "tests." It is hard to disbelieve the dominance of modernism in economics, though an objective, quantitative test would of course make it, or any assertion, more believable and would be worth doing. A proper sampling of referee reports of the *American Economic Review* would do the trick, watching out for the use of the modernist ukase ("Never ask business people what they are doing: they cannot tell the truth"; "Measure things regardless").

In any case, modernism rules: that is the main point. It will not do to say about the methodological rules of economists, as a professional philosopher might, "No one believes *that* stuff anymore." Maybe no one does in the higher reaches of sophistication in departments of philosophy. (Though even there, an outsider observes, the anger generated by Richard Rorty or Stephen Toulmin would seem to indicate some such faith.) But, to repeat, a modernist faith of the cruder and narrower sort thrives still in the harder sciences, such as economics.

Modernism Is a Poor Method

IT IS OBSOLETE IN PHILOSOPHY

There are many things wrong with modernism as a methodology for science, or for economic science.[5] The first is that the

---

5. The much-discussed question of whether there can be a value-free social science will not be much discussed here. That modernism puts moral argument outside rational discussion, though, is a failing.

The Poverty of Economic Modernism

philosophical arguments for it have long been known to be unpersuasive. Even philosophical economists appear to read about as much in
professional philosophy as philosophers do in professional economics.
It is not surprising, therefore, that the news of the decline of modernism
has not reached all ears. The logical positivists of the 1920s scorned in
their time what they called "metaphysics." From the beginning, though,
the scorn has refuted itself. If metaphysics is to be cast into the flames,
then the methodological declarations of the modernist family from
Descartes through Hume and Comte to Russell and Hempel and Popper will be the first to go. For this and other reasons philosophers agree
that strict logical positivism is dead. The length of time it has been dead
raises the question whether economists are wise to carry on with their
necrophilia.[6]

In economics the metaphysical position akin to logical positivism is
clumsily argued, probably because it derives more from the philosophizing of philosophical amateurs from Mach to Bridgeman than from
the parallel thinking of professional philosophers themselves. Mach,
Pearson, Duhem, and Ostwald—that is, scientists with an interest in the
history of science—revived positivism in the 1890s, but logical positivism, the philosopher's version, was a later development.

Modernist rules in economics, therefore, are asserted but seldom
argued. Consider the master rules. As often as they have been repeated,
it is hard to see on the face of it, or even beneath, the appeal of
"operationally meaningful statements" (Samuelson 1947, p. 3 and
throughout) or "valid and meaningful predictions about phenomena
not yet observed" (Friedman 1953) or "predictive value of hypothetical
generalization" (Machlup 1955, p. 1) as standards against which every
nonmathematical assertion is to be judged. No ordinary person follows a methodology like this in ordinary thinking, and its advocates
do not make an argument for treating some kinds of thinking as extraordinary.

The argument that Hutchison, Samuelson, Friedman, Machlup, and
their followers gave for adopting their metaphysics was an argument
from authority, at the time correct, namely, that this was what philosophers were saying. The trust in philosophy was a tactical error, for the
philosophy itself was changing as they spoke (e.g. Quine 1951). As a

6. See Passmore 1967. Karl Popper has played a role on both the modernist and the
antimodernist sides. He quotes Passmore with approval for the motto of a chapter of his
own entitled "Who Killed Logical Positivism?" (Popper 1976, pp. 87–90), in which he
confesses to the murder. "I," said the Popper, / "with my little chopper, / I killed Logical
Positivism."

philosopher of economics, Alexander Rosenberg, noted in 1976, "Many economists have described their views as positivist and have opened themselves to the discredit which in recent decades has accrued to this view in the philosophy of science."[7] Some philosophers now doubt the enterprise of epistemology, with its claim to give foundations for knowledge. And many more, as I have already said, doubt the confident prescriptions of modernist epistemology.

FALSIFICATION IS NOT COGENT

One prescription that economic modernists have in common, for instance, is an emphasis on the crucial falsifying test, supposedly the hallmark of scientific reasoning. Scientific Method narrows reasoning to logic and narrows logic to one proposition in logic, the so-called *modus tollens*. If H entails O, then not-O entails not-H.

True enough, one might say, though not much (Boland 1979, p. 505). Cartesian and especially Humean scepticism would make this the only real, fundamental, ultimate test. We can never affirm (it is said, even while affirming that the class will meet today), but only falsify. Such a crude way of speaking, as the philosopher J. L. Austin once pointed out (1975 [1955], p. 54), ignores the actual richness of scientific and other ordinary speech: "The truth of a statement may be connected importantly with the truth of another without it being the case that the one entails the other in the sole sort of sense preferred by obsessional logicians."

Philosophers have long recognized, however, that the doctrine of falsification, even in its own way of speaking, runs afoul of a criticism made by the physicist and philosopher Pierre Duhem in 1906. The criticism is apparent without philosophical study to any economist who has tried to use falsification. Suppose that the hypothesis H ("British businessmen performed poorly relative to Americans and Germans in the late nineteenth century") implies a testing observation O ("Measures of total factor productivity in iron and steel show a large difference between British and foreign steelmaking"). The one implies the other, that is, not by itself, but only with the addition of ancillary hypotheses H_1, H_2, and so forth that make the measurement possible ("Marginal productivity theory applies to Britain from 1870 to 1913"; "British steel had no hidden inputs offsetting poor business leaderships"; and so

---

7. Rosenberg 1976, p. x. Rosenberg goes on to say that "the notion that the failures of logical positivism should cast a pall over empiricism as a tenable epistemology is ludicrous" (p. xi). By "empiricism" he means a modernist scientific epistemology.

forth). Then of course not-O implies not-H, or not-H$_1$ or not-H$_2$ or not H$_3$ or any number of failures of premises irrelevant to the main hypothesis in question. The main hypothesis is insulated from crucial test by the ancillary hypotheses necessary to bring it to any test. The test may be worth doing, as it was in the example given. It is one good argument among several against the notion that British enterprise failed. But it is not the conversation stopper that it is supposed to be in the modernist methodology. It is not a certitude, not the crucial experiment, not the Only Real Test.

This insulation from crucial test is the substance of most scientific disagreement. Economists and other scientists will complain to their fellows, "Your experiment was not properly controlled"; "You have not solved the identification problem"; "You have used an equilibrium (competitive, single-equation) model when a disequilibrium (monopolistic, 500-equation) model is relevant." In sciences such as population biology or astronomy or economics, in which controlled experiment is expensive and not always convincing, the conversation can hardly begin without assuming the answers to numerous boundary questions. It cannot begin, that is to say, without assuming that the scientist knows the world pretty well and is engaged in fitting new facts into the existing theories. There is no "falsification" going on.

The chemist and philosopher Michael Polanyi describes a paper by Lord Rayleigh that had results too surprising to be credible: "When . . . I asked various physicists' opinions about it, they only shrugged their shoulders. They could not find fault with the experiments, yet they not only did not believe its results, but did not even think it worth while to consider what was wrong with it, let alone check up on it. . . . [Rayleigh] should have ignored his observation, for he ought to have known there was something wrong with it" (Polanyi 1966, pp. 64f.). Compare a remark by the physicist and historian of science Thomas Kuhn that "the scientist often seems rather to be struggling with facts, trying to force them into conformity with a theory he does not doubt" (1977, p. 193). At the level of broad scientific law the scientists simply use their theories. They seldom try to falsify them.

This is why simulation—trying out scientific arguments on paper to see if they are powerful enough—is important in economics and similar fields. Simulation is affirmative, not falsifying, asking whether one can make a case for such-and-such, not whether one can prove it wrong. It tests systems, not isolated hypotheses, and affirms a framework in which to test them. It tests the reasonableness of affirmation, not the possibility of doubt. In economics, for example, econometrics amounts to simulation. The doubting and falsifying method, enshrined in the official version of econometric method, is largely impractical.

And even if the one hypothesis in question could be isolated, the probabilistic nature of hypotheses, most especially in economics, makes crucial experiments noncrucial: chance is the ever-present alternative, the H_n that spoils falsificationism. This the falsificationists themselves have long recognized, and have long lamented. Falsification, near enough, has been falsified.

PREDICTION IS NOT POSSIBLE IN ECONOMICS

The common claim that prediction is the defining feature of a real science, and that economics possesses the feature, is also doubtful. It is a cliché among philosophers and historians of science, for instance, that one of the most successful of all scientific theories, the theory of evolution, makes no predictions and is therefore unfalsifiable by prediction. With fruit flies and bacteria, to be sure, one can test the theory in the approved manner; but its main facts, its dinosaur bones and multicolored birds, are things to be explained, not to be predicted. Geology and evolution, or for that matter an astronomy of objects many light years away, are historical rather than predictive sciences.

It is at least suggestive of something strange in prediction as a criterion for a properly modernist economics that Darwin's theory was itself connected to the classical economics of Smith, Malthus, and Ricardo (a system, as it happens, erroneous in most of the actual predictions it made). Strangely, it was in the midst of Milton Friedman's most famous piece of predictionist metaphysics that he cites Armen Alchian's (1950) revival of the connection. Friedman says (1953, p. 19) that the evolutionary theory of trees, like a Chicago theory of companies, supposes that "the leaves are positioned *as if* each leaf deliberately sought to maximize the amount of sunlight it receives." Alchian and Friedman are well known for their support of modernist methodology. Strangely, then, the nonpredictive, historical, evolutionary argument in economics—a variant of Dr. Pangloss's belief that whatever there is, is there for a reason—is most popular among the economists who think of themselves as most rigorous about prediction.

In any event, predicting the economic future is, as Ludwig von Mises put it, "beyond the power of any mortal man" (1948, p. 867). What says it is beyond his power is the very economics used to make the prediction. The economist for a big bank predicts that interest rates will fall after Christmas. If before making the prediction he has not placed his net worth in margin loans on bonds, properly hedged and insured against variance, he is behaving either irrationally or self-deceivingly. He claims to know the expected value of the future, yet for some reason chooses not to take the unlimited wealth that such Faustian knowledge can bring. He is willing for some reason instead to dissipate the opportunity by the act of telling others about it. If he does not really know the future, then he does not face such an opportunity. But then he has perhaps no business talking as though he does.

Predictionism cannot be rescued by arguing that the big bank economist makes merely conditional predictions ("If the government deficit continues to grow, the interest rate will rise"). Conditional predictions are cheap: if the sea were to disappear, a rock would accelerate in falling from sea level to the sea floor at about 32.17 feet per second per second. But a serious prediction has serious boundary conditions. If it does, then it must answer the American Question: If you're so smart, why ain't you rich? As an economist would put it, in his gnomic way, at the margin (because that is where economics works) and on average (because some people are lucky) the industry of making economic predictions, which includes universities, earns merely normal returns.

MODERNISM ITSELF IS IMPOSSIBLE, AND NOT ADHERED TO

The most damaging, though, of these lesser criticisms of modernist methodology is that if taken at its word the methodology is impossible. Consider again the steps to modernist knowledge, from predictionism through Kelvin's Dictum to Hume's Fork. If economists (or physicists) confined themselves to economic (or physical) propositions that literally conformed to such steps, they would have nothing to say. Cartesian or Humean scepticism is too corrosive a standard of belief for an actual human scientist, as Descartes and Hume both knew. As Polanyi put it (1962, p. 88), the methodology of modernism sets up "quixotic standards of valid meaning which, if rigorously practiced, would reduce us all to voluntary imbecility."

Modernism promises knowledge free from doubt, free from metaphysics, morals, and personal conviction. What it is able to deliver renames as scientific methodology the scientist's and especially the economic scientist's metaphysics, morals, and personal convictions. It cannot deliver what it promises. Probably it should not. One suspects, as have many who have thought about the matter in recent years, that scientific knowledge is not so very different from other knowledge.

I am arguing that the literal application of modernist methodology cannot give a useful economics. It remains to be seen whether actual arguments in economics use modernism as more than window dressing. In the meantime the best evidence is historical. In his *Against*

The Poverty of Economic Modernism

Method (1975) Paul Feyerabend uses an interpretation of Galileo's career to attack the claims of prescriptive methodology in physics, and the same point can be made about economics. Had the modernist criterion of persuasion been adopted by Galileo's contemporaries, Feyerabend argues, the Galilean case would have failed. A grant proposal to use the strange premise that terrestial optics applied also to the celestial sphere, to assert that the tides were the sloshing of water on a mobile earth, and to suppose that the fuzzy views of Jupiter's alleged moons would prove, by a wild analogy, that the planets, too, went around the sun as did the moons around Jupiter would not have survived the first round of peer review in a National Science Foundation of 1632, at any rate if that one (unlike ours) were wedded to modernist ideology. The argument applies widely to the history of physics: observational anomalies in the experiments testing Einstein's theories were ignored for many years, to be revealed as errors of measurement long after the theories had been embraced, embraced on grounds of "the reason of the matter," as Einstein was fond of saying (Feyerabend 1975, pp. 56-57).

Historians of biology have uncovered many cases of cooking the statistical results to fit modernist precepts of what counts as evidence, from Pasteur and Mendel down to the present. Gerald Geison has shown (Geison forthcoming; Farley and Geison 1974) that Pasteur, among other pieces of false speech, lied about the results of his experiments. It has been known for a long time that Mendel's experiments were too good to be true.[8] The measurement of IQ has from its beginning entailed fraud and self-deception in the name of scientific method (Gould 1981). Modernism appears to fit poorly the complexities of biology and psychology: straining after evidence of a sort available only in the simplest experiments in physics does not suit them well.

It suits economics poorly enough. For better or for worse, to take the leading case, the Keynesian revolution in economics would not have happened under the modernist legislation for science. The Keynesian insights were not formulated as statistical propositions until the early 1950s, fifteen years after the bulk of younger economists had become persuaded they were true. By the early 1960s the Keynesian notions of liquidity traps and accelerator models of investment, despite repeated

8. In "Mendel and Methodology" Robert Root-Bernstein (1983) rehabilitates Mendel in an interesting way. He argues that peas are hard to classify: some are obviously smooth, some obviously wrinkled, but some middling. Mendel got his too perfect results not by outright fraud but by doing what Kuhn and others describe as common in physics: defining the categories to suit his elegant mathematical theory. "These categories did not exist objectively or unambiguously in nature, but had to be invented by Mendel himself" (p. 289).

The Poverty of Economic Modernism

failures in their statistical implementations, were taught to students of economics as matters of scientific routine. Modernist methodology would have stopped all this cold in 1936: where was the evidence of an objective, controlled, and statistical kind?

Nor was the monetarist counterrevolution a success in fact for modernist methodology. Modernism dominated the minds of monetarist economists by the 1960s because their leader espoused it. They had convinced themselves that the main issues were issues of prediction and control. Yet it was not modernist certitudes that won the day for the view that money mattered. It was crude experiments and big books, by their crudeness and bigness, not the apparently modernist rituals performed in the professional journals.

The Kennedy tax cut, for example, raised the Keynesians to their peak of prestige; the inflation of the 1970s brought them down again, leaving the monetarists as temporary kings of the castle. Friedman and Schwartz's big book, *A Monetary History of the United States, 1867-1960*, was another important and nonmodernist victory for monetarism. It established a correlation between money and money income, though with many exceptions to be explained by various nonmonetarist epicycles. Keynesians and other opponents of monetarism do not deny the existence of such a correlation, but its importance. The correlation is important if money caused prices. It is unimportant if prices caused money. In particular, to go beyond the usual closed-economy framework of the debate, the monetarist argument supposes that money could be controlled by the monetary authority despite the openness of the American economy to trade in goods and in money itself. Friedman and Schwartz for the most part did not reply.[9] Yet what was telling in the debate was not the logical quality of their replies but the sheer bulk of their book, and the richness and intelligence of its arguments, however irrelevant most were to the main point. Modernist methodology had little to do with it.

A modernist methodology consistently applied, in other words, would probably stop advances in economics. Ask any economist. What empirical anomaly in the traditional tale inspired the new economic history of the early 1960s or the new labor economics of the early 1970s? None: it was merely a realization that the logic of economics had not exhausted itself at conventional borders. What observable implications justify the big investment of economic intellect since 1950 in mathematical general equilibrium theory? For all the modernist talk common among

9. One exception is Friedman's comment on McCloskey and Zecher (Friedman 1984, pp. 157–62).

its theorists, none; but so what? Could applications of economics to legal questions in the style of the emergent field of law and economics rely entirely on objective evidence? No; but why would one wish to so limit the understanding? And so forth. There is nothing to be gained and much to be lost by adopting modernism in economics.

The point is itself economic. In order for an economic assertion to be tested, Ronald Coase points out, some economist must care enough about it to bother. The economist will care only when the assertion is believed by other economists—by his allies or by some significant group of his opponents. Only when enough economists believe will there be a demand for tests. Fortunately, "economists, or at any rate enough of them, do not wait to discover whether a theory's predictions are accurate before making up their minds"; to wait in properly modernist style "would result in the paralysis of scientific activity" (Coase 1982, p. 14), since no one would have an incentive to choose one out of the infinite number of hypotheses for test. Even quantitative studies, Coase argues, rely heavily on prequantitative arguments founding belief, and he quotes with approval Kuhn's remark that "the road from scientific law to scientific measurement can rarely be traveled in the reverse direction" (ibid. p. 18, quoting Kuhn 1977, p. 219). The laws come from a tradition of conversation, and in physics as in economics "quantitative studies . . . are explorations with the aid of a theory" (Coase 1982, p. 17), searches for numbers with which to make specific a theory already believed on other grounds. Modernism, in other words, denying to scientists the mental devices they do in fact use, is impractical.

Economists follow a modernist line in their official methodology. In 1950 the line looked courageously up to date, suited to a band of revolutionaries in the mountains. By now, in part because its revolution has been successful, it looks oppressive, suited to a government in the coastal plains, squatting on the major ports and the radio station. Economists are not alone in adhering to the modernist revolution so long after its spirit has died. Perhaps it will be comforting to know that they would also not be alone if they repudiated its excesses.

2

FROM METHODOLOGY

TO RHETORIC

Any Rule-Bound Methodology Is Objectionable

The greater objection to modernism in economics, though, is that modernism supports a rule-bound methodology. It claims to deduce laws for science from the essence of knowledge or a rational reconstruction of the history of science. It claims that the philosopher of science can tell what makes for good, useful, fruitful, progressive science. It claims that he can limit the arguments that the scientists themselves make spontaneously, casting out some as unscientific, or at best placing them firmly in the "context of discovery." The philosopher undertakes to second-guess the scientific community. In economics a rule-bound methodology claims that the rulemaker is expert in all present economic knowledge and in all future economics, too, restricting the growth of the economic conversation to make it fit a philosopher's idea of the ultimate good.

Such claims from the easy chair are hard to take seriously. Einstein remarked (1953, p. 38) that "whoever undertakes to set himself up as a judge in the field of Truth and Knowledge is shipwrecked by the laughter of the gods." The modernist methodologist is a Red Queen ("Normative argument: off with his head"), and the gods are snickering behind their hands. Any methodology that is lawmaking and limiting will have this risible effect.

The maker of rules for economic science has, of course, the noblest intentions. Like the man from the government, he is here to help you. But economists like to remark of similar cases of interference in the spontaneous order that noble intentions are no defense against laughable results. The methodologist fancies himself the judge of the practitioner. His proper business, if any, is an anarchistic one, resisting the rigidity and pretension of rules. I. A. Richards made the point about the theory of metaphor: "Its business is not to replace practice, or to tell us how to do what we cannot do already; but to protect our natural skill from the interference of unnecessarily crude views about it" (1936, p. 116).

20

It is regrettable that modernist methodology, or any methodology consisting of rigid precept, is crude. It is worse that it is allowed to interfere with natural skill. The custom of methodological papers in economics is to scold economists for not allowing it to interfere more. Mark Blaug's useful book summarizing the state of play of economic methodology in 1980, *The Methodology of Economics*, is a recent case. Its subtitle promises to tell "How Economists Explain." It might better have been "How the Young Karl Popper Explained," for it repeatedly attacks extant arguments in economics for failing to comply with the rules Popper laid down in *Logik der Forschung* in 1934.

Blaug's exordium is typical of the best of the methodologists in economics: "Economists have long been aware of the need to defend 'correct' principles of reasoning in their subject; although actual practice may bear little relationship to what is preached, the preaching is worth considering on its own ground" (Blaug 1980, p. xii). Such words flow easily from a modernist's pen. Yet it is unclear why preaching unrelated to actual practice should be worth considering at all. Why do economists have to defend in the abstract their principles of reasoning, and before what tribunal? The methodologists—whether logical positivist or Popperian or Austrian or Marxist—should have an answer, but do not. Ancient common sense and recent philosophy of science suggest they cannot.

Blaug's peroration is frankly prescriptive, taking rules for economic speech directly from philosophy:

> What methodology can do is to provide criteria for the acceptance and rejection of research programs, setting standards that will help us to discriminate between wheat and chaff. The ultimate question we can and indeed must pose about any research program is the one made familiar by Popper: what events, if they materialize, would lead us to reject that program? A program that cannot meet that question has fallen short of the highest standards that scientific knowledge can attain. (p. 264)

It sounds grand, but Einstein's gods are rolling in the aisles. Why, the voice of pragmatism asks, should a dubious epistemological principle be a test of anything at all, much less of practice, much less the "ultimate" test? Doesn't science take place most of the time well short of the ultimate?

The operative word is "ultimate" and its numerous cousins in epistemology, such as "conceptually," "ideally," "in principle," "in the last analysis," "fundamentally," or "at the Second Coming." "Ultimately," says the epistemologist, "the only way we know is such and such." But this declaration does not persuade ordinary people and ordinary scientists. They take it as obvious that we know in many ways, not always reducible to sight or synthetic a priori. The "ultimate" way is not relevant. We need intellectual nourishment here and now, not epistemological pie in the sky.

The appeal of epistemological methodologists since Bacon to experimental facts as the "ultimate arbiter," for instance, will dismiss mere reflection as an idol, to be cast into the flames, or at least pushed off its altar. John Dewey, the voice of pragmatism, replies: "Such wholesale depreciation ignores the value inherent even in the most subjective reflection, for it takes the settled estate which is proof that thought is not needed, or that it has done its work, as if it supplied the standard for the occasions in which problems are hard upon us, and doubt is rife."[1] Dewey is here close to another friend of methodological breadth, Cardinal Newman, who hewed to broad-church reasoning. Thirty years earlier (1870, p. 150) the cardinal had written that "assent on reasonings not demonstrative is too widely recognized an act to be irrational, unless man's nature is irrational, too familiar to the prudent and clearminded to be an infirmity or an extravagance." By defending a catholicity of reasonings, of course, Dewey and Newman were not rejecting fact, or advocating the shutting down of laboratories. They were rejecting a restrictive methodism that narrows human reason to one particular kind of fact and puts most facts and most reasons beyond reasoning.

Anyone would commend the vision of scientific exploration that the best of the epistemological methodologists appear to have. It amounts to a dialectic, in the Continental sense foreign to the traditions of analytic philosophy. Dewey and Newman would have approved. Genuine exploration is brave and good. Refusing to offer hostages to evidence, though not rare even in modernist circles, is cowardly: so much one can take from the idea of falsification by evidence. Facing facts, we all agree, is good. In this modest sense we are all "empiricists." The problem comes, and the modernist shouting begins, with the words "empirical" and "evidence." Should it all be "objective," "experimental," "positive," "observable"? Can it be? One doubts it.

If the modernist commandments were stated as merely personal goals, no one, surely, would complain. The desire for Objectivity would be recognized as not wholly attainable, but worthy perhaps as a guide to the pilgrim, himself a modest fellow, who admitted freely that other

1. Dewey 1916, pp. 196f. The quotation comes from the essay "The Logical Character of Ideas," which was published separately in 1900. Its early date—by contrast, say, with *The Quest for Certainty* (1929)—is important to bear in mind, for elsewhere in the essay Dewey delivers encomia for positivism that might be read as inconsistent with his later views.

faiths might lead also to salvation. Let me, O Lord, not covet my neighbor's wife, even in imagination; furthermore, O Lord, let me try always to measure with objective experiment, even in imagination.

The modernist commandments, however, are not treated by the believers as a personal faith. They are a decalogue for our times, rules to govern me and thee, enforced by an intellectual hue and cry. And we shall stone thee if thou resisteth, and expel thee from the tribe.

Something is awry with an appeal for an open intellectual society, an appeal defending itself on liberal grounds, that begins by demarcating certain means of reasoning as forbidden and certain fields of study as meaningless. The intolerance of modernism can be best seen in its most tolerant earthly king. In *The Open Society and Its Enemies* (1945) Karl Popper, from whom much can be learned about the growth of knowledge, firmly closes the borders of his open society to psychoanalysts and Marxists, who are charged with violating all manner of modernist regulations. The difficulty is that on these grounds Popper would have to close the borders as well to a line of physicists from Galileo Galilei to the charmers of subatomic particles. During the 1890s some physicists did in fact reject atomism on the properly modernist grounds that such matters were not observable; and nowadays, as the physicist Steven Weinberg has noted (1983, pp. 9f.), no modernist would hunt for quarks. An economist wetback seized for working in such an open society would be deported summarily on the next truck (though pleading from the back his properly modernist credentials).

That adding methodological constraints to science cannot in general be wise will strike economists as obvious. Constraints, after all, constrain. The contrary notion that a rule-bound methodology is good for you has been much questioned recently by philosophers. Paul Feyerabend's demolitions of the philosophy of science and Richard Rorty's deconstructions of philosophy have left methodologists apoplectic. Rorty views the history of epistemology since Plato as an intellectual bet that did not come off: "People have, oddly enough, found something interesting to say about the essence of Force, and the definition of 'number.' They might have found something interesting to say about the essence of Truth. But in fact they haven't" (1982, p. xiv).

The philosophers are here following antimethodological findings from other fields. In particular the sociology and history of science over the past two decades have left the old rules of methodology looking unpersuasive. The sociologists and historians took to discovering what actually happened in science, favoring what happened over the Astounding Stories retailed in the opening chapters of science books. By this unremarkable device the methodological claims of modernism have been rejected, repeatedly. It might be tried in economics.[2]

Methodology Is Bourgeois

If it were not so damaging to the sense, Methodology, strutting around issuing orders to working scientists, would only be funny. In economics it stands in the middle of a meta-economical hierarchy from shop floor to board room. At the bottom is method with a small *m*, ever humble and helpful, about which no reasonable person would complain, or even joke much. It tells an economist what to do when the data have been selected in a particular sort of biased way or what to do when it is hard to think of reasons for price and quantity to change in a certain market. It tells, rather badly, how to write scientific prose; and it tells, rather well, how to grasp a situation in which profits remain to be earned by new entrants. Following Joan Robinson, economists call these their box of tools. The tools are economic theory in its verbal and mathematical forms, statistical theory and practice, familiarity with certain accounting conventions and statistical sources, and a background of stylized historical fact and worldly experience. The use of such tools to fashion sturdy little arguments is the métier of the economist, the economist's method.

Far above method with a small *m*, at the peak of the scholarly enterprise, stand the conversational norms of civilization. The German philosopher Jürgen Habermas and his tradition call these *Sprachethik* (Habermas 1973, p. 110). Don't lie; pay attention; don't sneer; cooperate; don't shout; let other people talk; be open-minded; explain yourself when asked; don't resort to violence or conspiracy in aid of your ideas. We cannot imagine good conversation or good intellectual life deficient in these. They are the rules adopted by the act of joining a conversation, whether among economists about how to manage the economy or between parents about how to manage the teenager. Socratic dialogue— at any rate when his interlocutors are permitted to say something be-

---

2. The founding rúle of Descartes himself has been scrutinized in this way by J. A. Schuster, who concludes that Descartes's "method-talk was not abstracted from successful practice in some area of mathematics [much less physics]; it was produced by a megalomaniacal performance of operations of analogical extension upon the terms of a discourse, universal mathematics [one of Descartes's projects], which itself could not do what it was purported to do" (1983, p. 19). Schuster refers to evidence internal to *Regulae ad directionem ingenii*, a work dated by Schuster earlier in Descartes's career than has been thought.

sides "So it would seem, Socrates"—has been the model of intellectual discourse. That we do not always follow the model is considered bad but not a reason to abandon it as a norm. The worst academic sin is not to be illogical or badly informed but to exhibit cynical disregard for the norms of scholarly conversation.[3]

Between the top and the bottom, a middle manager in a green suit, below the cool majesty of sprachethik and above the workaday utility of method with a small *m*, stands Methodology. Because it cannot claim the specificity of practical advice to economists, or to the lovelorn, it is not method. Because it does not claim the generality of how to speak well in our culture, or in economics, it is not sprachethik. It claims instead to be a universalization from particular sciences to a science of science in general. What makes Methodology comical is what usually makes the *bourgeois gentilhomme* comical. The joke is his dual position, at once master and servant, inclined therefore to hypocrisy and double-talk, 'umble and yet pompous.

The schools of economics have each their comical attachments to methodology. A Marxist economic methodology, for example, has rules such as:

The history of all hitherto existing society is the history of class struggle.
Use statistics, which are scientific.
Beware of remarks infected by false consciousness.

Neoclassical methodology, the dominant one in the English-speaking world, says among other things:

The history of all hitherto existing society is the history of interactions among selfish individuals.
Use statistics, which are scientific.
Beware of remarks that are nonfalsifiable or nonobservable.

Austrian methodology says:

The history of all hitherto existing society is the history of interactions among selfish individuals.
Use statistics gingerly if at all, for they are transitory figments.
Beware of remarks that do not accord with Austrian Methodological precepts.

3. My discussion of conversation comes from Richard Rorty 1982, pp. 165, 172; ibid. 1979, pp. 161, 170, 318, 371, and throughout; Polanyi 1966, pp. 84f. and throughout; and Habermas 1973.

From Methodology to Rhetoric

Similar rules pertain to other modern schools, or to more subtly divided subschools among them. They share the amusing Cartesian notion that practice according to the whatever-it-is below sprachethik and above plain method is possible, and will yield a harvest of truth.

Most defenses of methodology get what force they have by borrowing prestige from sprachethik or utility from method. The reply, for instance, that "you *must* have a methodology hidden *somewhere*" is true in practice only if the methodology pretends to be a practical rule of method, and is true in morality only if it takes over the moral rules of sprachethik. The point is that it is a poor thing when out on its own.

In practice methodology serves chiefly to demarcate Us from Them, demarcating science from nonscience. Once the modernists have founded a Bantustan for nonsciences such as astrology, psychoanalysis, acupuncture, nutritional medicine, Marxist economics, spoonbending, or anything else they do not wish to discuss, they can get on with the business at hand with a clear head. Methodology and its corollary, the Demarcation Problem (What is Science? How is It to be distinguished from nonscience?), are ways of stopping conversation by limiting conversation to people on our side of the demarcation line.

The replies to such scepticism about the uses of methodology and epistemology have been unpersuasive. Indeed, it has not usually been thought necessary to stoop so low as persuasion. The many traditional philosophers and the few remaining historians of science working by the old rules join in a prolonged if somewhat nervous sneer. Early in his penetrating exploration of the limits of analysis, Stanley Rosen (1980, p. xiii) observes that an appreciation of its limits is "not yet strong enough to prevent the typical practitioner of analytical philosophy from succumbing to the temptation of confusing irony for a refutation of opposing views." He remarks that the very "strengths of the analytical movement . . . have led to a general failure to understand the rhetorical nature of its own justification."

Various recent attempts have been made to rescue some residue of thinking about methodology. An economist, Bruce Caldwell, has contributed to the attempt, in his wide-ranging treatment in 1982 of the history of methodology in economics, *Beyond Positivism: Economic Methodology in the Twentieth Century*. Caldwell advocates methodological pluralism, as does Lawrence Boland, another economist, in his brilliant but opaque *The Foundations of Economic Method* (1982). These economists and others intend to carry on the conversation about the essence of Truth that Rorty finds so lacking in promise, albeit with a novel spirit of toleration and balance. One wonders whether people can in fact keep their toleration and balance for long in a conversation about my Truth and thine. As Rorty might say, they haven't yet.

A similar program is advocated most gracefully by a philosopher, Husain Sarkar, in *A Theory of Method*. He adopts an economic model of competing methodologies, following Stephen Toulmin in this, and anticipates that in a just world "a Darwinian competition among methods would ensue, until some methods became sound and stable" (Sarkar 1983, p. 163). He does not answer in detail why one would want a middle-ground methodology in the first place (as distinct from a concrete method for work on the day, and rules of decency enrolled in the sprachethik). An answer would have to argue that Rorty's Reservation had little force—that there *is* something worthwhile to say about the essence of Truth, in general.

Good Science Is Good Conversation

What distinguishes good from bad in learned discourse, then, is not the adoption of a particular methodology, but the earnest and intelligent attempt to contribute to a conversation. This is the oldest of philosophical doctrines. Plato was, as Cicero said, the best orator when making merry of orators, and his Socrates was the first and best conversationalist from the pen of a man trying to end conversation. The best modern statement is Michael Oakeshott's: "As civilized human beings, we are the inheritors, neither of an inquiry about ourselves and the world, nor of an accumulating body of information, but of a conversation begun in the primeval forest and extended and made more articulate in the course of centuries. . . . Education, properly speaking, is an initiation . . . in which we acquire the intellectual and moral habits appropriate to conversation" (1933, pp. 198-99).

Literal conversation is of course not the whole point, though part of it. In a broader sense, Cicero conversed with Aristotle and Marx with Adam Smith. True, one must not exaggerate the enthusiasm of intellectuals for real conversation. The lack of interest in what that idiot Jones has to say makes much intellectual dispute puerile. Durkheim and Weber were contemporaries at the birth of sociology, worked on similar subjects, and contributed largely to networks of conversation in their fields, yet neither so much as mentioned the other (Lepienes 1983). But such stories, like the passions about Jones, are felt to be violations of the intellectual sprachethik.

The notion of a conversation gives an answer to the demand for standards of persuasiveness. One recognizes with ease when a conversation in one's own field is working well. Most economists would agree, for instance, that at present the conversation about the real side of international trade is not working well, after a long period of excellence in the late 1950s and 1960s. Agricultural economics, likewise, has recently suffered a decline from a still longer period of brilliance. On the other hand, no economist familiar with the situation would doubt that the conversation in economic history improved radically from the 1950s to the 1960s, and continues at this higher level.

The conversations overlap enough to make one almost as sure about neighboring fields: examining the overlap is what editors, referees, and members of research panels do. The overlaps of the overlaps, as Polanyi once observed, keep all honest if some try to be. Q.E.D.: the overlapping conversations provide the standards. It is a market argument. There is no need for philosophical lawmaking or methodological regulation to keep the economy of intellect running just fine.

It is best to cite philosophers against methodological philosophizing. Habermas said it, though obscurely: "The expectation of discursive redemption of normative validity claims is already contained in the structure of intersubjectivity and makes specially introduced maxims of universalization superfluous" (1973, p. 110). He means to say, We don't need philosophers to tell us about ethics, because the ethics of conversing, sprachethik, will suffice. Another philosopher recently put it better, in answering how serious philosophers are themselves to be distinguished from system-making lunatics. Amelie Oksenberg Rorty writes that what is crucial is "our ability to engage in continuous conversation, testing one another, discovering our hidden presuppositions, changing our minds because we have listened to the voices of our fellows. Lunatics also change their minds, but their minds change with the tides of the moon and not because they have listened, really listened, to their friends' questions and objections" (1983, p. 562). One would wish for such a character of argument in economics. Perhaps when economists are disburdened of their philosophical baggage, and begin to look at how they converse, really converse, it will be so.

Rhetoric Is a Better Way to Understand Science

A way to get out of the modernist maze is to pick up a thread long separated from science: rhetoric. Rhetoric does not deal with Truth directly; it deals with conversation. It is, crudely put, a literary way of examining conversation, the conversation of economists and mathematicians as much as of poets and novelists. It can be used for a literary criticism of science. The humanistic tradition in Western civilization, in other words, is to be used to understand the scientific tradition. Much good can come of this.

The word "rhetoric" here does not mean a verbal shell game, as in "empty rhetoric" or "mere rhetoric" (although form is not trival either, and even empty rhetoric is full). Rhetoric is the art of speaking. More broadly, it is the study of how people persuade. In *Modern Dogma and the Rhetoric of Assent* Wayne Booth gives many useful definitions. Rhetoric is "the art of probing what men believe they ought to believe, rather than proving what is true according to abstract methods"; it is "the art of discovering good reasons, finding what really warrants assent, because any reasonable person ought to be persuaded"; it is "careful weighing of more-or-less good reasons to arrive at more-or-less probable or plausible conclusions—none too secure but better than what would be arrived at by chance or unthinking impulse"; it is the "art of discovering warrantable beliefs and improving those beliefs in shared discourse"; its purpose must not be "to talk someone else into a preconceived view; rather, it must be to engage in mutual inquiry" (Booth 1974a, pp. xiii, xiv, 59, xiii, 137).

The standards of "good" reasons and "warrantable" belief and "plausible" conclusions are to come, as I just said, from the conversations of practitioners themselves, in their laboratories or seminar rooms or conference halls. It is the sort of evaluation that economists and other dealers in ideas do anyway, by professional habit. As Booth says elsewhere (1967, p. 13), "We believe in mutual persuasion as a way of life; we live from conference to conference." Rhetoric is exploring thought by conversation.

The word "rhetoric" will be at first an obstacle to understanding, because it has become debased in common parlance. If "pragmatism" and "anarchism" had not already suffered too, falsely tied to the bottom line or the bomb, the argument might better be called "Pragmatism's Conception of Truth in Economics" (James 1907) or "Outline of an Anarchistic Theory of Knowledge in Economics" (Feyerabend 1975). But the enemies of sophisticated pragmatism and gentle anarchism, as of honest rhetoric, have felt no compunctions about slander, and the slander has discouraged onlookers from examining alternatives to coercion in philosophy, politics, or method. Yet "rhetoric" carries with it a tradition useful in understanding how economists speak. The word, like the other outcasts, is fine and ancient. Its ancient meaning should be more widely known among economists and calculators.

The rhetoric here is that of Aristotle, Cicero, and Quintilian. It has been relatively neglected since the seventeenth century, reduced to second best, second place in status well below the *logic* of inquiry that

From Methodology to Rhetoric

seventeenth-century philosophy claimed to have founded. Born long ago in a manger, away from the palaces of the philosophers, Rhetoric preached within and without the temple; but it was taken at last by the soldiers of the New Science and crucified on the Cartesian cross. Now in the third century after Descartes it has risen from the dead.

The faith built on these miracles is known in literary studies as the New Rhetoric, new in the 1930s and 1940s from the hands of I. A. Richards in Britain and Kenneth Burke in America (Richards 1936; Burke 1950). In philosophy John Dewey and Ludwig Wittgenstein, among others, had begun a little earlier to criticize Descartes's program of scepticism—though of course Descartes had earlier critics too. More recently Karl Popper, Thomas Kuhn, and Imre Lakatos, among others, have undermined the notion that science in fact uses the Cartesian rules of methodical doubt.

The literary, epistemological, and methodological strands have not yet combined into one cord. They belong together, in a study of how scholars speak, a rhetoric of inquiry. On the eve of the Cartesian revolution the French philosopher and educational reformer Peter Ramus (fl. 1550) brought to completion a medieval tendency to relegate rhetoric to mere eloquence, leaving logic in charge of all reasons. In some of the textbooks that Descartes himself read as a boy the merely probable argument was thus subordinated to the indubitable argument. Hostile to classical rhetoric, such a reorganization of the liberal arts was well-suited to the Cartesian program to put knowledge on foundations built by philosophy and mathematics.

Though the best minds followed it, believing for little reason that only mathematical argument was grounded, the program failed. Probable argument was in the meantime kept subordinate to certitude. Even statistics, the science of uncertainty, sought indubitable foundations, resisting at various times the rhetoric of Bayes and Wald. In Rorty's words, following Dewey, the search for the foundations of knowledge by Descartes, Locke, Hume, Kant, Russell, and Carnap was "the triumph of the quest for certainty over the quest for wisdom" (Rorty 1979, p. 61; cf. Dewey 1929, pp. 33, 227). To reinstate rhetoric properly understood is to reinstate wider and wiser reasoning.

The Jokes of Economists Tell

Economists know nothing of this, and would resent the suggestion that their talk is "rhetoric." That they cling to a somber modernist faith does not mean, of course, that in their actual scholarly practices they follow it. One sign of the tension between rhetorical practice and methodological faith is their joking. A memorandum circulated in May 1983 among the staff at the Council of Economic Advisors, for instance, included these pieces of encapsulated unease: "Mankiw's Maxim: No issue in economics has ever been decided on the basis of the facts." "Nihilistic Corollary I: No issue has ever been decided on the basis of theory, either." "Frisch's Restatement: Never let the facts stand between you and the right answer." "McCaleb's Policy Prescription Principle: All policy implications drawn from economics are matters of faith."[4]

Laboratory humor, of course, sustains all modernist scientists. The genre of the Humorous Law, after all, was invented by engineers, and even physicists have their fourth and fifth laws of thermodynamics: No piece of experimental apparatus works the first time it is set up; no experiment gives quite the expected result (Kuhn 1977, p. 184). Another, with an economic flavor, will later become relevant, the First Law of Particle Physics: The shorter the life of a particle, the greater it costs to produce. But the jokes in the physical sciences appear to corrode morale less than in economics. The *Journal of Irreproducible Results* and similar bulletins laugh regularly at the pomposities of Science (and pomposity is the target of similar pieces in the humanities, such as classics [Flory 1983]). The humor, however, takes a notably nasty turn only when it touches certain fields: sociology, medicine, and economics, in all of which methodology has assumed an unusually fetishistic form.

Neurosis comes from attempts to make life, and especially human life, fit into a methodology that did not describe well even the seventeenth-century physics for which it was designed. The neurosis breaks out from time to time in ways far from amusing, and among biological scientists, as I have noted, in occasional fraud. One wonders about similar pressures in economics. The jokes that young American economists tell around the water cooler appear to let out anxieties painful to tell. One might say: Freud knew. One is reminded of the jokes the Eastern Europeans tell about their masters. The situation is so comical that even the masters tell jokes. In 1967 George Stigler, a master of modernism in economics, lampooned the conversations of economics in a brilliantly funny "Conference Handbook" ("Introductory Remark number E: 'I can be very sympathetic with the author; until 2 years ago

---

4. I am indebted to Thomas McCaleb of Florida State University for letting me use this document. His "Capsule Contributions of Nobel Prize Winners in Economics" (example: "Paul Samuelson, 1970: Men are molecules and economics is thermodynamics") is hard to imagine in physics, mathematics, or other fields more sure of their methodological ground.

I was thinking along similar lines' "). It is significant that when confronting the tension between rhetorical practice and methodological faith Stigler wrote a comic essay, rather than a serious study in one of the several fields of economics he has influenced, the history of economic thought. The attitude of the "Handbook" is that the rhetoric of economics is mere game-playing in aid of ego gratification. The serious business of science is quite different, quite unrhetorical, as will be revealed on that happy day when the information theory of oligopoly or the vulgar Marxist theory of the state is brought to a critical test under the auspices of falsificationism.

Other Sciences Have Rhetorics

For all its claims to the scientific priesthood, then, economics is different from the man in the street's image of science, as economists recognize uneasily. But economists should be glad that their subject fits poorly with this image. It fits well with the New Rhetoric, as do studies long foreign to economics, such as the study of literature or of politics or law. Economists, especially neoclassical economists, will sometimes claim that their field is syllogistic, producing from "axioms" a series of "observable implications" by way of lengthy chains of reasoning. Their master Alfred Marshall said long ago that this is poor description and bad advice. Economics actually uses "short, stout links," in Marshall's way of putting it, or, in Aristotle's way, short and informal syllogisms. Economics, in other words, is not a Science in the way we came to understand that word in high school.

But neither, really, are other sciences. Economists can relax. Other sciences, even the other mathematical sciences, are rhetorical. Mathematics, to take the queen herself, appears to an outsider to be the limiting example of objectivity, explicitness, and demonstrability. Surely here only Truth counts, not human words. A long line of intellectuals has believed that here is bedrock, the ultimate authority. Yet standards of mathematical demonstration change. The last fifty years have been a disappointment to followers of David Hilbert, who intended to put mathematics on timeless and indubitable foundations. The historian of mathematics Morris Kline wrote recently that "it is now apparent that the concept of a universally accepted, infallible body of reasoning—the majestic mathematics of 1800 and the pride of man—is a grand illusion." Or again: "There is no rigorous definition of rigor. A proof is accepted if it obtains the endorsement of the leading specialists of the time and employs the principles that are fashionable at the moment. But no standard is universally acceptable today" (Kline 1980, pp. 6, 315).

Kline's point does not apply to the broad interior of mathematics, about which no one has serious doubts, but to its frontiers. An instance is the controversy a few years ago about a computerized proof of the four-color proposition (the proposition that maps can be drawn without ambiguity in four colors only, unproven since Moebius noticed it in 1840). The question was whether a calculation that could be done only by an electronic computer and not ever by a human mind could play a part in a "proof." The rhetoric of proof was in question.

Kline's opinions are somewhat loosely expressed and not accepted unanimously by mathematicians. Apparently more popular are those of Philip J. Davis and Reuben Hersh, whose book *The Mathematical Experience* (1981) was described in the *American Mathematical Monthly* as "one of the masterpieces of our age." Yet Davis and Hersh speak of the crisis of confidence in modern mathematical philosophy in terms nearly identical to Kline's. In the work of the Ideal Mathematician, they say, "the line between complete and incomplete proof is always somewhat fuzzy, and often controversial" (p. 34; cf. p. 40). They quote Solomon Feferman, who writes: "It is also clear that the search for ultimate foundations via formal systems has failed to arrive at any convincing conclusion" (p. 357). Without using the word, Davis and Hersh argue that what is required is a rhetoric of mathematics:

> The dominant style of Anglo-American philosophy . . . tends to perpetuate identification of the philosophy of mathematics with logic and the study of formal systems. From this standpoint, a problem of principal concern to the mathematician becomes totally invisible. This is the problem of giving a philosophical account . . . of preformal mathematics . . . , including an examination of how [it] relates to and is affected by formalization. (p. 344)

They assert that "informal mathematics *is* mathematics. Formalization is only an abstract possibility which no one would want or be able actually to carry out" (p. 349). Real proofs "are established by 'consensus of the qualified' " and are "not checkable . . . by any mathematician not privy to the gestalt, the mode of thought in the particular field. . . . It may take generations to detect an error" (p. 354). Compare again Cardinal Newman, *A Grammar of Assent* (1870): "Strange as it may seem, this contrast between inference [that is, formal demonstration] and assent is exemplified even in the province of mathematics. Argument is not always able to command our assent, even though demonstrative. . . . I am not speaking of short and lucid demonstrations; but of long and intricate mathematical investigations" (chap. 6, sec. 1, item

From Methodology to Rhetoric

6). Newman, who had studied mathematics at Oxford, was in a position to know—admitting that in 1816 mathematics had not yet embarked on the program of rigor that climaxed in Hilbert's school. At the end of the Hilbertian experiment, Davis and Hersh assert,

> The actual experience of all schools—and the actual daily experience of mathematicians—shows that mathematical truth, like other kinds of truth, is fallible and corrigible. . . . It is reasonable to propose a different task for mathematical philosophy, not to seek indubitable truth, but to give an account of mathematical knowledge as it really is—fallible, corrigible, tentative, and evolving, as is every other kind of human knowledge.[5]

Not much in this line has been done, though one astounding book has shown what can be: Imre Lakatos' *Proofs and Refutations: The Logic of Mathematical Discovery* (1976) gives a detailed account of the rhetoric of the Descartes-Euler theorem on polyhedra. The book is a model for how the historian of thought might pursue the rhetoric of knowledge. Lakatos makes clear that mathematicians do not "prove" theorems for ever and ever. They temporarily satisfy their interlocutors in a conversation.

It appears, then, that some problems facing even mathematics on its frontiers are problems of rhetoric, problems in "the art of probing what men believe they ought to believe." Similar points can be made about other sciences, such as paleontology or paleoanthropology or experimental psychology.[6] One can, it seems, make similar remarks even of physics, the favorite of those who seek a prescription for real, objective, positive, predictive science. The axiomatic, austere rhetoric that is supposed to characterize physics does not in fact characterize it well. Theoretical physicists know less formal mathematics than do mathematical economists, a peculiar reversal of the natural order of things. Thinking about physics from the outside has developed similar surprises. In the history and philosophy of physics, the sequence Carnap-Popper-Lakatos-Kuhn-Feyerabend represents a descent, accelerating recently, from the frigid peaks of scientific absolutism into the sweet valleys of anarchic

---

5. Davis and Hersh 1981, p. 406. In a paper for the Iowa Symposium on the Rhetoric of the Human Sciences in March 1984 Davis and Hersh carried these ideas a step closer to rhetorical self-consciousness.

6. On paleontology see the discussion of the Cambrian explosion of life in chapter 6, below, and Campbell 1984. On paleoanthropology, see Landau 1984, which discusses how aesthetic decisions about narrative determine the story of the descent from the trees. On experimental psychology, see Leary 1984 and Carlston 1984.

rhetoric. If economics should imitate other sciences, imitate even the majesty of physics and mathematics (to be sure, there is considerable doubt that it should), then it should perhaps open itself to a wider range of discourse.

Rhetoric, then, might be a way to look at economic talk, and a way to make it better. Better, not less rigorous, difficult, serious, weighty. A rhetoric of economics does not entail a Santa Monica approach to science ("Hey, man, how do you feel about the law of demand today?"). Were economists to give up their quaint modernism and open themselves officially to a wider range of discourse, they would not need to abandon data or mathematics or precision. They would merely agree to examine their language in action, and converse more politely with others in the conversations of mankind.

Mark Perlman, in a review of Terence Hutchison's revival of modernism in economics, put it well: "The essential methodological question is what does it take to convince oneself or others of the validity of an idea? . . . . [Economists] are unwilling to ask themselves the key question, 'What methods must I use in order to persuade an audience?' Economists' self-perception is as of 'an expert.' But economists are not experts; they are basically persuaders" (1978, pp. 528f.). As are we all, we scientists, mathematicians, and economists together.

3   ANTI-ANTI-RHETORIC

The Alternative to Modernism Is Not Irrationalism

It will perhaps be plausible by now that the "objectivity" of economics is exaggerated and, what is more important, overrated. The later explications of economic texts may make it more so. They will try to show, as Polanyi put it (1966, p. 62), that pregnant economic knowledge depends little on "a scientific rationalism that would permit us to believe only explicit statements based on tangible data and derived from these by a formal inference, open to repeated testing." A rhetoric of economics can expose what most economists know anyway about the richness and complexity of economic argument but will not state openly and will not examine explicitly.

The invitation to rhetoric is not, I emphasize, an invitation to "replace careful analysis with rhetoric," or to abandon mathematics in favor of name-calling or flowery language. The good rhetorician loves care, precision, explicitness, and economy in argument as much as the next person. Since he has thought more carefully and explicitly than most people have about the place of such virtues in a larger system of scholarly values, he may even love them more. A rhetorical approach to economic texts is machine-building, not machine-breaking. It is not an invitation to irrationality in argument. Quite the contrary. It is an invitation to leave the irrationality of an artificially narrowed range of argument and to move to the rationality of arguing like human beings. It brings out into the open the arguing that economists do anyway—in the dark, for they must do it somewhere, and the various official rhetorics leave them benighted.

The charge of irrationalism comes easily to the lips of methodological authoritarians. Their notion is that reasoning outside the constricted epistemology of modernism is no reasoning at all. Mark Blaug, for instance, charges that Paul Feyerabend's book *Against Method* "amounts to replacing the philosophy of science by the philosophy of flower power" (1980, p. 44). Feyerabend's flamboyance commonly attracts such dismissive remarks. Yet Stephen Toulmin and Michael Polanyi are nothing if not sweetly reasonable; Blaug lumps them with Feyerabend and attacks the Feyerabend-flavored whole. On a higher level of philosophical sophistication, Imre Lakatos' *Methodology of Scientific Research Programmes* repeatedly tars Polanyi, Kuhn, and Feyerabend with "irrationalism" (e.g., Lakatos 1978, 1:9 n. 1, 76 n. 6, 91 n. 1, 130, and 130 n. 3), emphasizing their sometimes aggressively expressed case against rigid rationalism and ignoring their moderately expressed case for wider rationality.

The tactic is an old one. Richard Rorty notes that "the charges of 'relativism' and 'irrationalism' once leveled against Dewey [were] merely the mindless defensive reflexes of the philosophical tradition which he attacked" (1979, p. 13; cf. Rorty 1982, chap. 9). The brave resolve taken up by the opponents of Dewey, Polanyi, Kuhn, and the rest is "if the choice is between science and irrationality, I'm for science." But that's not the choice.

Yet the doubt still remains. If we agree that rhetoric of various sorts plays a part in economic persuasion, and look on economic argument with a literary eye, are we not abandoning science to its enemies? Will not scientific questions come to be decided by politics or whim? Is not the routine of scientific methodology a wall against irrational and authoritarian threats to inquiry? Are not the barbarians at the gates?

The fear is a surprisingly old and persistent one. In classical times it was part of the debate between philosophy and rhetoric, evident in the unsympathetic way in which the Sophists are portrayed in Plato's dialogues. Cicero viewed himself as bringing the two together, disciplining rhetoric's tendency to become empty advocacy and trope on the one hand and disciplining philosophy's tendency to become useless and inhuman speculation on the other. The classical problem was that rhetoric was a powerful device easily diverted to evil ends, the atomic power of the classical world, and like atomic power the subject of much worrying about its proliferation.

The classical solution was to insist that the orator be good as well as clever: Cato defined him as "vir bonus dicendi peritus," the good man skilled at speaking, a Ciceronian ideal as well. Quintilian, a century after Cicero, said that "he who would be an orator must not only *appear* to be a good man, but cannot *be* an orator unless he *is* a good man" (*Institutio oratoria* 12.1.3).

We are accustomed by modernist presuppositions to talk of "good and bad rhetoric," contrasting Adlai Stevenson's splendid little jokes, say, with Joe McCarthy's vituperation. But it is people, not intellectual devices, that are good or bad. Good science demands good scientists— that is to say, moral, honest, hard-working scientists—not good methodologies. Rhetoric is merely a tool, no bad thing in itself. Or rather, it is the box of tools for persuasion taken together, available to persuaders good and bad. No surprise, then, that the classical world believed it took a "vir bonus" to use the tools right, just as cabala is not to be studied until those years of goodness beyond forty.

The classical worry about the power of rhetoric nonetheless looks quaint to moderns, who know well enough that regressions, computers, experiments, or any of the now canonized methods of persuasion can be used to deceive. The charge of deceit is commonly leveled at statistics, for instance, especially at the statistics most accessible to lay people, the statistical chart. It was a devil's invention of the late eighteenth century. Edward Tufte notes that "for many people the first word that comes to mind when they think about statistical charts is 'lie.' No doubt some graphics do distort the underlying data.... But data graphics are no different from words in this regard, for any means of communication can be used to deceive" (1983, p. 53). So said Aristotle:

> And if it be objected that one who uses such power of speech unjustly might do great harm, *that* is a charge which may be made in common against all good things except virtue, and above all against the things that are most useful.... it is plain that it is the function of one and the same art to discern the real and the apparent means of persuasion, just as it is the function of dialectic [that is, deductive, "compelling" reasoning] to discern the real and the apparent syllogism. (*Rhetoric* 1.1.1355^b.3.14)

There is nothing intrinsic in analogies, appeals to authority, arguments from contraries, or other recognizable pieces of classical rhetoric that make them more subject to evil misuse than the more obviously modern methods. One can only note with regret that the Greeks and Romans were more sensitive to the possibility of misuse and less hypnotized by the claims of method to moral neutrality.

This suspicion of rhetoric is as old as philosophy itself: we cannot use mere plausibility because an eloquent speaker could fool us:

> *Socrates:* And he who possesses the art [of rhetoric] can make the same thing appear to the same people just, now unjust, at will?
> *Phaedrus:* To be sure.
> (*Phaedrus* 261d)

We need something, it has been said, besides the mere social fact that an argument proved persuasive.

To such an objection the answers, then, are two. Science and other epistemologically pure methods can also be used to lie. Our defense must be to discourage lying, not to discourage a certain class of talk. Secondly, talk against talk is self-refuting. The person making it appeals to a social, nonepistemological standard of persuasiveness by the very act of trying to persuade someone that mere persuasion is not enough.

The Political Arguments for Methodology Are Weak

The twentieth century's attachment to limiting rules of inquiry solves, among other things, a German problem. In the German Empire and Reich it was, of course, necessary to propound a split of fact from values in the social sciences if something was to be accomplished free of political interference. And German speculative philosophy, one hears it said, warranted a logical positivist cure. Science had to be demarcated from nonsense, regardless of the cost in tolerance.

One can sympathize with the fixation on the Demarcation Problem among the older generation of observers of science, especially Europeans, and most especially German-speaking Europeans. Axel Leijonhufvud, an economist, and Earlene Craver, a historian, have together interviewed many of the Austro-Hungarian economists of the period before the Second World War. Leijonhufvud interprets positivism and other modernist impulses as reactions to interwar irrationalism. It was not strange, then, that those in close touch with German intellectual life should raise the alarm. In 1938 Terence Hutchison, a British economist sophisticated in the conversations of the Vienna School, could bring its positivism to economics with this justification: "The most sinister phenomenon of recent decades for the true scientist, and indeed to Western civilization as a whole, may be said to be the growth of Pseudo-Sciences no longer confined to hole-and-corner cranks . . . but organized in comprehensive, militant and persecuting mass-creeds. . . . [Testability is] the only principle or distinction practically adoptable which will keep science separate from pseudoscience" (pp. 10–11).

These German habits, though, have spilled over into a quite different world. It is said now that if we are to avoid dread anarchy, we cannot trust each scientist to be his own methodologist. We must legislate a uniform though narrowing method to keep scholars from resorting to figurative and literal murder in aid of their ideas. We ourselves can be trusted with methodological freedom, of course. But the others cannot.

The argument is a strange and authoritarian one, oddly similar to the argument of, say, the Polish authorities against Solidarity or of the Chilean authorities against free politics. It is odd to hear intellectuals raising the alarm against intellectual anarchy. Perhaps their low opinion of the free play of ideas comes from experience in the faculty senate.

Anti-Anti-Rhetoric

A literal anarchist, of course, would be delighted if an absence of methodology led to "anarchy." He views anarchy as no bad thing, merely a society free of the insolence of bureaucrats. The timorous authoritarian, to be precise, trembles not before *an-archos*, the lack of a leader, but before what he fears to be the inevitable result, *chaos*, the war of all against all, a bomb-throwing nihilism. But the inference that anarchism leads to chaos, though often drawn, is unsound. Supposing that chaos will result from the lack of a leader (and a leader's rules of methodological conduct) is a vulgar figure of speech, used most by people hostile in their official methodologies to vulgar figures of speech.

The methodological conservative believes that people will behave frightfully badly if not tamed by a religious belief or a literary canon or a scientific methodology. The notion has little to support it from intellectual history. Good and bad behavior have coexisted with loose and rigid rules of methodology in various times from Abraham to Goebbels. Richard Crosman, though using the word "anarchy" inexactly, attacks in such terms E. D. Hirsch's defense of a conservative canon of literature: "Amazingly enough, all we need to do to rigorously disprove the entire argument of Hirsch's book is to demonstrate that anarchy [by which he means chaos] does not necessarily result from 'subjectivism' and 'relativism.'[1] One may doubt that Hirsch is quite such a sitting duck as this, yet agree that the virtues of a methodology or a canon are doubtful. In an essay called "Anti-Anti-Relativism" Clifford Geertz has argued recently that the fear that chaos will come from abandoning rigid methodologies is unreasonable: "There may be some genuine nihilists out there, along Rodeo Drive or around Times Square," he says, "but I doubt very many have become such as a result of an excessive sensitivity to the claims of other cultures. . . . anti-relativism has largely concocted the anxiety it lives from" (1983, p. 8). And Richard Rorty, too, has joined the fun, philosophically speaking, in his essay "Relativism" (1984a). All of these literary and social scientific and philosophic people are making the same point, an obvious one by now but apparently still worth making: be of good cheer, for it is real politics, not professors' politics, that leads to chaos, or to the revolution.

---

1. Crosman 1980, p. 159. Gerald Graff (1983, pp. 604f.) argues forcefully that literary theories do not have specific "political implications." He wishes to "get beyond the whole dubious project of attaching specific political implications to theories independent of the way they operate in concrete social practice. A theory such as interpretive objectivism doesn't 'imply' any single politics. . . . Making political judgments and classifications of theories requires an adequate analysis of social practices. Is there any reason to think current literary critics possess such an analysis?" Judging from the level of political analysis in, say, Terry Eagleton's *Literary Theory* (1983), one would have to answer no.

To be sure, demarcating Truth from Error, Logic from Illogic, Science from Nonscience does at least clear a space for inquiry free from interference. This is again the German Problem, or nowadays the Slavic Problem. Demarcating science off from ordinary reasoning and claiming for it special epistemological status protects the scientist.

He needs protection nowadays in many countries from the local apparatchik, as in former days from the inquisitor. The official representative of a theocracy thinks he can see what is wrong, from the doctrinal point of view, with an open argument from analogy or an open argument from introspection. He knows about analogies and introspections. But he does not know about syllogisms and statistics (in particular he does not know that they are in fact analogies and introspections); latterly, indeed, he has even been ashamed that he does not know about them, so great has become the prestige of such figures of speech among us. When the Party man in charge of the scientist's soul points to deviationism, the scientist can pull out a sheaf of computer output and ask mildly, "Yes, perhaps I have made a mistake: please show it to me, comrade."

The argument, which is more than an armchair possibility, might justify the adherence to logical positivism and its coreligions in fascist countries between the wars and in certain workers' democratic republics and neofascist regimes since then. But it does not justify clinging to it in an open, plural, and pragmatic society.

An irrational fear that Western intellectual life is about to be overrun by nihilists grips many people. They are driven by it to the practice of Objectivity, Demarcation, and other regimens said to be good for toughening, such as birching and dips in the river on New Year's Day. They were not always so devoted to the strenuous life. The Second World War did it, another of the uncounted costs of Sarajevo, reparations, and all our woe. American historians in the 1940s and early 1950s, for instance, forswore their faith in relativism and took up an icy if unexamined Objectivity (Novick 1984, pp. 29–32). It was a premeditated act of ideology. The war against Fascist and Communist dictatorships, they as much as said, would be won or lost in the seminar room. The point is that these political arguments against an openly rhetorical history or biology or economics are weak.

The alternative to blindered methodologies of modernism, in other words, is not a mob warring against itself but a body of enlightened thinkers engaging in earnest conversation. Perhaps the thinkers would be more enlightened and more earnest when freed to make arguments that actually bore on the questions at issue. At any rate the supposition that this is true has underlain our civilization for quite some time, and the hour is late for abandoning it.

We Wish to Make Plausible Statements, Whether "Scientific" or Not

The other objection to an openly rhetorical economics is not so pessimistic as the fear that the barbarians are at the gates. It is the sunny view that scientific knowledge of a modernist sort may be hard to achieve, even impossible, yet all will be well if we strive in our poor way to reach it. We should, it is said, have a standard of Truth beyond rhetoric. We should aspire to more than mere persuasion.

A spatial metaphor is involved. The cheerful methodologist divides all possible propositions about the world into objective and subjective, positive and normative, scientific and humanistic, hard and soft, as in Figure 1.[2] He supposes the world comes neatly divided along the line of demarcation. The scientist's job is not to decide whether propositions are useful for understanding and for changing the world but to classify them into one or the other half, scientific or nonscientific, and to bring as many as possible into the scientific half.

scientific		humanistic
fact		value
truth		opinion
objective		subjective
positive	The	normative
rigorous	Demarcation	intuitive
precise	Line	vague
things		words
cognition		feeling
hard		soft
yang		yin
male		female

Figure 1. The Task of Science Is to Move the Line

But why? What would be the point of such an exercise? Whole teams of philosophical surveyors have sweated long over the placing of a demarcation line between scientific and other propositions, worrying for instance whether astrology can be demarcated from astronomy; it was the chief activity of the positivist movement for a century. It is unclear why they troubled themselves. The trouble is considerable: Kepler, for example, was a serious astrologer, Newton was a serious alchemist, and many modern scientists take seriously the claims of the paranormal, which causes much trouble for a view a priori that the

2. The diagram and the idea are Booth's (1974a, p. 17), but the idea has been expressed to me by many economists.

word "serious" cannot be spoken together with "astrology" and "alchemy" and "paranormal." We have fallen in love with the problem of finding out where God drew the boundary dividing scientific from nonscientific thinking. But there is no reason to believe that the term "scientific" occurred in God's blueprint of the universe at all.[3] People are persuaded of things in many ways, as will be shown presently for economic persuasion in detail. It is not clear why they should labor at drawing lines on mental maps between one way and another.

Modernists have long faced the embarrassment that metaphor, case study, upbringing, authority, introspection, simplicity, symmetry, fashion, theology, and politics apparently serve to convince scientists as well as they do other folk, and have dealt with the embarrassment by labeling these the "context of discovery." The way scientists discover hypotheses has been held to be distinct from the "context of justification," namely, justifications of a modernist sort. Thomas Kuhn's autobiographical reflections on the matter can stand for the puzzlement in recent years about this ploy: "Having been weaned intellectually on these distinctions and others like them, I could scarcely be more aware of their import and force. For many years I took them to be about the nature of knowledge, and .... yet my attempts to apply them, even *grosso modo*, to the actual situations in which knowledge is gained, accepted, and assimilated have made them seem extraordinarily problematic" (Kuhn 1970, p. 9).

The claim of the modernist methodologist is that "ultimately" all knowledge in science can be brought into the hard, objective part of the rectangle. Consequently, in certifying propositions as really scientific there is great emphasis placed on *"conceivable falsification"* and *"some future test."* The apparent standard is the modernist one that we must find plausible only the things we cannot possibly doubt. Yet even this peculiar standard is not in fact applied: a conceivable but practically impossible test takes over the prestige of the real test, free of its labor.

The silent substitution of a conceivable test left to the future for a present test left undone needs to be challenged. One is not doing science merely because one has promised ultimately to do it. The substitution is identical to the step taken in the "new welfare economics" of the 1940s. Economists wished to equate as morally similar *actual* compensation of those hurt during a Pareto optimal move with a *hypothetical* compensation not actually paid, as in the Hicks-Kaldor test. It

3. Lakatos 1976, pp. 67–68: "You have fallen in love with the problem of finding out where God drew the boundary dividing Eulerian from non-Eulerian polyhedra. But there is no reason to believe that the term 'Eulerian' occurred in God's blueprint of the universe at all."

was said that if conceivably we could compensate unemployed auto workers out of the gain from freer trade with Japan, then we should go ahead with freer trade. We do not actually have to pay the compensation.

The step is morally dubious, though much taken. Likewise, a properly identified econometric measurement of the out-of-sample properties of macroeconomic policy is "operational," that is, conceivable. Yet for all the scientific prestige the conceivability lends to talk about it, there are serious doubts that it is possible. While economists are waiting for the ultimate econometric test, they might better seek wisdom in the humanism of historical evidence on regime changes or of introspection about announcements of new monetary policies. And of course they do.

The point is that one cannot tell whether an assertion is persuasive by knowing from which portion of the scientific/humanistic rectangle it came. One can tell whether it is persuasive only by thinking about it. Not all regression analyses are more persuasive than all moral arguments; not all controlled experiments are more persuasive than all introspections. People should not discriminate against propositions on the basis of epistemological origin. There are some subjective, soft, vague propositions that are more persuasive than some objective, hard, precise propositions.

The economist is more persuaded that he will buy less oil when its price doubles than that the age of the universe is 16 billion years. He might even be more persuaded of it than he is that the earth goes around the sun. He has the astronomical facts only from the testimony of people he trusts, a reliable though not of course infallible source of useful persuasions.[4] The economic fact he has from looking into himself and seeing it sitting there smiling out at him. It is not because the law of demand has predicted well or has passed some statistical test that it is believed—although such further tests are not to be scorned. The "scientific" character of the tests is irrelevant.

It may be claimed in reply, and often is, that people can agree on precisely what a regression coefficient means but cannot agree precisely on the character of their introspection. This is false: people can converse on the character of their introspections, and do so habitually—about their aesthetic reactions, say, to a painting by Brueghel or a theory by Lucas. The conversations often reach conclusions as precise as human talk can. But even if it were true that regression is more precise, this

4. The "fact" that the earth goes around the sun is of course not a fact in a simple modernist sense at all. It depends on one's coordinates. As Nelson Goodman says (1983, p. 103), "That we can make the stars dance, as Galileo and Bruno made the earth move and the sun stop, not by physical force but by verbal invention, is plain enough."

would not be a good argument for economists to abandon introspection in economics. Introspections, even if imprecise, can be better than regression estimates infected with misspecifications and errors in the variables. That the regression uses numbers, precise as they look, is irrelevant. To speak precisely, precision means low variance of estimation; but if the estimate is greatly biased, it will tell precisely nothing.

Saying merely that an argument is "scientific" by some narrow canon does not say much. We know that the stealing of strips of land and sheaves of grain troubled the villager of medieval England. One way we know it is the confession of Avarice in *Piers Plowman:*

> If I go to the plough, I pinch so narrow
> That a foot's land or a furrow to fetch I would
> Of my next neighbor, take of his earth;
> And if I reap, overreach, or give advice to him that reap
> To seize for me with his sickle what I never sowed.
> (Langland, passus 13, lines 370–75)

Another is a properly scientific count of the percentage of cases in the manorial court dealing with strip and sheaf stealing, with due regard to what we know of the frailties of the statistics. There is no need to choose between the qualitative and the quantitative evidence: an intelligent rhetoric of economic history would give privilege to neither. Both have some weight, the one on account of the artistic excellence of the poem (a great poet sees well) and the other on account of the apparent definiteness of the offense (one case, one strip, usually). In view of our difficulty in saying much about the world, such catholicity in argument seems sensible.

An extreme case unnecessary for the argument here will make the point. You are more strongly persuaded that it is wrong to murder than that inflation is always and everywhere a monetary phenomenon. This is not to say that similar techniques of persuasion will be applicable to both propositions. It says merely that each within its field, and each therefore subject to the methods of honest persuasion appropriate to the field, the one achieves a greater certitude than the other.

To deny the comparison is to deny that reason and the partial certitude it can bring applies to nonscientific subjects, a common but unreasonable position. There is no reason why specifically scientific persuasiveness ("at the .05 level the coefficient on M in a regression of prices of 30 countries over 30 years is insignificantly different from 1.0") should take over the whole of persuasiveness, leaving moral persuasiveness incomparably inferior to it. Arguments like "murder violates the reasonable moral premise that we should not force other people to be means to our ends" or "from behind a prenatal veil of ignorance of which side of the murderer's revolver we would be after birth we would enact laws against murder" are persuasive in comparable units. Not always, but sometimes, they are more persuasive, better, more probable (Toulmin 1958, p. 34). Frank Knight, whose thinking is congenial to this rhetorical approach, made a similar point in similar words (1940, p. 164). Of the basic postulates of economics, attested by "sympathetic intro-spection," he said, "We surely 'know' these propositions better, more confidently and certainly, than we know the truth of any statement about any concrete physical fact or event . . . and fully as certainly as we know the truth of any axiom of mathematics."

We believe and act on what persuades us—not what persuades a majority of a badly chosen jury, but what persuades well-educated participants in the conversations of our civilization and of our field. To attempt to go beyond persuasive reasoning is to let epistemology limit reasonable persuasion.

The Philosophical Objections to Rhetoric Are Not Persuasive

Against this stands the ancient notion that we are all in pursuit of Truth—as against lower-case truths, such as the tempera-ture in Iowa City this afternoon or the quality of the president's judg-ment in foreign affairs. The pursuit of Truth is said to be very different from mere persuasion. Yet when set beside the actual behavior of scientists and scholars the notion looks strange.

The strangeness is not that the scientists and scholars in fact pursue Falsehood. They do not. They pursue other things, but things which have only an incidental relation with Truth. They do so not because they are inferior to philosophers in moral fiber but because they are human. Truth-pursuing is a poor theory of human motivation and nonoperational as a moral imperative. The human scientists pursue persuasiveness, prettiness, the resolution of puzzlement, the conquest of recalcitrant details, the feeling of a job well done, and the honor and income of office: as Nelson Goodman says (1983, p. 105), they pursue "varieties of rightness other than truth." It must be borne in mind that it is only a philosophical doctrine that we pursue Truth.

The philosophical doctrine is not so decisively True, furthermore, that it should be allowed to overwhelm our common sense in the matter of how much weight to place on rhetoric. The very idea of Truth—with a captial *T*, something beyond what is merely persuasive to all concerned—is a fifth wheel, inoperative except that it occasionally comes loose and hits a bystander. If we decide that the quantity theory of money or the marginal productivity theory of distribution is persuasive, interesting, useful, reasonable, appealing, acceptable, we do not also need to know that it is True. Its persuasiveness, interest, usefulness, and so forth come from particular arguments: "Marginal productivity theory, for one thing, is a consequence of rationality in the hiring of inputs" (and we think highly of rationality). "The quantity equation, for one thing, is a simple framework for macroeconomics" (and we think highly of simplicity).

These are particular arguments, good or bad. After making them, there is no point in asking a last, summarizing question: "Well, is it True?" It's whatever it is—persuasive, interesting, useful, and so forth. The particulars suggest answerable rhetorical questions that might matter, such as what exactly the use of the fact is or to whom exactly it is persuasive. There is no reason to search for a general quality called Truth, which answers only the unanswerable question "What is it that is in the mind of God?" Such and such and so and so accord with a human checklist of arguments persuasive to humans. That is all ye need to know.

The usual way of rebutting such an argument is to say that one *must* have a theory of truth, an epistemology. Recall the argument that one *must* have a methodology. How can one talk without one? (A light bulb goes on in the mind of the speaker.) Indeed, talking *against* epistemology is *itself* epistemological talk—talk *about* epistemology, which therefore *does* exist. (People who think they have discovered a neat philosophical argument favor italics.) Willard Quine calls the argument Plato's Beard, in honor of the man who got most famously tangled in it: "Nonbeing must in some sense be [or, in the italic style, *be*], otherwise what is it [or what *is* it] that there is not?" (Quine 1948, pp. 2f.). With it, he points out, one can prove the existence of nonbeings such as Pegasus, pigs with wings, and, here, epistemology: that is to say, the existence of an actual referent for any reference in the language. The point is a *reductio ad absurdum*. And if the reduction were not considered absurd, it would still not imply that serious people should spend much time thinking about the referent in question. The serious issues are rhetorical—how we become persuaded, in the actual case at hand—not epistemological.

Epistemology, as we have seen, has had its uses, and many uplifting sermons have been heard on pursuing Truth. They are more uplifting, to be sure, when the threat to the values thus celebrated is genuine: the preacher of the gospel facing death in the jungle looks more courageous than the same man thundering in Devon to a congregation of shepherds and military wives. The defenders of truth and rationality in the West have a habit of using the rhetoric of danger without really facing it. Listen to Lawrence Stone, that best of historians and worst of methodologists, issuing a call to arms from the letters column of *Harper's*:

> Today, we need to stand shoulder to shoulder against the growing army of enemies of rationality. By that I mean the followers of the fashionable cult of absolute relativism, emerging from philosophy, linguistics, semiotics, and deconstructionism. These . . . tend to deny the possibility of accurate communication by the use of language, the force of logical deduction, and the very existence of truth and falsehood. (1984, p. 5)

But the most serious minds doubt Truth's very existence, if it is construed as something standing there in the absolute, waiting to be observed by the lone scientist or historian. Nelson Goodman, no enemy of rationality, writes: "The scientist who supposes that he is single-mindedly dedicated to the search for truth deceives himself. . . . He seeks system, simplicity, scope; and when satisfied on these scores he tailors truth to fit. He as much decrees and discovers the laws he sets forth, as much designs and discerns the patterns he delineates" (1978, p. 18). Nor was Frank Knight prone to semiological fevers. Yet in his review of Hutchison's positivism in economics he declared, with many reasonable people since Gorgias of Liontini: "Testing observations is chiefly . . . a social activity or phenomenon. This fact makes all knowledge of the world of sense observation . . . itself a social activity. . . . A conscious, critical social consensus is of the essence of the idea of objectivity or truth" (1940, p. 156). These sober people, and many more, agree that Truth is a fifth wheel and persuasion social.

A specialization of the argument that we pursue Truth is that we pursue Logic. This, too, is questionable. In questioning it, again I do not mean to imply that it would be better to become illogical. Formal logic is fine, within its limits. What goes wrong is that formal logic is treated sometimes as all of reason.

The impulse to treat it this way shows up especially in lists of fallacies. Fallacy-mongering reveals a legislative attitude towards method. It is no surprise that Jeremy Bentham, confident of his ability to legislate for others in matters of method as in matters of education, prisons, and government, had compiled from his notes *The Book of Fallacies* (1824). David Hackett Fischer's book *Historians' Fallacies* (1970) has such a flaw: it takes as "fallacious" the many arguments that may be merely supporting, if by themselves inconclusive.

Elementary texts on logic exhibit this older attitude, that a form of words that cannot be fitted into a valid syllogism is to be judged fallacious—which is to say, bad argument. Irving Copi's fifth edition of *Introduction to Logic* (1978), for instance, praises Fischer's zeal in rooting out fully 112 different forms of fallacious heresy in the works of historians, and then turns to attack as "fallacies" (pp. 87, 91) the argument from authority, from the character of one's opponent, from equal ignorance, and many other arguments used daily by scientists, by historians, by judges (as Copi notes without realizing the significance), and, most significant of all, by philosophers themselves.[5] L. Susan Stebbing's little book, first published in 1943 but reissued many times since to successive generations of British students of philosophy, takes an even firmer stand against arguments merely persuasive to all concerned: "We can *know* our conclusions to be true only when we *know* both that the premises are true and that they imply the conclusion. For this purpose we *reason*" (1943, p. 160). Observe the force of her italics here, a bit of yelling in the cause of reason. She goes on to inveigh against "the orator," whose aim, she believes, "is to induce belief at all costs" and whose "appeal is not to reason but to uncontrolled emotion, not to considerations logically relevant but to prejudice."

It is notable that these logicians, committed presumably to the serious study of reason, do not exhibit serious understanding of rhetoric and its history. Copi sneers at rhetoric (pp. 75, 242), though he does admit (p. 255) that there were "older times when logic and rhetoric were more closely connected than they are today." Stebbing is less tolerant, but she first wrote in the decade in which rhetoric touched its nadir, and may be excused for using a little uncontrolled emotion and prejudice in defense of even a narrow idea of reasoning.

It is less excusable, though, that in narrow terms the defenses of narrowness are circular (the fallacy *petitio principii*). The rhetorical device is to use words like "true" or "correct" or "sound" or "what we know" (let us abandon "valid" for whatever uses the logician wishes to put it) to mean "obeying all the laws of a narrow logic as laid down by the local fallacymongerer" (Stebbing 1943, p. 161; Copi 1978, p. 87). Since the conclusion has been assumed, by definition, it is no trick to reduce truth, correctness, soundness, and what we know to formal logic

5. His Chapter 3, "Informal Fallacies," deals with such errors. A later chapter, "Analogy and Probable Inference," is strictly segregated, as is customary in philosophical exposition, from reasoning that is properly syllogistic (and therefore "demonstrative," "necessary," and so forth). There Copi admits charmingly that of course "most of our own everyday inferences are by analogy," presumably also the philosopher's own. He does not consider the possibility that his everyday deductions may also be analogies.

of a syllogistic sort, casting out the rest as fallacy.[6] It has taken a long time for Newman's reasoned complaint, written in 1841 (1870, p. 90), to become a common opinion among philosophers themselves: "Logicians are more set on concluding rightly, than on right conclusions."

Anti-Modernism Is Nice

The larger issue reaches well beyond technical philosophy, and beyond the philosophical misapprehensions of economists. The issue is modernism, economics being merely one field ready to shed it. Modernism served in earlier wars, I have said, and is not to be scorned. There were reasons for its long dominance. But modernism is decrepit now, and in its wild youth begat scientism, the doctrine that the only cognitive life is the scientific. Scientism has damaged the ability to understand. For unpersuasive reasons it has confined psychologists (until recently) to theories that do not use the unconscious mind and has confined economists (until recently) to theories that do not use psychology. Perhaps it is time to stop.

An economist who thinks so, and wishes a broader and more cogent conversation to begin in economics, does not have to join the antimodernists in everything they do. The antimodernists have been trying to revive certain writers long neglected, especially in the English-speaking world, who would not have accepted the modernist/scientistic orthodoxy as defined around 1950. These include such *bêtes noires* as the sophists, Cicero, scholastic philosophy, and Hegel. More recently they include the American pragmatists, long out of philosophical fashion, whose work was once viewed as an amusing but after all rather crude approximation to what was done properly in Vienna or Cambridge; of whom one might say,

> I write them out in a verse:
> James and Dewey and Peirce.
> Sweetness and light enough,
> Mathematically not up to snuff.[7]

---

6. This is the procedure, again, in J. L. Mackie's article "Fallacies" in *The Encyclopedia of Philosophy* (1967). Here the deduction of "ought" from "is" is described flatly as "an error exposed by Hume, but still frequently committed" (p. 178). In the past few decades, for instance, it has been frequently committed by Willard Quine, John Searle, J. L. Austin, and other notorious advocates of fallacy.

7. The arrival of intellectuals fleeing interwar Europe in fields as varied as philosophy, architecture, and painting killed off characteristically American, Midwestern, and milder versions of modernism in favor of a harsher European type.

The antimodernists themselves are as alarming as their heroes: they have included Continental philosophers such as Heidegger, Habermas, Adorno, Foucault, and other alarming people, certain unconventional observers of science (Polanyi, Koestler), renegade analytic philosophers such as Stephen Toulmin and Richard Rorty, social scientists using nonquantitative methods (from Freud to Piaget and Fraser to Geertz), sociologists of science after Robert Merton, philosophers and historians of science after Thomas Kuhn, and, most alarming of all, literary critics in profusion.

An attack on the narrowness of modernist rhetoric in economics does not depend on accepting such folk as allies. Richard Rorty has recently named them "the new fuzzies" (1984a), a term of affection (for he is one), evoking Winnie ille Pu discoursing on philosophy. In our actual practice in daily life and thought, though, we are all fuzzies, even we economists, however glinty and Darth Vaderish we think we are made by mastery of the identification problem and the Kuhn-Tucker conditions.

The economist inclined to snort at Heidegger and Dewey might reflect, too, on how he himself decides on allies. He does not check every new theorem devised by a mathematical economist or every new fact discovered by a historical economist. Yet he smiles on their conversations. It is not a good investment to doubt all testimony. Cartesian doubt, to put it economically, is inefficient. For some purposes it is enough for the economist to know that intelligent and honest economic scientists take such stuff seriously. Such authority often suffices, and should. In other words, the first lesson in antimodernist rhetoric is that the authority of serious conversations elsewhere should not be lightly obeyed, nor yet lightly scorned.

Rhetoric Is Good for You

The thinking about thinking that suits antimodernism is rhetoric. Rhetoric is not a new methodology. It is antimethodology. It points out what we actually do, what seems to persuade us and why. At the end of his treatment of the rhetoric of analytic philosophy (1980, p. 260) Stanley Rosen declared that his argument

> is not offered as a new theory or how to philosophize, but as an account of what we actually do. The positive task of the philosopher is to fecundate his analytic skills with dreams, and to discipline his dreams with analysis. I cannot provide him with a manual of rules and regulations governing this activity. There

are no rules and regulations for being reasonable, and certainly no rules and regulations for dreaming reasonable dreams.

To repeat: "There are no rules and regulations for being reasonable." Being reasonable is weighing and considering all reasons, not merely the reasons that some methodology or epistemology or logic claims to be stations of the cross along the one path to Justified True Belief. A methodology that claims the historical dialectic or the hypothetico-deductive model or phenomenology or historical *verstehen* or any one style of giving reasons to be The One is probably unreasonable. The reasonable rhetorician cannot write down his rules. They are numberless, because they cover all reasons, and bromidic, because they cover all circumstances. Above all, they change. The rhetorician demands a cheerful, mature, and sober clientele that can bear to face a world of hap without a drink in hand.

The modernist pedlar, on the other hand, makes large claims, and the rubes gather. If you will but be a modernist, says he to the amazed economists gathering at the tent, and scientistic and whatever else is current, following its rules, you will be a good economist, my friend, whether or not you are honest or imaginative or good. There's nothing to it, my lad.

Little wonder that youths in science are drunk with methodology: "Ale, man, ale's the stuff to drink / For fellows whom it hurts to think / . . . . / And faith, 'tis pleasant till 'tis past: / The mischief is that 'twill not last." One can understand the attraction of methodological formulas immediately potable. A textual critic equipped with the formula "the more sincere text is the better" or an economist with "the statistically significant coefficient should be retained" is ready for work. That his work will be wrong bothers him less than that he will not get the stuff out at all unless he possesses, as he is inclined to say, *some* methodology. Output, man, output's the stuff to get, / So deans and chairmen will not fret.

The ironic vocabulary of science reflects an uneasiness about taking methodology as against taking thought: the scientist speaks of "turning the crank" or "grinding it out." Taking thought would seem better than crank-turning, and a rhetorical criticism of economics is an invitation to take thought. What, one asks oneself in a rhetorical manner, is the root metaphor in my work? Do I really have evidence for its aptness? I have appealed to an authority here: is it a good one? There my formal language claims the Objectivity of Science: is the point I'm making really up to it? Here I am making a quantitative argument: what are my conversational standards of bigness? Should I simulate the results mathematically, to show that they have quantitative bite? I appeal to "theoretical reasons" in this argument: do I mean pretty diagrams? In what way exactly are they pretty? I depend heavily on introspection for that point: how can I increase my confidence that my audience has the same introspection? I appeal to symmetry at this point: have I appealed symmetrically? Is there another symmetry I might as well impose, too? What role do definitions play in my argument? How can I refine my appeal to the argument *a fortiori?*

Rhetorical criticism is an invitation to take thought but not, to repeat, a formula for good thinking. The very economics of the matter, to make an argument *ad hominem*, makes such formulas impossible. A scholar in possession of a scholarly formula more specific than Work and Pray would be a scientific millionaire. Scientific millionaires are not common. Methodology claims prescience in scientific affairs. The difficulty with prescience is that it is exactly "pre-science"—that is, knowing things before they are known, contradicting itself. Methodology entails this contradiction. It pretends to know how to achieve knowledge before the knowledge to be achieved is in place. Life is not so easy.

Even anarchists in methodology face this difficulty if they propose actual policies for science. No one can know what the scientific future will bring: it may be that the centralized, bureaucratized, methodized science that threatens to make the scientists into crank-turners, despite the evidence from the history of science that progress in science is seldom advanced and often retarded by such a structure, is just the ticket for the twenty-first century. Reasonable arguments can be made on both sides. The historical evidence is merely one strong argument among others, not the end of the conversation.

The best one can do, then, is to recommend what is good for science now, and leave the future to the gods. What is good for science now, to recur to an earlier theme, is good scientists, in most meanings of "good." A rhetorical criticism of economics can perhaps make economists more modest, tolerant, and self-aware, and improve one of the conversations of mankind.

4

THE LITERARY

CHARACTER OF

ECONOMIC SCIENCE

Science Uses Literary Methods

The French and German triads that correspond to our plain English "natural sciences, social sciences, and humanities" are "les sciences naturelles, les sciences sociales, et les *sciences* humaines" and "die Naturwissenschaften, die Sozialwissenschaften, und die Geistes-*wissenschaften*." In both the term for studies of poetry, language, and philosophy—studies humanistic and decidedly literary in form—includes a "science" word. But in French and German, and in other languages, the term is not properly understood as English "science," with what that august word connotes of numbers, laboratory coats, and decisive experiments publicly observed.

Although German usage, like German politics, has since the Second World War bent a little to the ways of Britain and America, the German speaker has on the whole less opportunity to use his word *Wissenschaft*, or the French speaker his *science*, as a club with which to beat word folk. Nor, on the other side, can it be so easily used the way it is by the English-speaking literati, as a curse against that blackest art, the anti-art, the bane of sweetness and light. It means merely "disciplined inquiry," as distinct from, say, journalism or common sense. It does not mean "quantitative" and does not warrant use as an epithet, wine-dark Science or the Scientist of the golden hair, as Lord Kelvin of Kelvin's Dictum used it in 1883: "When you cannot measure it, when you cannot express it in numbers, your knowledge is of a meagre and unsatisfactory kind"; and added, "It may be the beginning of knowledge, but you have scarcely in your thoughts advanced to the stage of *science*." In French and German—and, I am told, in Hungarian, Italian, Korean, Spanish, Swedish, and Turkish— the science word does not have this epistemological clout.

The word "science" began to be used in the honorific sense by the

English only in the nineteenth century. The earliest citation in sense 5b of the *Oxford English Dictionary* is 1867, from W. G. Ward in the *Dublin Review* for April, p. 255n (italics added): "We shall . . . use the word 'science' in the sense *which Englishmen so commonly give to it*; as expressing physical and experimental science, to the exclusion of theological and metaphysical." (The *Supplement* describes this 5b nowadays as of course "the dominant sense in ordinary use.") Earlier it meant "studies," as in "classical studies"—*Altertumswissenschaft* in German. In English one cannot imagine "classical science." The Wildhagen/Heraucourt German dictionary (1972) gives *die klassiche Wissenschaft* as "humanities" (clearly in the older sense of the English word) and *die philologisch-historische Wissenschaften* as "arts" (in the British academic usage, contrasted, again, with "science").

The point is that the damned foreigners, uncharacteristically, have gotten it right. "Literary criticism is a science" or (to get back to the issue at hand) "Economics is a science" should not be the fighting words they are in English. The fighting lacks purpose because, as our friends across the water could have told us, nothing important depends on its outcome. Economics in particular is merely a disciplined inquiry into the market for rice or the scarcity of love. Economics is a collection of literary forms, not a science. Indeed, science is a collection of literary forms, not a science. And literary forms are scientific.

These rude remarks, whispered by philosophers, sociologists, and historians of science in the past decade, do not imply that science is inconclusive or that literature is cold-blooded. The point is that science uses art for urgent practical purposes daily. The aesthetic judgments necessary before one out of the theories in particle physics is selected for the expensive experiment it requires for testing does not make science arbitrary or flimsy. As Steven Weinberg said recently about an experiment testing his piece of the physicist's art: "That experiment cost some $30 to $40 million dollars, not for the accelerator you understand, just for the experiment using the accelerator. . . . This is an enormous commitment of your money and our time, one that can only be made when the judgment has been made that the theory is worth testing, and that judgment is very often entirely a matter of how beautiful we think the theory is" (1983, p. 20). From 1967 to 1971 Weinberg's theory was considered too ugly to test. He points out that no one would have financed the British expedition to the South Seas in 1919 to test Einstein's theory had it been thought ugly. Kenneth Burke, coming from the literary side, speaks of the persuasiveness of elegant forms: "A yielding to the form prepares for assent to the matter identified with it" (1950, p. 58).

The Literary Character of Economic Science

And of course art, in turn, uses "scientific" figures of speech for urgent practical purposes too. Statistics, for example, are figures of speech in numerical dress. That textual criticism since the Renaissance has depended heavily on the logic of probability and the counting of frequencies does not make the improvement of our text of Manilius something foreign to its literary appreciation.[1] Wayne Booth attacks the pretensions of Popperian falsifiability to be the meaning of meaningfulness. Yet he notes (1974, p. 103) that "the test is a powerful one, in dealing with certain problems; I use it myself in trying to test my own guesses about how literary works are put together." The statistical and scientific tests, though, should not expand to take over all persuasions: "Stated as a universal dogma [falsifiability] is highly questionable." The only dogma worth promulgating is a broad-minded one, namely, that in a good argument the artistic and scientific modes of thought will interpenetrate each other. Modernists view the interpenetration of science and art as a contravention of God's law, likely to give birth to monsters. But in this they are mistaken.

The project here is to overturn the monopolistic authority of science in economics by questioning the usefulness of the demarcation of science from art. To show that economics resembles literary criticism, philology, and social theory as much as particle physics and dam-building can either thrill economists with a wild surmise or leave them trembling from identity outraged.

Though the project might outrage some economists, noneconomists will incline rather to fatigued indifference. They have never thought very much of the scientific claims of the subject anyway. All they know about economics is just what they read in the papers, but they know what they don't like, and besides, it ain't Science. But this approach is wrong. For one thing, it falls for demarcation, supposing, without thinking about it much, that science is demarcated from nonscience.

For another, economics *is* science, a successful sort at that. Economics explains as much about business people and resources as evolution explains about animals and plants, for identical reasons. No one who knows the subject will deny it; those who do not know it can become persuaded by reading Mancur Olson's *Logic of Collective Action* or Thomas Schelling's *Micromotives and Microbehavior* or another of the accessible jewels of the discipline. The claim here is not the vulgar figure of logic

1. See, for example, Willis 1972, p. 24, on stemmatic theory and p. 42 on the theory of errors. Anyone who believes the study of literature leads to a softening of the mind and mettle should be made to read this book, supplemented by Reynolds and Wilson 1974 and Housman 1961. The height of this sort of thing is John G. Griffith, "A Taxonomic Study of the Manuscript Tradition of Juvenal" (1968).

that economics is mere humanism because it is a failure as a science. The claim is that all science is humanism (and no "mere" about it) because that is all there is for humans.

Proofs of the Law of Demand Are Mostly Literary

Economics is scientific, then, but literary too. Saying that something is "literary" is saying that one can talk of it in ways that sound a lot like the things people say about drama, poetry, novels, and the study of them. Compare the performative character of the sentence "Economics is scientific." The sentence carries with it the implication that things can be said about economics and economies that use mathematics; that economists will emulate the rhetoric of controlled experiment; that economics will have "theorems" from the mathematics and "findings" from the experiments; that it will be "objective" (whatever the word might mean); and even that the world it constructs, to use Nelson Goodman's way of talking, will have a certain character, of maximizing and equilibrium, captured in the perspicacious phrase "the unreasonable effectiveness of mathematics." All these implications about economics are persuasive.

But equally persuasive are other implications, usually and erroneously thought to be antithetical, implied in the sentence "Economics is literary." The literary character of economics shows at various levels, from most abstract to most concrete, from Methodology down to the selling of diamonds.

The workaday methods of economic scientists, for example, are literary, an inescapable remark when one recognizes that the scientific paper is, of course, a literary genre with an actual author, an implied author, an implied reader, a history, and a form (see Bazerman 1981; Bazerman forthcoming). When an economist says, as he very frequently does, "The demand curve slopes down," he is using the English language; and if he is using it to persuade, as he very frequently is, he is a rhetor, whether he knows or likes it or not. A scientific paper, and an assertion within it such as this Law of Demand (that when the price of something goes up the demand for something goes down), does literary deeds. The economic scientist is self-evidently a linguistic actor, and to his performance can be applied the dramatistic notions of the literary critic Kenneth Burke, or of the philosophers J. L. Austin and John Searle. Scientific assertions are speech acts in a scene of scientific tradition by the scientist-agent through the agency of the usual figures of speech for purposes of describing nature or mankind better than the next fellow.

The error is to think that one is engaged in mere making of propositions, about which formal logic speaks, when in fact one is engaged—all day, most days—in persuasive discourse, aimed at some effect, about which rhetoric speaks. The pragmatists said this, too. Beliefs expressed in words are to be judged by their effects or, as it was put by William James with "disastrous felicity" (Burke), by their "cash value." Scientists are trying to persuade other scientists when they affirm a law.

The way they persuade others draws mostly on the usual arguments, arguments that one might see in *Areopagitica* or "A Modest Proposal for Preventing the Children of Ireland from Being a Burden to Their Parents or Country." Consider the good reasons that economists believe the Law of Demand to be persuasive:

1. Sometimes, certain very sophisticated statistical tests of the law applied to entire economies, in which every allowance has been made for bias and incompleteness, have resulted, after a good deal of hand-wringing and computer-squeezing, in the diagonal elements of certain matrices being negative at the 5 percent level of significance. And sometimes they have not. Even the inventors of fully identified, complete systems of demand equations, such as Hans Theil, have no great confidence in the result. A shift of one metaphor here, a shift of one appeal to authority there, and the "proof" would be valid no longer.

2. Less comprehensive but more numerous demonstrations of the law have been attempted market by market. Agricultural economists, especially, have for fifty years been fitting demand curves to statistics on corn and hogs. Again, the curves sometimes give the right slope, and sometimes don't. The most elaborate of such studies—Houthakker and Taylor's study of all commodities in the American economy (1970)— found that the law was weak. In any case the thought before calculation that forces the law to work (in other words, the specification) contains elements of introspection, analogy, and other sorts of common sense embarrassing to the claims of mindless Objectivity. Econometricians have begun to take heed (Leamer 1978; Cooley and Leroy 1981). But they need help in thinking about their before-calculation rhetoric.

3. Some economists have tried recently to subject the law to a few experimental tests. After a good deal of throat-clearing they have found it to be true for clearheaded rats and false for confused humans (Battaglio et al. 1981), an interesting result which no one worries about too much.

These three arguments are properly scientific, although only the third quite matches the received view of scientific method. The modernist arguments yield mixed results. Does this leave economists uncertain about the Law of Demand? Certainly not. Belief in the Law of Demand is the distinguishing mark of the economist, demarcating him from other social scientists more even than his other peculiar beliefs. Economists believe it ardently. Only some part of their ardor, therefore, is properly Scientific. The rest is below the demarcation line:

4. Introspection is an important source of belief. The economic scientist asks himself, "What would I do if the price of gasoline doubled?" If properly socialized in economics he will answer, "I will consume less." In similar fashion a poet might ask herself what she might do if she saw heather or a wave; a textual critic might ask himself how he would react to a line if "quod, o patrona virgo" were emended to "quidem est, patroni et ergo."

5. Thought experiments (common in physics) are persuasive too. The economic scientist asks in view of his experience of life and his knowledge of economics what other people might do if the price of gasoline doubled. A novelist, likewise, might ask how Huck would respond to Jim's request to come up on the raft; or a critic might ask how an audience would react to the sacrifice of Coriolanus.

6. Cases in point, though not controlled experiments or large samples, persuade to some degree. The biggest recent triumph for the Law of Demand was the oil embargo of 1973–74: the doubling of gasoline prices caused gasoline consumption to decline, although noneconomists predicted it would not. This is narrative, not statistical fit (although statisticians are moving towards a rhetoric that a literary person would recognize as narrative: Mosteller and Tukey 1977; Leamer 1978). The narrative tells. In the same way, Wayne Booth remarks, "The most sensitive book-length theological account we can imagine ... lacks something that men know together when in answer to the question, 'What is the life of man?' they answer, 'There was once in Bethlehem. . . .' " (1974, p. 186).

7. The lore of the marketplace persuades. Business people, for instance, believe that the Law of Demand is true, for they cut prices when they wish to raise the quantity demanded. They have the incentive of their livelihood to know rightly. What mere professor would dispute such testimony? To do so would in fact contradict a fundamental conviction among professors of economics (and among professors of ecology and evolutionary biology too) that opportunities for profit are not usually left lying about untaken. The argument is *ad hominem*, an argument from the character of its audience. In the same way a literary critic might try to defend the authority of the author—who, after all, has an incentive to know what he means—against the claims of the playful reader making his own text out of "Beauty is truth, truth beauty."

The Literary Character of Economic Science

8. The lore of the academy persuades too. If many wise economists have long affirmed the Law of Demand, what mere latecomer would dispute their testimony? All sciences operate this way, building on the testimony of forerunners. The argument from authority is not decisive, of course, but must be given weight. Scholarship could not advance if all questions were reopened every ten years. In the same way Keats followed the tradition of the pastoral as preparation for the epic; and New Criticism worked away in its tradition undisturbed by thoughts beyond the text.

9. Commonly the symmetry of the law will be a persuasive argument, because, to repeat, "yielding to the form prepares assent to the matter identified with it." If there is a Law of Supply—and there is ample reason to think there is—it is hard to resist the symmetrical attractions of a Law of Demand. At higher levels of the mathematical sciences the appeal to symmetry takes a higher percentage of conviction. In the same way the critic will search for structure in "Ode on a Grecian Urn" and find it in the symmetry of beautiful act and truthful scene.

10. Mere definition is a powerful argument, and is more powerful the more mathematical the talk. A higher price of gasoline, for instance, leaves less income to be spent on all things, including gasoline (at least by one definition of income, or of the law). In the same way the critic can define the elements of discourse dramatistically, leaving less for other metaphors.

11. Above all, there is analogy. That the Law of Demand is true for ice cream and movies, as no one would want to deny, makes it more persuasive also for gasoline. Analogy gives the law its majesty. If the law applied only to the trivial items for which it has been "proven" in modernist style, no one would care. That laboratory rats view cherry soda as a luxury good, though interesting, is not much of a basis for a science of mankind. But if the law applies to gasoline (or to rats), then it is easier to believe that it applies to housing; and if to housing, then to medical care; and then to political power; and then to love. Analogy is essential for science, but is of course the quintessential literary device.

These are all good reasons for believing the Law of Demand, but only the first three are scientific by the dichotomous definition of modernism. The other eight are artistic and literary. The modernist might try to reduce the eight to the three. "Analogy is based on a series of earlier experiments," he might say. But it is easier to see how the efficacy of general equilibrium, simultaneous equation, three-stage least squares methods of fitting complete systems of demand equations (reason 1) depends on the authority of the traditions about error terms (reason 8) or the appeal of symmetry as an aesthetic principle of specification (reason 9) than to see how analogy and introspection can be reduced to econometrics.

The modernist might say then, "Come, come: this introspection on which you rely for certain of the arguments would not be reliable unless our researchers had invisible lie detectors or perhaps mind-reading apparatus" (Machlup 1955, p. 488). It is a postulate of modernism, largely unspoken and therefore unargued, that minds do not exist. The puzzle is that a modernist who examines his mind when getting dressed in the morning and assumes the existence of other minds when driving to work claims to deny both as soon as he flicks on the lights at his laboratory. On the job he no longer believes he has a headache when his head hurts or that his daughter is sad when she cries.

The modernist might say in desperation, "These 'literary' arguments, as you call them, are in the end merely supportive and probable; the scientific arguments are the decisive ones." The proper response is, "Who says?" Anyone who actually runs experiments or fits curves knows that they too depend on analogies (the market is just like this demand curve), metaphysical propositions (the time series is a sample from all possible universes), and traditional authority (we have always assumed finite variance of the error term). And he knows that they, too, are merely supportive and probable. There is no certitude to be had, with any methodology.

The arguments fitting a modernist methodology are not in any case the whole story. As an empirical matter here they would be a rather small part of the story. Few economists would place more than 15 percent of their confidence in the Law of Demand on the first three reasons in total, leaving 85 percent to literary as against scientific rhetoric. One can test whether this is true by asking an economist, who will testify to its persuasiveness by introspection (then deny that persuasiveness comes sometimes from introspection). Or in properly modernist fashion one can observe what arguments an economist uses when trying to convince unbelievers, such as students. Much of his argument will rely on introspection, encouraging the students to examine theirs and improve it by critical thinking. He will exhibit the few cases in point he can remember, especially the more extreme cases such as the oil crisis, and will try to build on analogy with products that the students do believe follow the law. For the rest he will appeal to the identity of convex utility functions and the authority of the scientific tradition. No matter how sophisticated the class is, it will be a rare teacher, and a poor one, who relies much on the econometric results from the data mine and its miners.

The Literary Character of Economic Science

Economic scientists, then, persuade with many devices, and as speakers have an audience. They do not speak into the void: the rhetorical character of science makes it social. The final product of science, the scientific article, is a performance. It is no more separated from other literary performances by epistemology than pastoral poetry is separated from epic by epistemology. Epistemology is not to the point. But literary thinking is.

Linguistics Is an Appropriate Model for Economic Science

The strategies of argument that economists use, then, are "literary" in various senses. Economists can gain from looking at their subject with literary models in mind. To quantitative intellectuals it is evident that the great achievement of the nineteenth century was physics. To literary intellectuals [bracketing the perfection of the novel] it is equally evident that linguistics was. The styles of thought considered prestigious are determined by adherence to one or the other of these two models. Economics since Samuelson's *Foundations of Economic Analysis* (1947) has looked on nineteenth-century physics as its model. Perhaps is should try nineteenth-century linguistics.

Here is one reason. The founder of modern linguistics, Ferdinand de Saussure, devoted many pages of his *Course in General Linguistics* (1915, pp. 79ff., 115ff.) to the analogy between economics and his new linguistics. It is notable that a scholar as important for economics as Saussure was for linguistics, Leon Walras, flourished at the same time in the same nation, and had nearly identical ideas about the salience of what economists would call cross-sectional and comparative static thinking. The motto of both was "Everything touches everything else, today."

Saussure distinguished two approaches to understanding societies, the diachronic and the synchronic. The diachronic was the historical, dynamic, or (as economists would say) time-series approach typical of the linguistics of his day. It traced the history of words and grammar, showing how Latin *calidus* became by stages French *chaud*. Saussure noted that a speaker of French in 1910 did not need to know any of this to communicate with other speakers: he needed to know only the system of oppositions and analogies extant in 1910 that allowed one to distinguish *chaud* from *froid*. A historical linguistics, in other words, interesting though it was in its own right, could shed no light on how people used language at any one time.

What was needed to understand the way a language worked at a given time was a synchronic linguistics, an ahistorical, static, cross-sectional account of how one French speaker speaks to another. The two linguistics were, and had to be, distinct: it would make no difference to a French speaker if some chance had left him with the word *heiss* or *hot* instead of *chaud*, so long as he could keep the opposition of X against *froid* (and against various other things, such as *cabbage* or *cat*). Synchronic and diachronic linguistics, in Saussure's view, had to be separate sciences, one aligned along the "axis of successions" and the other along the "axis of simultaneities":

> For a science concerned with values the distinction is a practical necessity and sometimes an absolute one. In these fields scholars cannot organize their research rigorously without considering both co-ordinates and making a distinction between the system of values per se and the same values as they relate to time. . . .
> The opposition between the two viewpoints, the synchronic and the diachronic, is absolute and allows no compromise.
> (Saussure 1915, pp. 80, 83)

The point, which Saussure himself made quite clear (p. 79), is that economics, especially neoclassical and Austrian economics, *is* synchronic. Indeed, it fits his recommendation for a fresh organization of the linguistic sciences so closely that the economics of Menger and Jevons looks like his model. Both neoclassical economics and synchronic linguistics are theories of value—that is to say, theories of psychological attitudes attached to things (whether lexical or woolen things, whether *chaud* the word or sweater/pullover the object). In such an economics, as in such a linguistics, the exact matching of material and person does not matter: it does not matter that a particular grain of wheat from the Texas farm of George Hersh finds its way to the dinner table of David Mitch in Baltimore, no more than it matters that *chaud* rather than *heiss* represents in French the character of stoves that makes them painful for baby to touch; what matters is that *a* grain gets off the farm and onto the table, or that there is *some* sign for hotness.

Saussure's famous example of the 8:25 express from Geneva to Paris makes the point in a way that will elucidate it for economists (p. 108). He observed that "the" 8:25 is for purposes of travel "the" same train every day, even though it is never the same in physical makeup. The cars, the personnel, even the exact time of departure, may vary (the last not very much in the Switzerland of Saussure's day), and of course a car a day older is not the same car it was. Yet the train is the same, defined by its opposition to other trains and its uses in the mental worlds of its passengers. In like fashion, economics is oriented away from such matters as the exact makeup of pairings in the marketplace or the origin of a particular product. It will not digest ideas of embodied labor, the history of institutions, the dependence of a particular deman-der on a particular supplier, or anything else along the axis of succes-sions.

Economics has seen various projects to make the subject dynamic, to bring it into real time, to give it a historical perspective, to find out how much labor power is embodied in surplus value, to make it, in a word, diachronic. The comparison with synchronic linguistics suggests why the projects have failed to deflect economics from its static purity. Marxism, the German Historical School, Institutionalism new and old, have been trying to graft diachronic limbs onto a synchronic tree. The limbs keep falling off, to grow and flourish perhaps by themselves, but not as offshoots of the tree of analysis descended from Mandeville and Smith.

This does not mean that diachronic inquiries such as economic histo-ry are useless for economic studies as a whole, any more than historical linguistics is useless for linguistic studies as a whole. The same can be affirmed of the Marxist's political economy or the sociologist's history of institutions. Economic history is in this view the raw material for synchronic thinking. It becomes part of what the chemist and philoso-pher Michael Polanyi called the "tacit knowledge" about which the theorizing speaks. Synchronic theories such as neoclassical economics or Saussurean linguistics are suitable for mathematization. Polanyi wrote: "A mathematical theory can be constructed only by relying on *prior* tacit knowing and can function as a theory only *within* an act of tacit knowing, which consists in our attending *from* it to the previously established experience on which it bears. Thus the ideal of a compre-hensive mathematical theory of experience which would eliminate all tacit knowing is proved to be self-contradictory and logically un-sound."[2] In other words, the chemist or economist must start with some attractive-looking gunk in a test tube or some story about how a partic-ular economy has developed—that is to say, with conceptions on which he has a tacit, experiential, linguistic grasp. The experience (in literary terms, the narrative or in novelistic terms, perhaps, the dialogue) is the phenomenon to be theorized about. One must have a direct grasp of the subject in order to have something to be synchronic about.

2. Polanyi 1966, p. 21; tacit knowing is similar to Cardinal Newman's notion of the "illative sense" (the perception of that-ness). Cf. Newman 1870, chap. 9.

Literary Thinking May Improve Applied Economics

So much, then, for instances of literary thinking applied to how economists talk. There will be more. When confronted with the sentence "Economics is literary," however, only an economist would think first of applying it to the behavior of economists themselves or to the structure of economic theory. What occurs first and last to a noneconomist is that it could be used to characterize the economy. Surely here is an opportunity to get rid of that great stick of a character *Homo economicus* and to replace him with somebody real, like Madame Bovary.

It may be. The understanding of individual motivation in economics could use some complicating. The economist has from time to time inquired at the psychology shop for premises of behavior more complex than simple greed. He has not found much to his liking (though see Scitovsky 1976 and Akerlof and Dickens 1982). The experimental psychologists have stick figures of their own for sale, and few enough buyers.[3] It would seem reasonable that the economist might inquire instead at the English or the Communication shops. He might get them to sell a few behavorial assumptions on the sly, as for a while now they have been selling philosophy interdicted by the Department of Philosophy.

Some literary critics have been bold enough to begin. An economist hearing someone talking about "human action," distinct from "mere motion" such as the tides insensate have, attacking the behaviorist hallucination that man is a large rat, emphasizing the purpose-ness of human affairs, and bringing this together with a declaration that "the resultant of many disparate acts cannot itself be considered an act in the same purposive sense that characterizes each one of such acts (just as the movement of the stock market in its totality is not 'personal' in the sense of the myriad decisions made by each of the variously minded traders)"—an economist hearing all this would think himself in the presence of an Austrian economist: Hayek, perhaps, or von Mises, or some approximation *sui generis* such as Frank Knight. But he would in fact be in the presence of the doyen of American critics, Kenneth Burke

---

3. Though see the brilliant paper by Heiner (1983). In his "Prologue in Heaven" Kenneth Burke has the Lord, talking to his favorite angel, Satan, attack "a constant procession of solemn, humorless caricatures . . . [from] various oversimplified schemes that reduce human motives to a few . . . itches." Satan asks whether one must "shop around among the various caricatures" (1961, pp. 299f.).

The Literary Character of Economic Science

(1968, p. 447). The parallels between Burke's thinking and Austrian economics are notable, the more so because their politics otherwise do not match. But there do not appear to be any channels of mutual influence.

The places where literature and economics overlap are not otherwise much explored.[4] One can think of possibilities, though they are not wholly convincing and cannot be made so without more inquiry.

Here is an instance. Both economists and literary critics talk about "preferences." Economists mean by this, of course, simply "what people want," in the sense of wanting some candy when the price is right. With a few other economists, Albert Hirschman has recently observed that stopping at mere wants causes economists to overlook higher-level preferences, wants about wants (1984, pp. 89f.). Elsewhere these are known as taste, morality, or (west of the Sierras), lifestyle. Hirschman's notion is that if you wish to be the sort of person who enjoys Shakespeare, you will sit through a performance of *Two Gentlemen of Verona* as part of your education. You impose a set of preferences on yourself, which you then indulge in the usual way. You have preferences about preferences; metapreferences (cf. Elster 1979).

It would not be shocking if literary critics could teach economists a thing or two about metapreferences. Literary criticism, after all, is largely a discourse about them, and people like I. A. Richards, Northrop Frye, Wayne Booth, and Kenneth Burke are fair canny. One might think that the older line of critics—Sir Philip Sydney, Johnson, Coleridge, Arnold—would have in fact the most to teach, being more concerned than the recent kind with matters of value (matters of how well, as against simply how). A passage from the younger line, though, can illustrate how literary notions might be used to understand the economy of taste. Richards wrote in 1925:

> On a pleasure theory of value [that is to say, a theory using only preferences, not metapreferences] there might well be doubt [that good poetry is better than bad], since those who do enjoy it [namely, bad poetry, such as that collected in *Poems of Passion*] certainly appear to enjoy it in a high degree. But on the theory here maintained, the fact that those who have passed through the stage of enjoying the *Poems of Passion* to that of en-

4. A pioneer from the literary side is Kurt Heinzelmann, in *The Economics of the Imagination* (1980), which discusses at length how economic theory in the nineteenth century used language and how it, in turn, influenced the language of imaginative writers. Marc Shell has catalogued the use of (strictly) monetary metaphors in literature in his *Economy of Literature* (1978).

joying the bulk of the *Golden Treasury,* for example, do not return, settles the matter. . . . actual universal preference on the part of those who have tried both kinds fairly is the same (on our view) as superiority in value of the one over the other. (pp. 205f.)

An economist will notice that Richards' argument is the same as the economics of "revealed preference" or, on a national level, the "Hicks-Kaldor test of welfare improvements." To use the reasoning developed by Paul Samuelson, an early economic exponent of austere modernism in testing, one bundle of groceries is revealed preferred to another if you could buy either bundle (could afford to buy either) but in fact chose one. In your view, the bundle you could afford but did not take must be inferior.

The point is that Richards' test is a revealed preference test for (good) taste. In other words, it is a way of ranking metapreferences. You could have read the classic comic book, but in fact chose to read Dostoevski, because you wanted to be that sort of person. The Dostoevski-reading persona is revealed to be preferred by you. That someone passes through the stage of enjoying "The Love Boat" on television to that of enjoying the bulk of modern drama and does not return settles the matter. That someone passes through the stage of enjoying modern drama to that of enjoying the bulk of Shakespeare and does not return settles it again: Shakespeare is metapreferred to modern drama, which is in turn metapreferred to "The Love Boat."

The same applies to nonliterary preferences, which is why Richards' notion can be used by economists. To be sure, it's more complicated than that. We do drift slowly from one metapreference to another, and sometimes, gyrelike, return to elementary pleasures. But the notion is a good beginning. People who learn French cooking may never return to German. The style of life in Iowa City—that is, the preferences one chooses to indulge—may be revealed to be preferred to those in Hyde Park, and those in Hyde Park to those in Stanford. It would be so if one observed people with free choice trekking from Stanford to Hyde Park and thence to Iowa City but never back again. In like fashion, a capitalist democracy may be revealed to be preferred to a workers' democratic republic, by the direction in which the guns on the border point.[5]

5. Milton Friedman uses this very figure of speech to support his argument against conscription in peacetime: "I have observed many persons initially in favor of the draft change their opinions as they have looked into the arguments and studied the evidence; I have never observed anyone who was initially in favor of a volunteer force reverse his position on the basis of further study. This greatly enhances my confidence in the validity of the position I have taken" (1975, p. 188).

The Literary Character of Economic Science

What is attractive about the test is that it replies in a suitably modernist way to the modernist argument that "you can't say anything about ranking tastes." The Richards test is similar to Rawls' test of political constitutions from behind a veil of prenatal ignorance; it is similar likewise to the tests of social preferences proposed before Rawls by the economists Harsanyi, Sen, and others; and these are, in turn, extensions from the individual to the society of the leading novelty in economic theory since the 1940s, expected utility. The Richards test, in short, may be literary criticism, but it is also economics. Even by the economist's narrow standard of sayability, there is nothing intrinsically can't-sayable about changes in preferences guided by taste. Or at any rate it is no more can't-sayable than ordinary remarks about ordinary choice, the usual sayings of economic theory.

Economics, then, can be seen as an instance of literary culture. That it can also be seen as an instance of scientific culture is no contradiction. It shows merely how the official rhetoric of science narrows the field, demanding that it honor the one and spurn the other. The unofficial, workaday rhetoric takes a broader view, and a more persuasive one.

5

FIGURES OF

ECONOMIC SPEECH

Even a Modernist Uses, and Must Use, Literary Devices: The Case of Paul Samuelson

Obscured by the official rhetoric, the workaday rhetoric of economics has not received the attention it deserves. The knowledge of it is therefore contained only in seminar traditions, advice to assistant professors, referee reports, and jokes. Economists can do better if they will look soberly at the varieties of their argument.

The task of an economic criticism would be to dissect samples of economic argument, noting in the manner of a literary or philosophical exegesis exactly how the arguments sought to convince the reader. It is not obvious a priori what the categories might be; in view of the range of modern economics they would doubtless vary from author to author. A good place to start might be the categories of classical rhetoric. A good place to continue would be the procedures of modern literary critics, bright people who make their living thinking about the rhetoric of texts.

The purpose of a literary scrutiny of economic argument is not to hold the authors up to ridicule or to attack the nonliterary parts of economics. It is rather to see beyond the received view on its content, by examining its form. As is said of poetic traditions so also may be said of economic writing, that the form "is often an adaption of tradition" and the content "contains the substance of the poet's immediate inspiration" (Williams 1969, p. 8). Form carries the tradition of the discipline; the content (where it can be distinguished from the way of speaking, which is seldom) is merely what is new. But what is old is most of what we think, after all. Kenneth Burke discusses at length a phrase of Coleridge: "Language thinks for us." Indeed. Do we speak the language, or does the language speak us? Language is no tool to be picked up and set down: it flies to our hand, or leaps out of it, like some sorcerer's broom.

Consider two pages (pp. 122–23), chosen literally at random, from that premier text of the received view, Paul Samuelson's *Foundations of*

Figures of Economic Speech

Economic Analysis. Published in 1947, a few years before Friedman's modernist manifesto, it was a local maximum in economic scholarship. Besides its reduction of economics to the mathematics of nineteenth-century physics, brilliant reading even now, the book contains much modernist legislation for economic science. On the page preceding the selection, for example, Samuelson boasts that such and such "is a meaningful, refutable hypothesis which is capable of being tested under ideal observational conditions" (p. 121; cf. pp. 3–5, 84, 172, 221, 257). Consider, though, how he actually achieves persuasion:

1. To begin with, he gives a general mathematical form from which the results in comparative statics can be obtained by reading across a row. The implication of the lack of elaboration is that the mathematical details are trivially easy (leading one to wonder why they are mentioned at all). An "interesting" special case is left "as an exercise to the interested reader," drawing on the rhetorical traditions of applied mathematics to direct the mind in the right direction. The mathematics is presented in an offhand way, implying that we can all read partitioned matrices at a glance (and fitting poorly with the level of mathematics in other passages).

It is notable that when speaking of mathematics Samuelson is "we," but when speaking of economics, "I." Mathematical results are to be laid out for inspection. They are impersonal. Their truth is apparent to "us," if we are not dunces. Economics, by contrast, is viewed as personal and arguable (Samuelson is unusual among economists in the boldness with which he introduces "I"; most economists use in this case the passive voice). Here as elsewhere in the book Samuelson's persona alternates between the cool stater of mathematical truth and the excited propounder of economic argument.

The air of easy mathematical mastery was important for the influence of the book, by contrast with the embarrassed modesty with which British writers at the time (J. R. Hicks most notably) pushed mathematics off into appendices. Samuelson's skill at mathematics in the eyes of his readers, an impression nurtured at every turn, is itself an important and persuasive argument. On good grounds, he presents himself as an authority. That the mathematics is sometimes pointless, as here, is beside the point. Being able to do such a difficult thing (so it would have seemed to the typical economist reader in 1947) is warrant of expertise.

The argument is similar in force to that of a classical education conspicuously displayed. To read Latin like one's mother tongue and Greek like one's aunt's tongue is difficult, requiring application well beyond the ordinary. Therefore—or so it seemed to Englishmen in the 1890s—

men who have acquired such a skill should have charge of a great empire. Likewise—or so it seems to economists in the 1980s—those who have acquired a skill at partitioned matrices and eigenvalues should have charge of a great economy. The argument is not absurd or a "fallacy" or "mere rhetoric." Virtuosity *is* some evidence of virtue.

2. There are six appeals to authority—to C. E. V. Leser, Keynes, Hicks, Aristotle, Knight, and P. A. Samuelson (appeal to authority is something of a Samuelsonian specialty). Appeal to authority is often reckoned as the worst kind of "mere" rhetoric. Yet it is a common and often legitimate argument, as here. No science would advance without it, because no scientist can redo every previous argument. We stand on the shoulders of giants (or at least a big pyramid of midgets), and it is a perfectly legitimate and persuasive argument to point this out from time to time. In 1888 Francis Ysidro Edgeworth, an authority on economics, philosophy, and statistics worth paying attention to, justified appeal to authority on statistical grounds: "The Doctrine of [Offsetting] Errors supplies the *rationale* of the common-sense practice of deferring to authority. . . . All that authority can do is—what, according to Horace, all that philosophy can do—to get rid of a large portion of error."[1]

3. There are several appeals to relaxation of assumptions. The demand for money, writes Samuelson, is "really interesting . . . when uncertainty . . . is admitted." Again, the implicit assumption in Hicks that money bears no interest is relaxed, unhitching the interest rate from the zero return on money. Relaxation of assumptions is the essay-maker of modern economics. In the absence of quantitative evidence on the importance of the assumption relaxed, mere speculation of this sort is not (for the modernist) evidence at all. Samuelson is careful to stick to the subjunctive mood of theory (money *"would* pass out of use"), but he no doubt wants his strictures on a theory of the interest rate based merely on liquidity preference (that is, on risk) to be taken seriously as comments on the world as it is. They are, surely, but not on the operationalist grounds he articulates when preaching methodology.

4. There are several appeals to hypothetical toy economies, constrained to one or two sectors, from which practical results are said to be derived. Since Ricardo this has been among the commonest forms of economic argument, the Ricardian vice. The modern theory of international trade indulges in it the most; labor economics, perhaps, the least. It is no vice if done reasonably, but neither does it prove much in the narrow sense of proof. "It would be quite possible to have an economy in which money did not exist, and in which there was still a substantial rate of interest." Well, yes, of course.

1. Quoted in Stigler 1978, p. 293. Edgeworth seems to have in mind *Epist.* 1.1.41–42.

Figures of Economic Speech

5. There is, finally, one explicit appeal to analogy, which is said to be "not . . . superficial." Analogy, as will be shown in detail in a moment, pervades economic thinking, even when it does not think of itself as analogical: transaction "friction," yield "spread," securities "circulating," money "withering away," are inexplicit examples here from one paragraph in Samuelson of live or half-dead metaphors. Yet analogy and metaphor, like most of the other pieces of Samuelson's rhetoric, have no standing in the received view.

Two of the five devices are literary and rhetorical. The appeal to authority and the appeal to analogy are figures of speech that a poet would use. The other three are rhetorical alone—that is to say, figures of speech used to persuade. They are "figures of speech" because they are ways of talking that do not reduce to syllogism or experiment. Figures of speech are not in strict Cartesian doctrine persuasive at all. None prove by deduction or falsification. Yet *The Foundations of Economic Analysis* used them all, with hundreds of others, in rich array.

Most of the Devices Are Only Dimly Recognized

The range of persuasive discourse in economics is wide, ignored in precept while potent in practice. Economists are unselfconscious about their rhetoric. Most of it is dead in the way that a polite cliché is dead to writers without self-conscious skill. Economists use a have-a-nice-day rhetoric that does not know itself or care.

At the broadest level it is worth noting that the practice of economic debate often takes the form of legal reasoning, because, as Booth put it, "the processes developed in the law are codifications of reasonable processes that we follow in every part of our lives, even the scientific" (1974a, p. 157). Economists would do well to study jurisprudence, then, with some aim other than subordinating it to economic theory. In his penetrating book *What's Wrong with Economics* (1972) Benjamin Ward has examined the legal analogies of economic reasoning. They are many. Like jurists, for instance, economists argue by example, by what Edward Levi calls "the controlling similarity between the present and prior case" (1948, p. 7).

The details of the pleading of cases at economic law have little to do with the official scientific method. Without self-consciousness about workaday rhetoric they are easily misclassified. A common argument in economics, for example, is one from verbal suggestiveness. The proposition that "the economy is basically competitive" may well be simply an invitation to look at it this way, on the assurance that to do so will be illuminating. In the same way a psychologist might say "we are all neurotic": she does not mean that 95 percent of a randomly selected sample of us will exhibit compulsive handwashing; she merely recommends that we focus attention on the neurotic ingredient "in us all" (Passmore 1966, p. 438). To misunderstand the expression as a properly modernist hypothesis would be to invite much useless testing. The case is similar to the monetarist equation $MV = PT$ understood as an identity. The equation is the same, term for term, as the equation of state of an ideal gas and has the same status as an irrefutable but useful notion in economics as it has in chemistry. The identity *can* be argued against, but not on grounds of "failing a test." The arguments against it will deny its capacity to illuminate, not its modernist truth.

Another common argument in economics with no status in the official rhetoric is philosophical consistency: "If you assume the firm knows its own cost curve, you might as well assume it knows its production function too: it is no more dubious that it knows one than the other." The argument, usually inexplicit though signaled by such a phrase as "it is natural to assume," is in fact characteristic of philosophical discourse (in the style of Passmore 1961). It is analogous to symmetry as a criterion of plausibility and comes up in many forums. A labor economist tells a seminar about compensating differentials for the risk of unemployment, referring only to the utility functions of the workers. An auditor remarks that the value of unemployment on the demand side (that is, the value to the firm) is not included. The remark is felt to be powerful, and a long discussion ensues of how the demand side might alter the conclusions. The argument from "the other side is empty"—which is to say, an appeal to theoretical tidiness and symmetry—is persuasive in economics. But economists are unaware of how persuasive it is

Likewise (and here we reach the border of self-consciousness in rhetoric), "ad hoccery" is universally condemned by seminar audiences. An economist will cheerfully accept a poor R^2 and terrible and understated standard errors if only he "has a theory" for the inclusion of such and such a variable in his regressions. "Having a theory" is not so open and shut as it might seem, depending, for instance, on what reasoning is prestigious at the moment. Anyone who before 1962 threw accumulated past output into an equation explaining productivity change would have been accused of ad hoccery. But after Arrow's essay "The Economics of Learning by Doing" (which, as it happened, had little connection with maximizing behavior or other higher-order hypotheses in economics), there was suddenly a warrant for doing it.

An example of the rhetoric of economics which falls well within the border of self-consciousness is simulation. Economists will commonly make an argument for the importance of this or that variable by showing its potency in a model with back-of-the-envelope estimates of the parameters. Common though it is, little writing is devoted to its explication (but see Zeckhauser and Stokey 1978). Students learn simulation entirely by studying examples of it, and by studying the examples without being told what they are examples of. The accidental teaching contrasts with the self-conscious way in which econometrics and theory are taught.

Economists have developed few rhetorical standards for assessing simulation. Between A. C. Harberger's modest little triangles of distortion and Jeffrey Williamson's immense multiequation models of the American or Japanese economies since 1870 is a broad range. Economists have no vocabulary for criticizing any part of the range. They can deliver summary grunts of belief or disbelief but find it difficult to articulate their reasons in a disciplined way.

Models Are Nonornamental Metaphors: The Case of Gary Becker

The most important example of economic rhetoric, however, falls well outside the border of self-consciousness. It is the language economists use, and in particular their metaphors. To say that markets can be represented by supply and demand "curves" is no less a metaphor than to say that the west wind is "the breath of autumn's being." A more obvious example is "game theory," the very name being a metaphor. It is obviously useful to have in one's head the notion that the arms race is a two-person, negative-sum cooperative "game." Its persuasiveness is instantly obvious, as are some of its limitations (some malicious wit remarked once that game theory has a nice name but no results).

Noneconomists find it easier to see the metaphors than do economists, habituated as the economists are by daily use to the idea that of course production comes from a "function" and that of course business moves in "cycles." Certain of the metaphors are perfectly self-conscious, as revealed, for instance, by the exultation or irony with which the "invisible hand" is handled. And everyone understands that a metaphorical question is at issue when it is asked whether a mechanical or a biological analogy best suits the economy as a whole (Boulding 1975; Georgescu-Roegen 1975; Kornai 1983). Some economists, again quite self-aware, make their contributions to the field by thinking metaphorically in ways that no one can mistake: Albert Hirschman, for instance, with his exits and voices; or J. K. Galbraith with his countervalences.

But few economists recognize the metaphorical saturation of economic theories believed to be quite literal. One economist doing so recently is Willie Henderson, who has written most illuminatingly on the subject (1982). Observers of other fields are more aware of the metaphoric saturation of thought: a recent volume of essays by philosophers, linguists, and psychologists is entitled simply *Metaphor and Thought* (Ortony 1979). In the physical sciences the case is plain. Jacob Bronowski noted (1965, p. 36) that the scientist needs "the exploration of likenesses; and this has sadly tiptoed out of the mechanical worlds of the positivists and the operationalists, and left them empty. . . . The symbol and the metaphor are as necessary to science as to poetry." One might better say that even positivists and operationalists are tied to metaphor too—the metaphor of "objectivity," for instance, and in any case the metaphors of their discipline. Richard Rorty had it more right (1979, p. 12): "It is pictures rather than propositions, metaphors rather than statements, which determine most of our philosophical [and economic] convictions."

Each step in economic reasoning, even the reasoning of the official rhetoric, is metaphoric. The world is said to be "like" a complex model, and its measurements are said to be like the easily measured proxy variable to hand. The complex model is said to be like a simpler model for actual thinking, which is in turn like an even simpler model for calculation. For purposes of persuading doubters, the model is said to be like a toy model that can be manipulated quickly inside the doubter's head as he listens to the seminar. John Gardner wrote:

> There is a game—in the 1950s it used to be played by the members of the Iowa Writers' Workshop—called "Smoke." The player who is 'it' [thinks of] some famous person . . . and then each of the other players in turn asks one question . . . such as "What kind of weather are you?" . . . Marlon Brando, if weather, would be sultry and uncertain. . . . To understand that Marlon Brando is a certain kind of weather is to discover something (though something neither useful nor demonstrable) and in the same instant to communicate something. (Gardner 1978, pp. 118–19)

On the contrary, I shall argue, in economics the comparable discovery is both useful and, by recourse to rhetorical standards, demonstrable. What kind of a curve is a market? What kind of a material is a worker?

Figures of Economic Speech

Metaphor, though, is commonly viewed as mere ornament. From Aristotle until the 1930s even literary critics viewed it this way, as an amusing comparison able to affect the emotions but inessential for thought. "Men are beasts": if we cared to be flat-footed about it, the notion was, we could say in what literal way we thought them beastly, removing the ornament to reveal the core of plain meaning underneath. The notion was in 1958 common in philosophy, too: "With the decline of metaphysics, philosophers have grown less and less concerned about Godliness and more and more obsessed with cleanliness, aspiring to ever higher levels of linguistic hygiene. In consequence, there has been a tendency for metaphors to fall into disfavour, the common opinion being that they are a frequent source of infection" (Horsburgh 1958, p. 231). Such suspicion toward metaphor is widely recognized by now to be unnecessary, even harmful. That the very idea of "removing" an "ornament" to "reveal" a "plain" meaning is itself a metaphor suggests why. Perhaps thinking is metaphorical. Perhaps to remove metaphor is to remove thought. The operation on the metaphoric growth would in this case be worse than the disease.

The question is whether economic thought is metaphorical in some nonornamental sense. The more obvious metaphors in economics are those used to convey novel thoughts, one sort of novelty being to compare economic with noneconomic matters. "Elasticity" was once a mind-stretching fancy; "depression" was depressing; "equilibrium" compared an economy to an apple in a bowl, a settling idea; "competition" once induced thoughts of horse races; money's "velocity" thoughts of swirling bits of paper. Much of the vocabulary of economics consists of dead metaphors taken from noneconomic spheres.

Comparing noneconomic with economic matters is another sort of novelty, apparent in the imperialism of the new economics of history, law, politics, crime, and the rest, and most apparent in the work of the Kipling of the economic empire, Gary Becker. Among the least bizarre of his many metaphors, for instance, is that children are durable goods, like refrigerators. The philosopher Max Black points out that "a memorable metaphor has the power to bring two separate domains into cognitive and emotional relation by using language directly appropriate to the one as a lens for seeing the other" (1962, p. 236). So here: the subject (a child) is viewed through the lens of the modifier (a refrigerator).

A beginning at literal translation would say, "A child is costly to acquire initially, lasts for a long time, gives flows of pleasure during that time, is expensive to maintain and repair, has an imperfect second-hand market. . . . Likewise, a durable good, such as a refrigerator. . . ." That the list of similarities could be extended further and further, gradually revealing the differences as well—"children, like durable goods, are not objects of affection and concern"; "children, like durable goods, do not have their own opinions"—is one reason that, as Black says, "metaphorical thought is a distinctive mode of achieving insight, not to be construed as an ornamental substitute for plain thought" (p. 237). The literal translation of an important metaphor is never finished. In this respect and in others an important metaphor in economics has the quality admired in a successful scientific theory, a capacity to astonish us with implications once unseen.[2]

But it is not merely the pregnant quality of economic metaphors that makes them important for economic thinking, and not mere ornaments. The literary critic I. A. Richards was among the first to make the point, in 1936, that metaphor is "two thoughts of different things *active together*, ... whose meaning is a resultant of their interaction" (Richards 1936, p. 93 [italics added]; cf. Black 1962, p. 46; Barfield 1947, p. 54). A metaphor is not merely a verbal trick, Richards continues, but "a borrowing between and intercourse of thoughts, a transaction between contexts" (p. 94). Economists will have no trouble seeing the point of his economic metaphor, one of mutually advantageous exchange. The opposite notion, that ideas and their words are invariant lumps unaltered by combination, like bricks (see again Richards 1936, p. 97), is analogous to believing that an economy is a mere aggregation of Robinson Crusoes. But the point of economics since Smith has been that an island full of trading Crusoes is different from and often better off than the mere aggregation.

Another of Becker's favorite metaphors, "human capital," invented at Chicago by Theodore Schultz, illustrates how two sets of ideas, in this case both drawn from inside economics, can thus mutually illuminate each other by exchanging connotations. In the phrase "human capital" the field in economics treating human skills was at a stroke unified with the field treating investment in machines. Thought in both fields was improved—labor economics by recognizing that skills, for all their intangibility, arise from abstention from consumption; capital theory by recognizing that skills, for all their lack of capitalization, compete with other investments for a claim to abstention. Notice, by contrast,

---

2. A good metaphor depends, too, on the ability of its audience to suppress incongruities, or to wish to. Booth gives the example of " 'All the world's a stage' . . . (The reader must make a choice only if the incongruities—failures of fit—come too soon). Usually they arrive late and without much strength. . . . we have no difficulty ruling from our attention, in the life-stage metaphor, the selling of tickets, fire insurance laws, the necessity for footlights" (1961, pp. 22f.).

that because economists are experts only in durable goods and have few (or at any rate conventional) thoughts about children, the metaphor that children are durable goods has, so to speak, only one direction of flow. The gains from the trade were earned mostly by the theory of children, gaining from the theory of durable goods (fertility, nuptiality, inheritance), not the other way around.

What is successful in economic metaphor is what is successful in poetry, and the success is analyzable in similar terms. Concerning the best metaphors in the best poetry, comparing thee to a summer's day or comparing A to B, argued Owen Barfield, "We feel that B, which is actually said, ought to be necessary, even inevitable in some way. It ought to be in some sense the best, if not the only way, of expressing A satisfactorily. The mind should dwell on it as well as on A and thus the two should be somehow inevitably fused together into one simple meaning" (Barfield 1947, p. 54). If the modifier B (a summer's day, a refrigerator, a piece of capital) were trite—in these cases it is not, although in the poem Shakespeare was more self-critical of his simile than economists usually are of theirs—it would become, as it were, detached from A, a mechanical and unilluminating correspondence. If essential, though, it fuses with A to become a master metaphor of the science, the idea of "human capital," the idea of "equilibrium," the idea of "entry and exit," the idea of "competition." The metaphor, quoth the poet, is the "consummation of identity."

Few would deny that economists frequently use figurative language. Much of the pitiful humor available in a science devoted to calculations of profit and loss comes from talking about "islands" in the labor market or "putty-clay" in the capital market or "lemons" in the commodity market. The more austere the subject the more fanciful the language. We have "turnpikes" and "golden rules" in growth theory, for instance, and long disquisitions on what to do with the "auctioneer" in general equilibrium theory. A literary man with advanced training in mathematics and statistics stumbling into *Econometrica* would be astonished at the metaphors surrounding him, lost in a land of allegory.

Allegory is merely long-winded metaphor, and all such figures are analogies. Analogies can be arrayed in terms of explicitness, with simile ("as if") the most explicit and symbol ("the demand curve") the least explicit; and they can arrayed by extent, from analogy to allegory. Economists, especially theorists, frequently spin "parables" or tell "stories." The word "story" has in fact come to have a technical meaning in mathematical economics, though usually spoken in seminars rather than written in papers. It means an extended example of the economic reasoning underlying the mathematics, often a simplified version of the situation in the real world that the mathematics is meant to characterize. It is an allegory, shading into extended symbolism. The literary theories of narrative could make economists self-conscious about what use the story serves. Here the story is the modifier, the mathematics the subject. A tale of market days, traders with bins of shmoos, and customers with costs of travel between bins illuminates, say, a fixed point theorem. "Tales well told endure forever," as an economist and poet put it.

Both Mathematical and Nonmathematical Reasoning in Economics Rely on Metaphor

The critical question is whether the opposite trick, modifying human behavior with mathematics, is also metaphorical. If it were not, one might acknowledge the metaphorical element in verbal economics about the "entrepreneur," for instance, or more plainly of the "invisible hand," yet argue that the linguistic hygiene of mathematics leaves behind such fancies. This indeed was the belief of the advanced thinkers of the 1920s and 1930s who inspired the modernist conception of economic method. When engaging in verbal economics, we are more or less loose, it is said, taking literary license with our "story"; but when we do mathematics we put away childish things.

But mathematical theorizing in economics is metaphorical, and literary. Consider, for example, a relatively simple case, the theory of production functions. Its vocabulary is intrinsically metaphorical. "Aggregate capital" involves an analogy of "capital" (itself analogical) with something—sand, bricks, shmoos—that can be "added" in a meaningful way; so does "aggregate labor," with the additional peculiarity that the thing added is no thing, but hours of conscientious attentiveness; the very idea of a "production function" involves the astonishing analogy of the subject (the fabrication of things, about which it is appropriate to think in terms of ingenuity, discipline, and planning) with the modifier (a mathematical function, about which it is appropriate to think in terms of height, shape, and single-valuedness).

The metaphorical content of these ideas was alive to its nineteenth-century inventors. It is largely dead to its twentieth-century users, but deadness does not eliminate the metaphorical element. The metaphor got out of its coffin in an alarming fashion in the Debate of the Two Cambridges in the 1960s. The debate is testimony, which could be multiplied, to the importance of metaphorical questions in economics. The very violence of the combat suggests that it was about something

Figures of Economic Speech

beyond mathematics or fact. The combatants hurled mathematical reasoning and institutional facts at each other, but the important questions
were those one would ask of a metaphor: Is it illuminating, is it satisfying, is it apt? How do you know? How does it compare with other
economic poetry? After some tactical retreats by Cambridge, Massachusetts, on points of ultimate metaphysics irrelevant to these important
questions, mutual exhaustion set in, without decision. Daniel Hausman,
a philosopher of economics, noted this in his brilliant book on the
subject (1981) and nearly saw why. The reason there was no decision
reached was that the important questions were literary, not mathematical or statistical. The debate was equivalent to showing mathematically
or statistically that a woman cannot be a summer's day. Yet no one
noticed. The continued vitality of the idea of an aggregate production
function (in the face of mathematical proofs of its impossibility) and the
equal vitality of the idea of aggregate economics as practiced in parts
of Cambridge, England (in the face of statistical proofs of its impracti-
cality), would otherwise be a great mystery.

Even when the metaphors of one's economics appear to stay well and
truly dead there is no escape from literary questions. The literary man
C. S. Lewis pointed out in 1939 that any talk beyond the level of
the-cow-standing-here-is-in-fact-purple, any talk of "causes, relations,
of mental states or acts . . . [is] incurably metaphorical" (1939, p. 47). For
such talk he enunciated what may be called Screwtape's Theorem on
Metaphor, the first corollary of which is that the escape from verbal into
mathematical metaphor is not an escape: "When a man claims to think
independently of the buried metaphor in one of his words, his claim
may . . . [be] allowed only in so far as he could really supply the place
of that buried metaphor. . . . this new apprehension will usually turn
out to be itself metaphorical" (p. 46). If economists forget and then
stoutly deny that the production function is a metaphor, yet continue
talking about it, the result is mere verbiage. The phrase "production
function" will be used in ways satisfying grammatical rules, but will not
signify anything.

The charge of meaninglessness applied so freely by modernists to
forms of argument they do not like or understand sticks in this way to
themselves. Lewis's second corollary is that "the meaning in any given
composition is in inverse ratio to the author's belief in his own literal-
ness" (p. 27). An economist speaking (she believes) literally about the
demand curve, the national income, or the stability of the economy is
engaging in "mere syntax." Lewis cuts close to the bone here, though
sparing himself from the carnage: "The percentage of mere syntax
masquerading as meaning may vary from something like 100 percent

in political writers, journalists, psychologists, and economists, to something like forty percent in the writers of children's stories.... The mathematician, who seldom forgets that his symbols are symbolic, may often rise for short stretches to ninety percent of meaning and ten of verbiage" (p. 49). If an economist is not comparing a social fact to a one-to-one mapping, thus bringing two separate domains into cognitive and emotional relation, she is not thinking:

> I've never slapped a curved demand;
> I never hope to slap one.
> But this thing I can tell you now:
> I'd rather slap than map one.

Self-consciousness about metaphor in economics would be an improvement on many counts. Most obviously, unexamined metaphor is a substitute for thinking—which is a recommendation to examine the metaphors, not to attempt the impossible by banishing them.[3] Richard Whately, D.D., archbishop of Dublin, publicist for free trade as for other pieces of classical political economy, and author of the standard work in the nineteenth century on the elements of rhetoric, drew attention to the metaphor of a state being like an individual and therefore benefiting like an individual from free trade. He devoted some attention, however—not all of it ironic—to the question of the aptness of the figure:

> To this is it replied, that there is a great difference between a Nation and an Individual. And so there is, in many circumstances.... [he enumerates them, mentioning, for instance, the unlimited duration of a nation] and, moreover, the transactions of each man, as far as he is left free, are regulated by the very person who is to be a gainer or loser by each—the individual himself; who, though his vigilance is sharpened by interest, and his judgment by exercise in his own department, may chance to be a man of confined education, possessed of no general principles, and not pretending to be versed in philosophical theories; whereas the affairs of a State are regulated by a Congress, Chamber of Deputies, etc., consisting perhaps of men of extensive reading and speculative minds. (Whately 1846, pp. 101–2)

The case for intervention cannot be better put. And the metaphor is here an occasion for and instrument of thought, not a substitute.

---

3. An example of a naive attack on economic metaphors, and of a failure to realize that economic theory is itself armed with metaphor, is the first page of D. N. McCloskey (1970).

Figures of Economic Speech

Metaphors, further, evoke attitudes that are better kept in the open and under the control of reasoning. This is plain in the ideological metaphors popular with parties: the invisible hand is so very discreet, so soothing, that we might be inclined to accept its touch without protest; the contradictions of capitalism are so very portentous, so scientifically precise, that we might be inclined to accept their existence without inquiry.

But even metaphors of the middling sort carry freight. The metaphors of economics often carry in particular the authority of Science and often carry, too, its claims to ethical neutrality. It is no use complaining that we didn't *mean* to introduce moral premises. We do. "Marginal productivity" is a fine, round phrase, a precise mathematical metaphor that encapsulates a most powerful piece of social description. Yet it brings with it an air of having solved the moral problem of distribution facing a society in which people cooperate to produce things together instead of producing things alone. It is irritating that it carries this message, because it may be far from the purpose of the economist who uses it to show approval for the distribution arising from competition. It is better, though, to admit that metaphors in economics can contain such a political message than to use the jargon innocent of its potential.

A metaphor, finally, emphasizes certain respects in which the subject is to be compared with the modifier; in particular, it leaves out the other respects. Max Black, speaking of the metaphor "men are wolves," notes that "any human traits that can without undue strain be talked about in 'wolf-language' will be rendered prominent, and any that cannot will be pushed into the background" (1962, p. 41).

Economists will recognize this as the source of the annoying complaints from nonmathematical economists that mathematics "leaves out" some feature of the truth or from noneconomists that economics itself "leaves out" some feature of the truth. Such complaints are often trite and ill-informed. The usual responses to them, however, are hardly less so. The response that the metaphor leaves out things in order to simplify the story only temporarily is disingenuous, occurring as it often does in contexts where the economist is simultaneously fitting fifty other equations. The response that the metaphor will be "tested" eventually by the facts is a stirring promise, but seldom fulfilled.

A better response would be that we like the metaphor of, say, the selfishly economic man as calculating machine because of its prominence in earlier economic poetry or because of its greater congruence with introspection than alternative metaphors (of men as religious dervishes, say, or as sober citizens). In *The New Rhetoric* (1958, p. 390), Perelman and Olbrechts-Tyteca note that "the acceptance of an analogy

. . . is often equivalent to a judgment as to the importance of the charac-teristics that the analogy brings to the fore." What is remarkable about this unremarkable assertion is that it occurs in a discussion of purely literary matters, yet fits so easily the matters of economic science.

This is in the end the significance of metaphors and of the other rhetorical machinery of argument in economics: economists and other scientists are less isolated from the concerns of civilization than many think. Their modes of argument and the sources of their conviction—for instance, their uses of metaphor—are not very different from Cicero's speeches or Hardy's novels. This is a good thing. As Black wrote (1962, p. 243), discussing "archetypes" as extended metaphors in science, "When the understanding of scientific models and archetypes comes to be regarded as a reputable part of scientific culture, the gap between the sciences and the humanities will have been partly filled."

The Master Tropes Rule Economics:
The Case of Robert Solow

The best way to show the metaphorical character of economics is to show it working in the economics apparently most far removed from literary matters. A good instance is a famous essay of 1957 on the production function and productivity change by Robert Solow, a president of the American Economic Association and in other ways eminent in the field (most surprisingly, in the dismal science, for his fluency and wit).

The paper has been extraordinarily important, as any economist knows from his knowledge of the conversation. Solow's paper, together with some related ones he wrote about the same time, inaugurated virtually a new field of economics. If on this point introspection or questionnaire does not entirely persuade, the importance of the paper is plain enough in the statistics of citations in other economic papers. Ten years after its publication it was still receiving over twenty-five citations a year on average, and still over twenty a decade and a half later (Table 1).

Solow was trying to understand the rising income of Americans from 1909 to 1949. He wished to know in particular how much was caused by more machinery, buildings, and other physical "capital" and how much by other things—chiefly, perhaps, the increasing ingenuity of people. He began:

> In this day of rationally designed econometric studies and
> super input-output tables, it takes something more than the

Figures of Economic Speech

Table 1. Annual Citations, 1966–1982, of Solow's 1957 Article

1966	25	1972	23	1978	14
1967	22	1973	24	1979	16
1968	28	1974	24	1980	27
1969	28	1975	25	1981	25
1970	30	1976	30	1982	17
1971	21	1977	19		

Source: *Social Science Citation Index.*

usual "willing suspension of disbelief" to talk seriously of the aggregate production function. . . . The new wrinkle I want to describe is an elementary way of segregating variations in output per head due to technical change from those due to the availability of capital per head. . . . Either this kind of aggregate economics appeals or it doesn't. Personally I belong to both schools. . . . It is convenient to begin with the special case of *neutral* technical change. . . . In that case the production function takes the special form $Q = A(t) f(K,L)$ and the multiplicative factor $A(t)$ measures the cumulated effect of shifts over time. (Solow in Zellner 1968, pp. 349f.)

He then uses a mathematical twist and the assumption of economic competition to derive a measure of $A(t)$.

The four master tropes discussed at length by literary theorists such as Kenneth Burke (e.g., 1945, pp. 503–17) are here at work: metaphor, metonymy, synecdoche, and irony. The argument depends at once on a metaphor. The "aggregate production function" that Solow diffidently introduces asserts that the making of our daily bread is like a mathematical function. The jumble of responsibility, habit, conflict, ambition, intrigue, and ceremony that is our working life is supposed to be similar to a chalked curve on a blackboard. Economists are habituated to such figures of speech, as I have said, to the point of not recognizing that they are, but noneconomists will agree that they are bold. No wonder Solow thinks this one requires willing suspension of disbelief.

The K and the L in the equation are metonymies, letting a thing merely associated with the thing in question stand as symbol for it, as the White House does for the presidency. The L reduces the human attentiveness in making bread to an hour of work. The hour is a mere emblem, no more the substance of the matter than the heart is of emotions, or a bottle is of the wine. The K reduces the material inheritance of the workplace to a pile of shmoos. Solow is aware of the boldness of this figure, too; though defending it as conventional, he "would not try to justify what follows by calling on fancy theorems on aggregation and index numbers," and refers in a footnote to Joan Robinson's exploration of "the profound difficulties that stand in the way of giving any precise meaning to the quantity of capital" (p. 350 and note).

The identification of *A(t)* with "technical change" is another of the master tropes, a synecdoche, taking a part for the whole; and on it the paper turns. The notation says that the multiplier *A* depends on time, rising as technologists get smarter. But as Solow admits, "slowdowns, speedups, improvements in the education of the labor force, and all sorts of things" will also cause it to rise. Critics of the calculation—such as Evsey Domar, Theodore Schultz, and Solow himself—have called it a mere "measure of our ignorance." Calling it "technical change," as Solow does apologetically though persistently, is a bold synecdoche indeed, taking the part for the whole and running with it.

Solow runs with it into a paragraph containing a little simple mathematics and a clever exploitation of the conventions of the economic conversation. By the second page of the article he has made his main point and persuaded most of the economists listening. He persuades them with the symmetry of the mathematics and the appeal to the authority of scientific traditions in economics, and with the perspectival tropes: metaphor, metonymy, and synecdoche.

Especially he persuades them with irony, the "perspective of perspectives" (Burke 1945, p. 512). Observe his ironical bow to "rationally designed econometric studies" (he knew as did part of his audience that their rationality was in doubt, though in 1957 the econometricians were humorlessly unaware). He describes his notion as a mere "wrinkle" and as "elementary," so elementary a wrinkle that no one had thought of it before and after Solow an intellectual industry arose to exploit it.[4] He protects himself from criticism by mocking the sobersides: "Personally I belong to both schools." The synecdoche of "technical change" is protected when in doubt by ironical quotation marks, though the marks fall away as the doubt fades.

Irony is the most sophisticated of the master tropes. Hayden White, a historian who has treated the master tropes in the writing of history

---

4. Literally speaking, it had in fact been thought of before, by G. T. Jones in 1933 in his *Increasing Returns*. Solow was not aware of Jones, an economic historian, though he was aware of several attempts in the 1950s by historically oriented economists such as Valavanis-Vail, Schmookler, and Abramovitz to measure the same thing. The others were less influential because they did not use the metaphor of the production function as explicitly as Solow did.

in the nineteenth century, put the matter of the sophistication of irony this way:

> It presupposes that the reader or auditor already knows, or is capable of recognizing, the absurdity of the characterization of the thing designated in the Metaphor, Metonymy, or Synecdoche used to give form to it.... Irony is in one sense metatropological, for it is deployed in the self-conscious awareness of the possible misuse of figurative language.... Irony thus represents a stage of consciousness in which the problematical nature of language itself has become recognized. It points to the potential foolishness of all linguistic characterizations of reality as much as to the absurdity of the beliefs it parodies. It is therefore "dialectical," as Kenneth Burke has noted. (1973, p. 37)

The most sophisticated economists, like the most sophisticated novelists, favor irony (Booth 1974b). Irony presupposes an existing conversation off of which one can score; in this and in other ways it is mature. George Stigler, for instance, the constant intellectual companion of Solow, wrote of the guiding metaphor of consumer preferences: "It would of course be bizarre to look upon the typical family—that complex mixture of love, convenience, and frustration—as a business enterprise. Therefore, economists have devoted much skill and ingenuity to elaborating this approach" (1966, p. 21).

Economic metaphors, then, are important for economic rhetoric, and not mere frills. No economist could speak without metaphor and the other master tropes. Economists make more appeals to their audience than simply their appeals to The Facts or The Logic, though facts and logic, of course, figure in from time to time as well.

6

THE RHETORIC OF

SCIENTISM

HOW JOHN MUTH PERSUADES

Muth's Article Was Ill-Written But Important

Economic science, then, must use rhetoric and might as well be aware that it must. Consider another example in detail, less charming than Solow's but as important. In 1961 John Muth published a paper in *Econometrica* (the leading journal of statistical and mathematical economics, and the very embodiment of modernism in economics) entitled "Rational Expectations and the Theory of Price Movements." For many years economists ignored it. Robert Lucas and Thomas Sargent, who were chiefly responsible for its subsequent fame, wrote in 1981 (p. xi) that the paper had "a remarkably quiet first decade," which is no rash assessment. Though early accorded, like Solow's paper, the honor of inclusion in Arnold Zellner's *Readings in Economic Statistics and Econometrics* (1968), the paper was for a long time little read and less understood. The pattern of citations to the paper is unusual in a field that models itself so self-consciously on the urgent bustle of physics (Table 2). Seventy-four citations in 1982: even such an important paper as Solow's reached, at most, thirty in a year. There was a tiny flash, and long afterwards a boom.

Table 2. Annual Citations, 1966–1982, of Muth's 1961 Article

1966	5	1972	9	1978	47
1967	3	1973	10	1979	44
1968	2	1974	10	1980	71
1969	2	1975	20	1981	56
1970	4	1976	33	1982	74
1971	2	1977	41		

Source: *Social Science Citation Index*. The index begins in 1966.

The Rhetoric of Scientism

The paper took a long time to be recognized as important because it was badly written. The case illustrates by an argument from contraries the importance of successful writing in successful science. Galileo was a master of Italian prose; Poincaré, Einstein, and Keynes influenced science and society as much with their pens as with their mathematics.

Even by the undemanding standards of American academic life Muth's prose was not masterful or influential. It was badly organized, with ill-motivated digressions and leaps from large claims to lame examples. Little distinction was made between minor points of form and major revisions of economic thinking. Though no reader of *Econometrica* would have stumbled over the inelegant mathematics involved, he probably did wonder what exactly it was supposed to prove.

The paper bore some of the marks of professional excellence, such as an easy familiarity with mathematical statistics at a time when not many economists could claim it, and a wide-ranging bibliography. But even a serious reader of the journal could easily have dismissed it as mere muttering. Apparently most did. While richer in invention even than it appeared, it was too obviously clumsy in arrangement and style—the two other categories of classical rhetoric—to warrant much investment by its readers.

Yet the paper was important (and I believe persuasive). The argument begins with the simple point that what people think the future will bring is an important reason why they act as they do. Any explanation of economic action requires some explanation of how economic actors think about the future. Before Muth's theory the prevailing explanation was that people are slow to change their opinions, that they get a more or less correct idea of what the future will bring and then gradually adjust to it.

The trouble with the prevailing explanation was that it implied that economic actors are less perceptive than economics professors. The actors were supposed to be slow to change, but the professors were said to know they are slow, and to be able to trace their slow adjustment. The audience claimed to know the lines better than the players. What was troubling about the claim was that it implied the unnatural assertion that a professor of economics knows more about the future of sales and costs in steelmaking, publishing, or insurance than do the steelmakers, publishers, or insurance companies. If he did, he would be—or could be—rich. The claim to know how economic actors predict is a claim to superior foreknowledge of the predicted outcome. It runs up against the American Question, which is always, as we have seen, an objection to claims of foreknowledge: If you're so smart, why ain't you rich?

Muth's notion was that the professors, even if correct in their model of man, could do no better in predicting than could the steelmaker or publisher or insurance company. Or, to put the same point the other way, the economic actors, even if inspired, could do no better than the best conceivable economic model.

The notion is one of intellectual modesty and should be considered with the discussion earlier of the methodological impossibility of prediction in economics. Under Muth's constraint the professors admit that they are expert only in the social science of economics, not in the markets for high carbon steel or hail insurance. The professors then have an answer to the American Question: they admit they ain't so smart, which explains why they ain't rich. They declare themselves willing to attribute to economic actors at least as much common sense as is embodied in professional theories.

The common sense is "rationality": therefore Muth called the argument "rational expectations." No longer are the actors viewed as automata cut off from knowledge of the playwright's intent or the audience's understanding. They are to be taken as fully human, on a par with professors and playwrights. They have imperfect and mutable but rational expectations.

The idea of rational expectations is an extension of an older and broader principle of economic reasoning, the principle of entry. Economists have long asserted that business people follow the call of profit. In this they differ from most other observers of society. Wherever there is profit, the economists say, there will be entry: into French restaurants in Iowa City if there really is a market there for good food; into oil production if there really is a large gap between price and cost. Of course, the entry itself eliminates its cause. As more enter the industry of food preparing or oil drilling, the prevailing price will fall (or rise not so fast as it would have). The profit and the further incentive to enter will be eroded.

The same, said Muth, holds for the industry of producing information about the future. If an economist equipped with a few courses in economic theory and statistics could actually produce valuable information about the future of the housing industry, one might expect him to become fabulously wealthy.

Information on some economic variables is not valuable and is therefore no road to wealth. It is not valuable to know that there will be 2,567,000 housing starts next year, unless the number of housing starts enables one to predict *better than other people can* some price, such as the price of number 3 interior softwood plywood or the price of six-room duplexes on suburban lots. By itself knowledge of next year's housing starts is useless. The hypothesis of rational expectations might still apply: it may still make sense to suppose that builders and economists will reach about the same conclusions as to how many housing starts there will be. But unless a price is affected, and unless money is to be made in exploiting rare information about the effect, there is less reason to think so. There is then no compelling reason of self-interest to arrive at forecasts that are on average correct.

The valuable information is information on future prices that is on average correct and is not already embodied in the market's expectations (embodied in futures prices of plywood, say, or the present price of houses). With it one can speculate profitably. The information exceeds in value the normal return to its production—the salary, perhaps, of an assistant professor. If it did, though, other economists would set up shop, since the first economist on the scene would not by assumption be the only one who could produce the information: the others could take the courses and read the books. Taking courses and reading books cannot be a source of fabulous wealth. A widely dispersed skill in economic theory and statistics is what is supposed to make it possible to predict the future of the economy. But, in the long run, according to economic theory itself, widely dispersed skills do not earn much. Likewise, the entry of new economists continues until a fresh entrant at the margin earns no more than the usual reward for a usual education.

Muth's notion was not entirely unprecedented. Before Muth wrote, and well before he was read, the idea of entry had been applied even to the industry of predicting. The "Austrian" economists had long emphasized that economists could not predict better than, or as well as, the entrepreneur (e.g., von Mises 1949, p. 867). Muth's version was more precise. During the 1960s in finance some mathematically inclined students of the Austrian economists established the propositions that investment tip-sheets are useless, that a dartboard does as well as a stockbroker in choosing stocks to buy, that stock prices follow a random walk, and that in general the professors and pundits on Wall Street were paid for their tongues, not for their prescience. Muth's version was broader in applicability. During the 1960s and 1970s the mathematical theory of growth, which plainly needed a theory of expectations, had lit on the mathematically convenient one of assuming that the economic agents correctly anticipated what was going to happen. Muth's formulation required them to be correct only on average.

What made Muth's version of the argument especially important was its application, at first by Stephen Turnovsky and Robert Lucas and later by many others, to the matter of macroeconomics. Muth's paper became the holy writ for one of the sects that sweep macroeconomics every five years. Whatever the ultimate fate of the sect, the good news transmitted to macroeconomics is likely to remain a part of economic thinking permanently. The message, elaborated in scores of difficult and penetrating papers during the 1970s (see Lucas and Sargent 1981), was that the human rationality of the economic actor in his thinking about the future was to be taken seriously. He was to be viewed, for a change, as nobody's fool.

He was no longer to be taken as a fool, especially, in his understanding of the policy of governments. He was to recognize, for instance, that the federal government reduces taxes eventually when times are bad, in an attempt to make them good. When the tax reduction did in fact happen, such a student of practical politics would not be surprised. He would have rationally come to expect it. Wall Street has long had the idea: the investor would long since have discounted the tax reduction, and would react not at all to its accomplishment. He would have spent the money months before.

In the Keynesian or monetarist models of the 1960s and before, by contrast, the economic actor was perpetually astonished, the perfect rube: [Seizes newspaper.] "My word! The government has just reduced taxes in depression!" [Eyes bug out.] "Holy cow! The government has trimmed the growth of money after a long period of inflation! Gosh!" [Faints.] It would be trivially easy to manipulate such a dunce, from which grew the conviction in the 1940s and 1950s that it was trivially easy to manipulate the economy—to "fine-tune" it, as the journalists said. The models of rational expectations in the 1970s went to the opposite extreme. They viewed the economic actor as a man of the world: "Oh, yes, a tax cut." [Yawns, lights cigarette in a golden holder.] "Hmm: I see that inflation has been going on for some months." [Settles into club chair.] "About time for the Fed to do its tight money act." [Calls broker, sips scotch; dozes off under his copy of *Barron's*.]

Muth's Main Points Can Be Expressed in English

The essay by Muth, then, is influential. By what means does it persuade? The question is a critical not a historical one. It is not of much interest here to know who influenced Muth's paper, how it circulated in draft, what circumstances in macroeconomics made it an idea whose time had come, and whether it was anticipated in Austrian economics, Chicago-school finance, or growth theory. Its history is to the point only to the extent that the history illuminates the way it achieves its effect now.

The Rhetoric of Scientism

To use again Saussure's jargon, the issues here are synchronic not diachronic. One can approach "The Waste Land" in two ways. One way, literary history, would ask how the poem came to be written, what influences it felt, what influence it had. The other, literary criticism, would ask what claims the poem makes on the reader, what myths it uses and creates, how it is arranged for its effects. The history would be of use to the criticism and the criticism to the history. But they are distinct undertakings.

The reasons for studying Muth's paper, then, are not historical, as interesting as these would be for other purposes. It is more persuasive to use important examples than to use trivial ones to show that rhetorical techniques are important in economics (and Muth's paper, it must be clear, is important). Further, it is more persuasive to use mathematical papers than literary ones to show that economics is literary (and Muth's paper was mathematical by the standard of 1961 and has spawned papers mathematical by the standard of today). The interest here lies not in the history of thought surrounding Muth's paper but in the way the prose works, or tries to work.

Below are reproduced the crucial sentences in the paper. In the interest of general intelligibility the selection does not include the many mathematical arguments, but these were for the most part mere instances of the verbal arguments and often strayed from the main point. This is not to say that the mathematical arguments were without purpose. They added persuasive weight to the paper in various ways: by exhibiting a relevant virtuosity; and by showing in a number of particular cases how rational expectations might look, showing how they would differ from other sorts of expectations, and, by methods of simulation common in applied mathematics, showing how much the difference matters.

It would be easy to persuade economists that the selection here is the core:

Muth	*Translation*
[A] The objective of this paper is to outline a theory of expectations and to show that implications are—as a first approximation—consistent with the relevant data.	The paper asks how people guess about what the future will bring. The answer is tested against some of the facts in agricultural markets.
[B] I should like to suggest that expectations, since they are informed predictions of future events, are essentially the same as the predictions of the relevant economic	The guesses people make are probably no better or worse than the guesses economists would make. I'll call such guesses "rational," to distinguish them from the

theory. At the risk of confusing this purely descriptive hypothesis with a pronouncement as to what firms ought to do, we call such expectations "rational." It is sometimes argued that the assumption of rationality in economics leads to theories inconsistent with, or inadequate to explain, observed phenomena, especially changes over time (e.g., Simon 1959). Our hypothesis is based on exactly the opposite point of view: that dynamic economic models do not assume enough rationality.

[C] The hypothesis asserts three things: (1) Information is scarce, and the economic system generally does not waste it. (2) The way expectations are formed depends specifically on the structure of the relevant system describing the economy. (3) A "public prediction," in the sense of Grunberg and Modigliani (1954), will have no substantial effect on the operation of the economic system (unless it is based on inside information). This is not quite the same thing as stating that the marginal revenue product of economics is zero, because expectations of a single firm may still be subject to greater error than the theory.

[D] It *does not* assert that the scratch work of entrepreneurs resembles the system of equations in any way; nor does it state that predictions of entrepreneurs are perfect or that their expectations are all the same.

[E] If the prediction of the theory were substantially better than the expectations of the firms, then there would be opportunities for the "insider" to profit from the

irrational—i.e., unreasonable, foolish—guesses that present theories posit. Hostility to "rationality" is common among the critics of economics. I wish to go in the other direction: to see how far one can get by supposing that people are as rational in guessing about the future as in buying bread in the present.

In other words, I'm saying that people take appropriate care with their guesses, and economists should credit them with such caretaking. If people take care in guessing, talk about the future will be pointless: people will have allowed for the effects being talked about. For instance, declarations that prosperity is just around the corner will have no impact, unless the declarer really does know something we all don't know. Economists do know something, though not as much as their present notions about guessing imply: they know that a bunch of guesses by individuals average out over a large group to less quirky guesses.

Business people do not have to be trained in mathematical economics to do about as well as economists can do in guessing the future. Nor do they have to guess perfectly or all in the same way.

The notion of rational guessing makes a lot of sense. If economists could do better than business people, the economists would be rich. They are not. A farmer

The Rhetoric of Scientism

knowledge—by inventory speculation if possible, by operating a firm, or by selling a price forecasting service to the firms. The profit opportunities would no longer exist if the aggregate expectation of the firms is the same as the prediction of the theory: . . . . The expected price equals the equilibrium price.

[F] It is rather surprising that expectations have not previously been regarded as rational dynamic models, since rationality is assumed in all other aspects of entrepreneurial behavior. From a purely theoretical standpoint, there are good reasons for assuming rationality. First, it is a principle applicable to all dynamic problems (if true). Expectations in different markets and systems would not have to be treated in completely different ways. Second, if expectations were not moderately rational there would be opportunities for economists to make profits in commodity speculation, running a firm, or selling the information to present owners. Third, rationality is an assumption that can be modified. Systematic biases, incomplete or incorrect information, poor memory, etc., can be examined with analytical methods based on rationality.

[G] The only real test, however, is whether theories involving rationality explain observed phenomena any better than alternative theories. In this section we shall therefore compare some of the empirical implications of the rational expectations hypothesis with those of the cobweb "theorem." The effects of rational expectations are particularly

guessing about the price of hogs will arrive on average at the price the market does: he'd better.

It is asymmetric for economists to treat people as rational economic men in buying bread or building ships but not in guessing the future. On aesthetic grounds it would be better to use one principle of rationality. As I said, if economists were so smart as to know how business people were failing to be rational, the economists would be rich. Furthermore, rationality is usually a good place to start thinking about human affairs, especially economic affairs. You can add later whatever allowance for ignorance or foolishness seems justified in each case.

But these arguments I've made so far are just frosting, and are not good scientific method. The cake is the ability of my notion to make better sense of the world than some competing notion. In agricultural markets especially (though also in the study of general booms and busts) the competing notion is called the "cobweb theorem." No one actually takes the "theorem" very important because the cobweb theorem has often been regarded as one of the most successful attempts at dynamic economic theories (e.g., Goodwin 1947). Few students of agricultural problems or business cycles seem to take the cobweb theorem very seriously, however, but its implications do occasionally appear. For example, a major cause of price fluctuations in cattle and hog markets is sometimes believed to be the expectations of farmers themselves. . . . As a result, the prediction of the cobweb theory would ordinarily have the sign opposite to that of the firms.

seriously, perhaps because they recognize without thinking about it much that it's not rational. In any event, it says that each single farmer thinks prices will stay high when they are high, and that he will therefore raise lots of hogs to take advantage of the high price. By the time the little hogs become big hogs, however, every other farmer has also raised lots of hogs; the price is in fact low, contrary to what he expected. The farmer, poor fool, never learns.

[H] There is some direct evidence concerning the quality of expectations of firms. Heady and Kaldor (1954) have shown that for the period studied, average expectations were considerably more accurate than simple extrapolation.

Heady and Kaldor showed that the firms do learn, or at least that they learn better than this.

[I] It often appears that reported expectations underestimate the extent of changes that actually take place. . . . Such findings are clearly inconsistent with the cobweb theory, which ordinarily requires a negative coefficient.

Other writers have found that farmers do not expect prices to move as much as the prices actually do move, but that they at least predict the right direction: the cobweb theorem says they would predict the wrong direction.

[J] The evidence for the cobweb model lies in the quasi-periodic fluctuations in prices of a number of commodities. The hog cycle is perhaps the best known, but cattle and potatoes have sometimes been cited as others which obey the "theorem." . . . That the observed hog cycles were too long for the cobweb theorem was first observed in 1935 by Coase and Fowler (1935, 1937). The graph of cattle prices given by Ezekiel (1938) as evidence for the cobweb theorem implies an extraordinarily long period of

The whole notion of the cobweb is based on the ups and downs of, say, hog prices. But hog prices take much longer to go up and down than it takes to raise hogs. Something is wrong. What is wrong, I'll venture, is that the irrational theory of how farmers make guesses about the future is mistaken.

production (5–7 years). The interval
between successive peaks for other
commodities tends to be longer than
three production periods.

Muth's Article Engages in the Usual Appeals to Scientific Method

The question is how Muth's argument achieves cre-
dence. Now of course it did not achieve credence easily, because it was
obscurely written. Its obscurity, however, became a rhetorical advantage once it had been made the holy writ of a faith. It is composed in
a foreign language, but the language is a sacred one, like Old Church
Slavonic. Its style is the key to its rhetorical appeal, because it is the
style of scientism.

Lucas and Sargent, the most prominent users of the argument, are
persuaded that it is "one of the most carefully and compactly written
papers of recent vintage: every sentence in the introduction [not reproduced here] counts, and many have since been expanded into entire
articles. Muth introduces the hypothesis at a general, verbal level, motivating it as a corollary of the general principles of economic equilibrium, and then turns to specific, certainty-equivalent examples" (Lucas
and Sargent 1981, p. xvii). The praise is itself scientistic and draws on
the stylistic rhetoric of modernism. The language of "introduc[ing] the
hypothesis at a general, verbal level, motivating it as a corollary of . . .
general principles" is undiluted modernism. One deduces lower-level
hypotheses from general principles, the test of the lower hypothesis
being therefore an indirect test of the principles. The talk of corollaries
is part of the same tradition (and so too, incidentally, is the special
virtue attributed to care and compactness, the virtues of mathematics).
The hypotheses come from the context of discovery, before the rigor of
justification. One "motivates" a proof in mathematics—the language
used here—by stepping for a little while outside the rigorous mode of
proof-making to show the groundlings what is afoot.

Muth himself makes similar remarks, also couched in modernist language, about what should warrant belief. In the first sentence of the
selection he implicitly declares that most of his arguments to follow in
the paper are by his own standards epistemologically lame. Showing
that "the implications are . . . consistent with the relevant data" (paragraph A) is indeed the positivist criterion of truth in science, but little
of the paper does it. He does show that if he is careful his notion does
not lead to manifest absurdity, such as a condition that speculators in

hogs entered the business to lose rather than to gain money. These are the quality of the "data" he shows "consistent" with his argument.

Towards the end, after much argument that would find no place in the epistemology of positivism, he turns impatiently on himself with a positivist *ukase*: "The only real test, however, is whether theories involving rationality explain observed phenomena any better than alternative theories" (paragraph G). The words are redolent of the received view. The richness of scientific persuasion is to be reduced to a crucial experiment, a "real test" (*pace* Duhem and the dilemma that no test is crucial). Since the alternative views are "theories," the job of science is to upend or uphold them (*pace* Kuhn and the history of normal science fitting fact to invariant theory). The relevant test depends on "observed phenomena," the hard, objective data so much to be desired (*pace* Polanyi and the notion that scientific knowledge is not epistemologically special).

The appeals to the method of science in Muth's paper are mainly matters of style, arising out of a modernist conversation. The paper does not achieve credence by axiomatic proof or statistical curve-fitting, though written in the genre recommended by modernism. What is modernist in it is not the turns of argument but the style.

The conflict between the "nonrhetorical" ideology of modernism and the actual practice of modernists has been apparent from the beginning, showing up repeatedly in matters of style. Amelie Oksenberg Rorty points out of Descartes that "despite his austere recommendations about the methods of discovery and demonstration, he hardly ever followed those methods, hardly ever wrote in the same genre twice" (1983, p. 548). She notes that his attacks on the common topics of argument, such as authority or the appeal to common knowledge, have an ironic air, for he "found himself using the very modes he intended to attack." Since Bacon and Descartes and the creators later in the seventeenth century of the scientific paper, any scientist who wished to persuade had to adopt the modernist style, as Muth did. Darwin is the leading case. The student of rhetoric John Campbell has argued that Darwin took "care to redescribe his path to discovery so that it appeared to conform with conventional standards of Baconian inductionism"; and Edward Manier writes that "the early drafts of the theory do not conform to the 'hypothetico-deductive model' of scientific explanation, although they indicate Darwin's intent to represent his views as if they did conform to that model" (Campbell 1984, p. 15 and p. 13, where Manier is quoted).

The style of Muth's article makes an ethical and emotional appeal, an appeal to his character as a Scientist and to the self-image of his

The Rhetoric of Scientism

audience as fellow scientists. The word "I" occurs twice only (once in the selection), in keeping with the convention that kings, editors, people with tapeworms, and honest-to-goodness scientists are permitted to use the more dignified "we" instead. The style is often indirect in other ways, as suits a Scientist (one can make insecure scientists still more insecure by violating such stylistic conventions).[1] Ten of the thirty sentences in the selection have their main clauses in the passive voice. Amidst much that is self-confident and even cocky there are soothing words of proper scientific modesty: "as a first approximation" (A) the theory works; "I would like to suggest" (B), not assert; "it is rather surprising" (F) that the theory has been overlooked; "it often appears" (I) that behavior is inconsistent with the alternative theories. And throughout the essay the reader is treated to dollops of scientific vocabulary from the classical languages: "purely descriptive hypotheses," "observed phenomena," "objective probability distributions of outcomes," "analytical methods," and the like.

Northrop Frye observes that "much of the difficulty in a philosophical [and scientific] style is rhetorical in origin, resulting from a feeling that it is necessary to detach and isolate the intellect from the emotions" (1957, p. 330). He examines a characteristically opaque sentence from James Mill, translates it in the style of the translation of Muth above, and wonders, as one does about Muth, "why, if James Mill meant that, he could not have said it." The answer is that "the style is motivated by a perverse, bristling intellectual honesty. *He* will not condescend to employ any of the pretty arts of persuasion, sugar-coated illustrations or emotionally-loaded terms; he will appeal only to the cold logic of reason itself—reinforced, to be sure, by a peculiarly Victorian sense that the more difficult the style, the tougher the moral and intellectual fibre one develops in wrestling with it." On the page before he remarks, "All of these are clearly at least in part endeavours to purify verbal communication of the emotional content of rhetoric; all of them, however, impress the literary critic as being themselves rhetorical devices."

Well, of course. The form of Muth's article seeks to persuade. Not to fool: persuade. Put clearly or modestly or, above all, Unscientifically, it would not have been in the end a success as a scientific paper. In a word, the article, like any other piece of scientific work, is rhetorical, even in its stylistic appeal to a rhetoric of not having a rhetoric.

1. More sophisticated stylists in economics (compare the discussion of George Stigler and Robert Solow above) play off the conventions of scientific writing, making disquieting little jokes about this or that item in the creed. Naive readers do not get the jokes, or even note them, and sophisticated readers are correspondingly charmed.

Muth's Appeal Is in Fact to the Community of Scholars

The theory of knowledge put forward by the objective, data-respecting, sober style of modernism in Muth's paper is that the privileged form of knowing is knowing by the lone person himself, *solus ipse*. That is, real knowing is said to be individual and solipsistic, not social. No one needs to *say* anything to you, the Cartesian says, to persuade you of the ancient proof of the irrationality of the square root of 2. There is nothing social about your assent to it. So too the metaphor of facing fact. One turns towards it (the Cartesian professor now turns and talks in the direction of an imagined object), and there it is. We face "observations" for "the real tests." No need to talk. To be sure, we are not called on daily to face the observations or reexamine the tests of planetary motion or the synthesis of protein. We accept astronomers and chemists when they claim to have done so. Yet, the modernist asserts, armed with his solipsistic theory of truth, the important thing is that we *could* do so ourselves if we wished. That's truth: what we could come to believe after lonely study.

Though not much developing the point, Wayne Booth suggests that the crux of modernism is its solipsistic theory of truth. He quotes Tom Paine, that archetype of man in modernism's late adolescence, declaring stoutly: "I do not believe in the creed professed by . . . any church I know of. My own mind is my own church" (1974a, p. 86). On the same page he quotes Kenneth Burke, the John the Baptist of a newer dispensation, as though answering Paine's solipsism: "A man is necessarily talking error unless his words can claim membership in a collective body of thought." Booth remarks that the joke is on the man who tries to organize a discussion group for solipsists. When economists strain to use modernist methods, their discussions take on this character of shadow boxing. The result, says Booth, is a division of propositions into articles of faith held for no reason and reasons held without solid faith. One thinks of the strange mix of ideological fervor and disinterested inquiry in economics. The result of a solipsistic epistemology consistently applied must be the breakdown of the conversation of scholarship: "All the many allies who might work together to discover what can be legitimately believed are thus encouraged simply to affirm *at* each other. . . . Passionate commitment has lost its connection with the provision of good reasons. And reason has been reduced to logical calculation and proof about whatever does not matter enough to encourage commitment" (1974a pp. x–xi).

The Rhetoric of Scientism

But persuasive knowledge is social. It is a social event that Muth's arguments came to be credible. Certain of the arguments were persuasive to certain people. The arguments were not written in the heavens or, as Descartes imagined, in the soul of the self-regarding man. The astronomer relies for his convictions on "a sequence of instrument makers and astronomers and nuclear physicists, specialist in this and that, each of whom he must trust and believe. All this knowledge, all our knowledge, has been built up communally. . . . The fallacy which imprisons the positivist and the analyst [in philosophy] is the assumption that he can test what is true and false without consulting anyone but himself" (Bronowski 1965, p. 57). Aristotle had said "a statement is persuasive and credible . . . . because there is someone whom it persuades" (*Rhetoric* 1, 2, 1356b 27), no trivial truism, though from the *trivium*, and true. At the other end of the Western philosophical tradition, exhausted from the repeated attempts to leap to a higher-than-social level of truth, one finds Charles Morris and Nelson Goodman, among others, making the same point (Morris, quoted in Rorty 1979, p. 376; Goodman 1954, p. 57).

The evidence for the social character of knowledge in the present case is that not everyone of Muth's society has been persuaded. A particular society of economists, not the ages, was to be persuaded. Not all were persuaded, and those who were have identifiable characteristics. His arguments, to use the modernist word, were not altogether "compelling." They did not compel assent the way some (but not all) of the simplest and oldest proofs in mathematics do, or the way some (but not all) of the simplest and most dramatic controlled experiments in physics do. This may be seen in the refusal of such intelligent economists as Robert Gordon, James Tobin, and Benjamin Friedman, among many others, to give their assent to Muth's arguments.

The official rhetoric of the paper allows no room for anything but unanimous assent, since the paper claims to be a certified piece of positivism "consistent with the facts." But noncompulsion in scientific argument is, of course, commonplace. When honest and well-informed biologists disagree about the strength of a tendency to inherited altruism among human blood relatives or when honest and well-informed physicists disagree about the significance of Bell's Theorem, they must be using arguments that do not compel assent in the conclusive way required by modernist method.

Muth's paper has in fact few modernist certitudes. The main argument, as I have said, is that rational expectations applies more widely a principle of entry used daily by economists elsewhere. The usual models "do not assume enough rationality" (B); "rationality is assumed in all other aspects of entrepreneurial behavior" (F), so why not here? It is an appeal to a figure of speech discussed earlier, philosophical consistency. Muth is simply pointing to an oversight in the application of economic theory. It is as though for some reason astronomers in possession of Newton's theory had not noticed that the motions of the earth's moon could be brought under it. A paper pointing out that this too could be fitted into a theory that explained the motions of the earth, Jupiter, and Mars, and even of Ganymede and Phobus, would be instantly plausible to many. Likewise in Muth's case.

The analogy was by no means persuasive to all economists, I have noted. Yet it had magical power over others. Some of Muth's audience were convinced as much as they were ever going to be as soon as they understood the argument, that is to say (if they were among the tiny group who saw through its "compactness"), by about the second page. Compare the rapidity with which Solow persuaded his audience, or at least the part of it that believed anyway the metaphor of the production function. There is nothing unscientific about such ready if partial assent.

Nor did Muth break with the traditions of science when he turned to little mathematical simulations that seemed to behave well—not simulations that "predict well" in properly modernist style, but that compute and fit and lie still beside the existing theory without exploding. Thomas Kuhn, in contrasting his views on the "logic of discovery or psychology of research" with Popper's, argued that for the most part a scientist is concerned rather with evaluating his "best guesses about the proper way to connect his own research problem with the corpus of accepted scientific knowledge. . . . the scientist must *premise* current theory as the rules of the game" (Kuhn 1977, p. 270). Science, to repeat, is not "testing" its theories against predictions. The attempts at simulation are mostly puzzles the scientist poses which are "like crossword puzzles, challenges only to his ingenuity. *He* is in difficulty, not current theory" (ibid., p. 271n).

The role of simulation in science is evident in the conversation about the extinction of the dinosaurs. The new explanation argues that a comet hit the earth scores of millions of years ago, creating a natural version of the nuclear winter. As a reviewer of a book on the subject wrote, "The chief difficulty is in rendering it quantitative. We must hope that someone will now produce a numerical simulation that extinguishes/perpetuates all the right species in all the right numbers" (McCrea 1983). A related conversation is taking place in astronomy, using identical rhetorical devices. The astronomical argument, beginning with the observation that there are regular mass extinctions, is that the sun has a mate, a star called Nemesis, whose orbit periodically disturbs the comet fields surrounding the sun, causing comets to rain into the solar system. Or perhaps the disturbing body is a Planet X:

> Although the Planet X model also appears to explain the periodic mass extinctions adequately, Mr. Whitmire says he does not consider it to be better than the Nemesis model. Nemesis, he noted, has so far withstood many detailed calculations. But if the Planet X model can withstand similar calculations, "I think it will be a better model than Nemesis" for two reasons, he added. The most important reason, he said, is that the existence of Planet X has long been postulated, so scientists "would not be inventing anything new." The second reason is that the orbit of the planet is closer to the sun than that proposed for Nemesis, which means it would be much more likely to be stable. (*Chronicle of Higher Education*, February 20, 1985)

When the puzzle is solved, the scientific community applauds, but it is not applauding an event in the hypothetico-deductive model of science. The situation is similar in economics and in Muth.

The Explicit Arguments Are Rhetorically Complex

Having shown that his instance can be simulated without gross violation of the facts, Muth is ready to make more direct arguments for it. Early on he remarks that "information is scarce, and the economic system generally does not waste it" (paragraph C; compare the remark on the "marginal revenue product of economics" in the same paragraph, which makes the same point). Such remarks are common in economics: economists delight in posing deep but tough little examination questions for their colleagues, just as classicists delight in posing for theirs apt but difficult quotations from the Greek Anthology. The correct reaction is a show of effortless understanding.

In Muth's case the understanding is that he is comparing information about the future of hog prices with any other good that can be bought and sold. If the analogy persuades, then one will believe that business people buy information to the optimal extent—or at any rate to the extent of optimality that they exhibit in their other and more ordinary purchases. Their purchases of trucking services or space in feedlots do not leave any gaps between the cost of the last units of such things and the value in use. There is no waste, no misallocation. Nor, Muth is saying, is there misallocation in purchasing information about the future, which implies that there is no gap for mere economists to exploit. When business people have done their jobs, the future will in fact bring what *on average* they had expected it would bring. The argument does not "state that the predictions of entrepreneurs are perfect" (C). They do not hit the bull's-eye every time. But at least their hits are distributed around the bull's-eye in such a way that no economist could profitably advise them to aim higher in shooting (E, F near the middle).

His three further arguments "from a purely theoretical standpoint" (F) are revealing. They are purely aesthetic, which is what economists mean when they call an argument "theoretical." As I have noted, when economists are asked why almost all of them believe in free trade, they will say that it is a "theoretical" argument that convinces them. Further inquiry will reveal that it is in fact a pretty diagram that convinces them. Evidence that would convince a consistent positivist is wholly absent. So here, which probably explains why Muth immediately turns on himself with the stern injunction to seek positive virtue and "explain observed phenomena."

The arguments are arguments from symmetry and suitability and personal character, very distant from the rules of modernism. His notion of rational expectations would be a unified theory of expectations, Muth argues, symmetrical in all its applications. The appeal is to a uniformity in social nature—or, more accurately, to a desire to understand social nature uniformly. He argues again that economists would be rich if they were as smart as alternative theories posit (E again). The argument is practically *ad hominem* and has the reflexive character that the Frankfurt School of philosophers associates with critical as against scientific theories.

He argues finally that rational expectations can be conveniently modified to fit the imperfections of the social world. Flexibility is frequently praised in scientific theories and of course should be. But flexibility is simply a promise that the theory will be able to evade crucial tests, surviving unscathed from positivist tortures. Nothing could be further from naive falsification. All the arguments he uses are, as Muth says, "good reasons"; but they do not fit with the narrowing epistemology that many scientists still believe.

Even when he has jerked himself back to "real tests," Muth cannot follow the modernist line. His "observations" (H, I, J) are all reports of other people's work, once removed from the virtue of primary experiment. They are, in fact, mainly attacks on the plausibility of one among the infinite number of possible alternatives to rationality, not the full, fair horse race among alternatives imagined in positivist folklore. The Heady and Kaldor paper cited by Muth used self-reporting of expectations by the farmers themselves, which is forbidden in the economist's version of positivist method. The regression coefficients discussed in paragraph I are open to numerous objections, as Muth well understood. And the observation in J that cycles in hog prices are in fact much longer than the gestation period of hogs (the gestation period is important to the other theories of expectation) is hardly decisive, as Muth himself remarks: "positive serial correlation of the exogenous disturbances" means that farmers may have a series of several bad years in a row, lengthening the apparent cycle beyond the period it takes to raise a hog. The rejection of the nonrational hog cycle may be merely apparent. The test Muth proposes, to put it technically, is underidentified.

To say that Muth's "observations" would not persuade consistent modernists is not, however, to say that they do not persuade reasonable economists. Economists, as was argued at length above, cannot be consistent modernists and remain reasonable. The persuasiveness of Muth's paper comes from the richness and catholicity of its unofficial arguments, well beyond the official narrowness. Among economists an argument from axiomatic demonstration, statistical test (regression in particular), or appeal to the competitive model all have prestige. None is logically compelling, nor even very persuasive by itself. One can object to each that garbage in implies garbage out. Yet the most hostile economist, if properly socialized, will want to yield to the form. He will be pleased by their success at a formal level—"Gosh, what a clever argument that is: What a neat proof / statistical test/ appeal to the intellectual traditions of economics"—even if he wants to disbelieve their substance.

To claim that Muth persuades by rhetorical means is not of course a criticism. Quite the contrary: it is inevitable, and even good. Outside of a rather small group of specialists in speech, communication, theatre arts, and related fields the study of the rhetoric of a text is usually a preface to debunking it. There is a rhetoric of the analysis of rhetoric. An outsider reading "Sweet Talk: The Moral Rhetoric against Sugar" by Elizabeth Walker Mechling and Jay Mechling, published in 1983 in the *Central State Speech Journal*, aches for the demonstration that the diatribes against sugar, analyzed rhetorically in the paper, are in fact misled. But the demonstration does not come. The expectation that it must come is naive. Critical thinking is not necessarily "critical" in the usual sense.

Muth's article is typical of the literature of economics, with its rich and unexplored rhetoric. That is the point: economists are not aware of the rhetorical riches buried in their style of talk. The richness is not astonishing, of course. That economists persuade the way other professional arguers do is no more astonishing than that arguers now use much the same common topics as were current in Cicero's time (Burke 1950, p. 56). True, one might be equally astonished by both facts, and study them with wondering respect. An anthropologist, for instance, would do well, as some have, to study rhetoric among the Sherpa or the Ilongot, to see if the same figures of argument carry conviction there as with us. In any case a study of rhetoric among the Econ need not encourage bad rhetoric any more (or less) than the study of econometrics encourages bad econometrics.

Muth's Rhetoric Is Indistinguishable from That in Other Fields

Muth's rhetoric ought to be familiar, because it uses figures of speech common to our civilization. Different fields of study pick from the same list of figures of speech. The list is issued with an education.

Imagine the figures of speech stuffed into a storeroom: twelve dozen appeals to authority here, a gross of syllogisms there, 157 metaphors (few of them fresh) on the top shelf, a dozen urn models stuck in behind the metaphors, and one argument from design, apparently secondhand, over by the window. These and others are available for use. A field such as economics will at one time make large use of the argument from design, say, and little use of appeals to the character of Scientist; at another time it will use a different bundle, having put the used ones back in the storeroom. None of the items are epistemologically privileged. To be proud that one achieves human persuasion by using existence theorems as against analogies does not make much sense, especially considering that the bundle of figures used is not permanent. Today's user of an argument from experiment will be tomorrow's user of an appeal to authority.

In short, any field, such as economics, differs from another, such as history or physics, in two respects. It uses for a while a somewhat different selection from the common store of figures of speech. Much overlap can be expected. And it studies different objects. A science is a class of objects and a way of conversing about them, not a way of knowing truth.

The overlap of argument especially requires factual demonstration. One does not after all see engineers using the metaphor of the invisible hand every day or theologians using Brouwer's fixed-point theorem (though each could). The plan is to see the overlap by getting down into the details of argument in fields different from economics, showing the similarity point by point to Muth's argument.

Three fields that among them must surround economics, whatever coordinates one might use, are paleontology, pure mathematics, and the study of Latin literature. If we accept the modernist notion that correlates what is out there with how we know, these surely will be, respectively, the realms of plain fact, indubitable proof, and mere opinion. It will develop that they are not.

For paleontology I have already remarked on how the conversation about mass extinctions uses simulation, a figure of speech whose use in economics has grown as the price of computer time has fallen. Even when away from their computers, the economists use it, to think about the effect of withholding the grain crop on prices, for example. It is mathematical analogizing. In this, unsurprisingly, economists are not different from other scientific poets.

Another case in point is described by Stephen Jay Gould. The sudden proliferation of species at the beginning of the Cambrian period, one of the great puzzles in evolution, was explained by Steven Stanley in 1973 by positing the sudden arrival of forms of life that fed on other forms of life, single-celled herbivores, as it were, in a grassy sea. Their grazing on the dominant forms allowed the new forms to survive the competition from the previously dominant ones, which in turn resulted in new grazers. For the similarity of Stanley's explanation to the analysis of Muth, Gould's description is worth quoting at length:

> Stanley did not develop his theory from empirical studies of Precambrian communities. It is a deductive argument based on an established principle of ecology that does not contradict any fact of the Precambrian world and seems particularly consistent with a few observations. In a frank concluding paragraph, Stanley presents four reasons for accepting his theory: (1) "It seems to account for what facts we have about Precambrian life"; (2) "It is simple, rather than complex or contrived"; (3) "It is purely biological, avoiding *ad hoc* invocation of external controls"; and (4) "It is largely the product of direct deduction from an established ecological principle."
>
> Such justifications do not correspond to the simplistic notions about scientific progress that are taught in most high schools and advanced by most media. Stanley does not invoke proof by new information obtained from rigorous experiment. His second criterion is a methodological presumption, the third a philosophical preference, the fourth an application of prior theory.

Only Stanley's first reason makes any reference to Precambrian facts, and it merely makes the weak point that his theory "accounts" for what is known (many other theories do the same). But creative thought in science is exactly this—not a mechanical collection of facts and induction of theories, but a complex process involving intuition, bias, and insight from other fields. Science, at its best, interposes human judgment and ingenuity upon all its proceedings. (Gould 1977, p. 125)

That the theory "accounts for what [few] facts we have" (as Stanley put it, in the usual phrase) is exactly Muth's claim too, buttressed immediately—lest we pause too long over the paucity of these facts and become depressed—by appeals to the traditions of reasoning in the field and the aesthetic pleasure of the simpler argument. It is not strange to find evolution and economics using identical rhetorical devices, for they are identical twins raised separately. In any case, Muth's and Stanley's theories are similar in the rhetorical appeals they make.

In pure mathematics the case is one described by Mark Steiner in 1975 (Steiner 1975), suggested in turn by George Polya's remarkable book on the rhetoric of number and quantity, *Induction and Analogy in Mathematics* (1954). The great Swiss mathematician Leonhard Euler wished to find a simple expression, supposing one existed, for the infinite sum $1 + 1/4 + 1/9 + 1/16 + \ldots$ and so forth forever, the sum of the reciprocals of successive squares of the positive integers. To those unfamiliar with infinite sums, the logic of which was not developed in full rigor until long after Euler wrote, there is no obvious reason why the sum should exist (although a little calculation makes it very plausible that it does and is somewhere around 1.64). What Euler showed is typical of the rabbits that eighteenth-century mathematics was always pulling out of hats half consciously: that the sum is exactly $\pi^2/6$. To nonmathematicians it is astonishing that π turns up so often in expressions apparently unrelated to circles.

The argument that Euler developed depended on many things, among them, as Steiner puts it, precisely that "he knew that a constant like π on the basis of past experience, was likely to show up in such a context" (1975, p.105). Likewise, Muth knew on the basis of past experience that rational models were easy to manipulate and likely to give especially simple results. Euler felt his result to be "simple and esthetic" (Steiner's words, p. 105), as Muth did. Euler could see no alternative, as Muth could see no merit and many demerits in the cobweb theorem. Euler, a famous calculator, showed the formula to be empirically correct to twenty decimal places. Muth had less precise material, but made an

The Rhetoric of Scientism

identical argument, dressed up for purposes of modernist epistemology as "the only real test."

The most important strand in Euler's web of persuasion was an algebraic derivation of the equality. But the derivation depends on a crucial "inductive 'leap' . . . unjustified by anything so far presented" (Steiner 1975, p. 103). The leap was an analogy between finite equations like $0 = 3 + 4x - 10x^2$, of the second degree, and equations like

$$0 = x/1 - x^3/(3)(2) + x^5/(5)(4)(3)(2) - x^7/(7)(6)(5)(4)(3)(2) + \ldots .$$

Euler imagined that these should be called equations of the infinite degree, yet as Steiner notes (p. 106), "no axiomatization, or even formalization, of 'infinite addition' existed at the time." It was "Euler's genius and his painstaking verifications" by numerical simulation that made fruitful this notion of "exploiting the analogy between finite and infinite." Even by the standards of eighteenth-century mathematics "Euler had not proved his results." But—and this is the crucial point— "we must admit that Euler had a right to be confident in his discovery, beyond any doubt."

So too Muth. His discovery, though clearly more doubtful than Euler's, also rested on an unproven analogy, between ordinary goods and information about the future. He claimed, with approximately as much prior warrant as Euler, that both were objects of production, allocation, and lucid plan. The analogy, like Euler's, carried much of the weight of persuasion. Like Euler, Muth had a warrant for using the analogy that in other applications a similar analogy "yields other results that are also verified to many decimal places," and that it is "an analogy that brings forth previously proved theorems" (Steiner 1975, p. 107). This is the burden of Muth's use of the word "rational." He is pointing out that other applications of the analogy between human action and methodical calculation have proven fruitful in understanding. And of course they have. The mathematician, like the paleontologist, does not argue in a way much different from the economist.

Another theorem of Euler, as I have noted, was the subject of Lakatos' experiment in the rhetorical study of mathematics (it would have irritated Lakatos and the Lakatosians to describe it as a "rhetorical study"). The conversation about the Descartes-Euler theorem on polyhedra witnessed many correct but contradictory proofs, though a purely modernist line would demand only one. As the Teacher in Lakatos' dialogue says, "Proofs, even though they may not prove, certainly do help to improve our conjecture" (Lakatos 1976, p. 37). Muth's demonstrations do not "prove" the theorem of rational expectations in any final, ultimate, modernist sense, any more than Euler's proved his theorem: they illuminate it and improve it, with an audience in mind. In Latin literature the example is a striking new understanding of the arrangement of poetry books in the late republic and early empire. Helena R. Dettmer (1983) has discovered that the poets arranged their books with methodical care (one might say rationality), going so far as to impose numerical patterns on the sums of lines in corresponding sections. Her treatise on the structure of Horace's *Odes*, for instance, discovers in them an immense structure of nested rings, linking poems hundreds of lines distant from each other. *Odes* 1.1 corresponds (as has long been known) to *Odes* 3.30 in theme and meter, *Odes* 1.2 to *Odes* 3.29 in theme (as has not been suspected, significant though it is for understanding Horace's attitude to the peace-giver and liberty-taker Octavius Augustus Caesar). Likewise, 1.3 corresponds to 3.27 (a slight irregularity), 1.4 to 3.28, 1.5 to 3.26, and so on and on in dazzling and unsuspected symmetry.

Certain poems stand out by their tightness of symmetry in the arrangement as "structural," and for these Dettmer discovers dozens of astonishing arithmetical truths: the fourteen structural poems in the first half of the book have in sum (not individually) exactly the same number of lines as the fourteen corresponding ones in the second half (348 lines); the five structural poems on one side of the midpoint have in sum 124 lines, as do the five corresponding ones on the other side. As Dettmer says, difficult though it may be to believe, "The mathematical symmetry is highly significant because it furnishes clear and compelling evidence that all the structural poems have been identified."[2] Other Latin poets of late republican and early imperial times used similar artifice. In Catullus' little book, for example, Dettmer has discovered a series of numerical theorems no less astonishing than Euler's and more precise than Muth's (Dettmer 1984a). Divide the middle (long) poems on the basis of theme and evident verbal echoes into sets labeled A (which is poem 64), B (poems 61 and 62), B' (68a and 68b), A' (65 and 66), C (63), and C' (67). Note a lemma (which like Euler's algebra, Stanley's cropping theory, and Muth's rationality "yields other results that are also verified") that Roman poets arranged their poetry in balanced rings, as Dettmer has shown to be true of Horace, Vergil, Propertius, Ovid, and others. Signify the number of lines in a section by its letter. THEOREM: $A - B + A' - B' = C + C'$.

It takes the breath away. One can believe almost anything about

2. Dettmer 1983, pp. 525, 531. Note that Dettmer, though lacking training in statistics, here uses the word "significant" in exactly its statistical sense, as a low probability of rejecting the hypothesis of no symmetry if it were true. Note, too, her use of the modernist word, "compelling" evidence.

π, precambrian organisms, or hog farmers, but had imagined that poets were of different stuff.[3] This and many scores of other instances detailed by Dettmer change the conception of Latin poets, increasing admiration for their artfulness, if not their art. The embedding of the poetry in verified structures can resolve numerous textual and interpretative doubts, from the validity of the conjecture "o patrona virgo" in line 9 of "Cui domo lepidum novum libellum" to the understanding of how the Romans thought.

What is chiefly important here is the character of the argument. Dettmer's book on Horace is 550 pages long and assesses methodically hundreds upon hundreds of verbal echoes and thematic clues, embedding them in the two-thousand-year-old conversation of scholarship about Horace. It is wholly "scientific" if the word means "precise, numerical, thorough, crushingly persuasive." Dettmer realizes that she will have trouble making the numerical symmetries believable to many classicists, who identify as dogmatically with the literary half of the modernist dichotomy as most economists identify with its mathematical half:

> Whether one likes numbers or not (and many do not), the fact remains that they exist. It is true that numbers and their implications, the [poet indulging in] addition or deletion of verses to make patterns, do indeed destroy our romantic illusions of a poet posed with stilus and wax tablet sitting beneath a spreading plane tree, invoking the Muse for inspiration. . . . [But numerical patterns] furnish an invaluable tool for the literary critic. (Dettmer 1983, pp. 7–8)

Their use can be denied only by an epistemological theory that forbids numerical figures of speech in the study of poetry. The official epistemology gets in the way of the science. Similarly, on epistemological grounds economists like Muth deny official status to arguments from introspection and authority.

Dettmer's scientific precision, though expressed more in "numbers" than most, is characteristic of the best classical scholarship. Steele Commager in "Notes on Some Poems of Catullus" (1965) or Ronald Syme on "Piso and Veranius in Catullus" (1956) argue in a similarly exact way. They argue, to be sure, about literary and historical matters, such as the impression that a certain line of poetry makes in view of the linguistic evidence on usage in republican Rome or the identity of

3. Unless one were familiar with the reinventions of such devices in Anglo-Saxon poetry and in French and English poetry of the sixteenth century.

a certain governor of Macedonia in 60/59 B.C. in view of the political evidence on families and parties. But in their use of figures of speech they might as well be arguing about the usages of hog farmers in A.D. 1950 or the identity of a herbivore in 600,000,000 B.C. Subjects, as I have said, do not entail epistemologies. If "science" means "indubitable," then there is no science in science. If it means "very persuasive," then much clear and honest thinking is scientific.

The contrary notion, shared by literary and scientific modernists, is that only certain subjects can be scientific, and that their study will always depend on certain invariant figures of speech. Modernist methodism, exhibited in Muth's paper, asserts that only experiment, statistical procedures, or axiomatization are "scientific."

Methodism infects classical textual criticism too and is as unhelpful there as it is in economics. One methodological rule in textual criticism, for example, embodied in various Latin maxims, is to honor the text. Every surviving manuscript of Macrobius' *Saturnalia* 1.6, line 14, speaking of an article of clothing, reads "totam." A thoughtless scientism, of the sort that measures regardless or axiomatizes regardless, would therefore resist the emendation "togam," the well-known article of male clothing, even though this other, alleged "totam" would be the sole occurrence of such a word in Latin literature.[4]

Such voluntary imbecility in the application of Rules of Methodology infuriated the poet and textual critic A. E. Housman. On the rule that "The More Sincere Text is the Better" (even if erroneous and senseless), he wrote:

> The best way to treat such pretentious inanities is to transfer them from the sphere of textual criticism . . . into some sphere where men are compelled to use concrete and sensuous terms, which force them, however reluctantly, to think. . . . I ask him to tell me which weighs most, a tall man or a fat man. . . . *Tall* and *fat* are adjectives that transport even a textual critic from the world of humbug into the world of reality, a world inhabited by comparatively thoughtful people, such as butchers, grocers, who depend on their brains for their bread. (Housman 1922, p. 1063)

The best way to treat such pretentious inanities as that economics is distinct from other fields by virtue of a unique methodology is to translate them into comparatively concrete and sensuous terms. Which is the

4. James Willis 1972, p. 7, who is eloquent on the point.

more persuasive evidence, a correlation coefficient of .90 or an uncontroversial piece of introspection? A rule of methodology claims to say, in general. But there is no point in knowing such a thing in general. An economist does not do economics in general. He does it in particular. Surely if he does it well he uses particular figures of speech from the common store.

7

THE PROBLEM OF

AUDIENCE IN

HISTORICAL ECONOMICS

ROBERT FOGEL AS RHETOR

It is mildly surprising, perhaps, to find that Muth's paper on rational expectations does its work rhetorically. It will be less surprising to find that Robert W. Fogel's book on the economic history of railroads does, too. As must any attempt at scholarly persuasion, economic history is rhetorical. But the conflict in Fogel between two official rhetorics of economic history—the historical and the economic—sharpens the edge of argument, one blade against another. In contrast with Muth and macroeconomics, the rhetoric in this field of economics (no less precise and mathematical nowadays) stands out in plain view.

By now it is clear that the word "rhetoric" is no insult. Classically and properly, to repeat, rhetoric is critical inquiry, not merely "giving effectiveness to truth but . . . creating truth" (Robert Scott 1967, p. 9). The writing of history has a rhetoric (Hexter 1971; White 1973), no small matter: it limits the historian in what sorts of evidence and what sorts of logical appeals he can make if he wishes to retain an audience. And economics surely has a rhetoric. Fogel's book is a good text in point.

The Text Was Important

Railroads and American Economic Growth, published in 1964, was a revised version of Fogel's Ph.D. dissertation in economics at Johns Hopkins. It is relevant to the book's rhetoric that Fogel had started the advanced study of economics rather late, at thirty years of age, after a youth devoted to radical politics. By his own account the events of 1956, a year of rethinking by the left, turned him towards the

The Problem of Audience in Historical Economics

academic as against the political study of economic-historical problems. The book was his second: he had published his M.A. thesis from Columbia as *The Union Pacific Railroad: A Case in Premature Enterprise* (1960). He was by 1964 well known among "cliometricians," a then-tiny band of economists such as Douglass North, William Parker, Brinley Thomas, Rondo Cameron, Robert Gallman, Lance Davis, and J.R.T. Hughes attempting to reinvent economic history as economics. His 1964 book made him more widely known to historians and economists, although the center of its argument had already stirred specialists in economic history at conferences and had been published by itself two years before (Fogel 1962). What stirred them was its powerfully argumentative form and its startling conclusion: that railroads did *not* have very much to do with American economic growth.

The conclusion was in the air. Albert Fishlow published the next year his own Ph.D. dissertation, from Harvard, which made a point for the 1850s very similar to the one Fogel made for his year, 1890. The simultaneous discovery was motivated by a simultaneous stimulus, namely, W. W. Rostow's claim a few years earlier that railroads had begun America's "take-off into self-sustained growth." Fogel wrote his dissertation under the premier student of national income, Simon Kuznets, and began the study, as can be seen from his preliminary thesis proposal, expecting Rostow's enthusiasm for the railroads to be confirmed. It was not, and with characteristic vigor Fogel turned to attacking it.

The vigor displayed itself in dense argument and massed statistics. Fishlow's book made effectively the same point, was better written than Fogel's, used techniques of persuasion more familiar to historians, and was reviewed much more genially, yet was in the end less influential. Fogel's novelty of argumentative form attracted the attention of the young and the anger of the old, a combination of stimuli bound to succeed in intellectual life. The attention and anger inspired methodological declarations and denunciations.

Fogel was the Napoleon of the cliometric revolution in economic history. Napoleonic precepts adorned the study walls of his troops: "An army of economic historians marches on its computer"; "The career of historian is open to mathematical talent"; and "There is only one step from the sublime to the ridiculous." Barry Supple, noting in 1970 the spread of Général Fogel's army to Britain and the world, recalled Wordsworth's lines on the French Revolution as it appeared to enthusiasts: "Bliss was it in that dawn to be alive, / But to be young [and numerate] was very heaven!"

Fogel's book is the archetype of cliometrics. Through twenty years it has worn well, and still inspires imitators and respectful critics. It was more than a methodological advance. The theme that one innovation cannot explain much of economic growth has converted many from *simpliste* romanticism about the Iron Horse, or the Big Steel Mill.

Its argument was largely concentrated in a brilliant display in the first fifty pages of the book. The enemy is the "axiom of indispensability," that is, the notion that the railroad could not be dispensed with. The assault proceeds so: Fogel on pages 10 and 11 translates the axiom into an assertion that the coming of the railroad increased national income. He points out on page 12 that if there were good substitutes for the railroad, then its coming might have increased income very little. A good substitute—say a canal—might still have required a big shift in the location of production, Denver declining and St. Louis rising. But if it was indeed a good substitute the impact on the whole would have been small.

On pages 19 and 20 he labels the increase of income from the railroad as against the next best alternative, the "social saving." On page 20 and in a long footnote he notes that forcing hypothetical canals to carry goods in the same pattern as on the railroads would make his measure an upper bound on the truth. That is, his measure of social saving would always have to be *higher* than the true but unmeasurable amount. By an argument *a fortiori*, then, if he finds the measured social saving from the railroad to be small, the true social saving would be smaller still. On pages 22, 23, and 24 he examines the substitutes for rail—namely, wagon and water—arguing that if water was widely feasible, the social saving would be small. After a diversion into linear programming (p. 26), and another repetition of his *a fortiori* argument that his procedure gives a lower bound (p. 28), he turns to estimating the costs of water (pp. 44–47), breaking the cost into its parts. The costs of the higher stocks of grain and meat that would be required when the canal water froze in winter, for instance, is only a small amount (pp. 44–46). Page 47 modestly describes these ruminations as "casual," yet puts forward a sharp conclusion: on this score railroads increased national income by only 0.6 percent.

The figure relates to transport among the major regions of the nation, most particularly between the granary of the Midwest and the cities of the East and Europe. In chapter 3 Fogel calculates the amount that was saved within the Midwest. It too was small. In chapter 4 he argues (contra Rostow again) that the secondary effects of railroad construction were small, not large. In chapter 5 he attacks in particular the Rostovian idea that the demand for railroad iron greatly stimulated the iron industry. Chapter 6, finally, is a concluding movement allegro, with crescendo and cymbal clash, drawing wide conclusions about the role of theory and statistics in history.

The Problem of Audience in Historical Economics

The core of the book is the first fifty pages: it was this exercise that most stimulated the imagination of imitators and most infuriated the critics. In a few pages Fogel showed to the satisfaction of some that the railroad did not dominate American economic growth, and to the satisfaction of most that the question needed rather more study than was earlier believed. It is a characteristic bit of Fogeliana, and of cliometrica.

Fogel's Book Poses a Rhetorical Puzzle

A puzzle arises from this fact: to an audience consisting of a certain species of professional economist the entire point of Fogel's book, and one of the two main points made in Fishlow's book, comes down to a three-line proof.[1] It goes as follows:

1. Railroads are supposed to have been a large factor in American growth.
2. From the railroad, canal, and wagon rates for transportation, however, one can see that railroads were about half as costly as the alternatives and carried half the transport; transport is 10 percent of national income.
3. If Adam Smith is in heaven and all is right with the world, then a 50 percent cost saving $\times$ 50 percent of transport $\times$ 10 percent of national income = 2.5 percent of national income, no large change.

A suitably trained audience, to repeat, will consider such an argument decisive. The three-line proof of smallness (known to some economists as Harberger's Law) was crafted in virtually this form by Peter McClelland (1975) to apply to the economic history of the Navigation Acts, and it has become a cliometric routine.[2]

The puzzle is, why did Fishlow and Fogel go beyond the three-line proof? To ask the question is to answer it: no one except the pre-prepared audience would have been persuaded by it, and even the pre-prepared audience would not have noticed it. A half-page in the *American Economic Review* entitled "A Simple Proof of the Insig-

---

1. The other point in Fishlow's book was in a way more important. It was that the problem of spillovers in benefits from railways could be solved, and in the event was solved, by local initiative. The solution calls into question the interdependencies of investment that have worried many economists, such as Scitovsky, Rosenstein-Rodan, and Chenery.

2. For example, Gary Hawke's masterful replication of Fogel's calculation for England and Wales in 1865 gives the three-line proof in a paragraph on p. 173 (Hawke 1970).

nificance of Railways to American Economic Growth" would have looked idiotic in the rhetorical world of economics circa 1964 (it is indicative of change, for better or for worse in twenty years, that it would have looked less idiotic circa 1984). In the rhetorical world of mathematics or biology, by contrast, such brevity has weight: the paper by Watson and Crick announcing the structure of DNA was two pages long, a good bit of it given over to thanking the agencies that funded the research. In other words, the rhetorical world that Fogel and Fishlow inhabited determined how much and what exactly they felt impelled to write. If they were to succeed, they had to go well beyond the three-line proof. Their success, in other words, was a rhetorical matter, not written in the stars or in the Nature of Science.

A related puzzle is, why did Fogel have more impact than Fishlow? Both wrote hefty books filled with much craft and art. But only Fogel's has spawned a large literature. If at bottom the two books have the same point, and if the point is so simple, and if both are skillfully done, why did Fogel's hit harder? For anyone familiar with the case, this question, too, answers itself: it is a matter of the rhetoric of Fogel's book, or rather a matter of the differences in rhetoric between the two. In general, then, the solutions to the puzzles lie in rhetoric. To be particular—and the particulars are illuminating—one must study Fogel's rhetoric.

Since, as I have already noted, the traditions of intellectual life seem to demand that a rhetorical analysis be hostile, a declaration of allegiance even more full than those already made about the earlier texts will be useful. I am wholly sympathetic with Fogel's methods and conclusions. I choose Fogel's piece as one of several of which I approve to show that even good economics is rhetorical, and choose an example from economic history to show how important multiple audiences are. No condescension is involved. Had modesty not forbidden I might have illustrated the point about audiences with an example from my own historical work, which is similar to Fogel's in rhetorical style and about which I can hardly condescend. The example is purposely chosen as one of which I wholly approve from the pen of a man with whom I have been associated in the vulgar mind for nearly twenty years.

The problem is that an unsympathetic rhetorical analysis is liable to cheapen the meaning of "rhetoric" into "evil rhetoric," a cheapening, as must be apparent by now, I wish especially to avoid.[3] But someone

---

3. Albert Hirschman points out to me that an ideological analysis has the same difficulty. If "ideology" is something that only those other, bad people have, then the notion cannot be developed fully.

The Problem of Audience in Historical Economics

who was unsympathetic to Fogel's book could easily arrive at the same observations about its rhetoric. Understood as the art of argument, the "charge" that a piece is "rhetorical" is not a charge at all, but a remark true of all speech acts. To note that in making his point Fogel uses legal procedures, scornful asides, scientific jargon, statistics, simulation, thought experiment, and the traditions of economic argument does not bury or praise him. It describes him and anyone else who tries to move the reason. Rhetoric in the sense used here, to say it once more, is reason writ large.[4]

Fogel's Book Is Self-Consciously Rhetorical

The rhetoric of the piece is so varied and thick that it obscures itself. One cannot see how the argument persuades or fails to persuade without disentangling the rhetorical parts from each other, laying them out for separate inspection.

The first point about Fogel's rhetoric is that it is unusually aware of itself as rhetoric. The rhetoric of the book is rhetorical. The prose has many charms and a few flaws, but above all it has force: no urbane indirection here; just bang, bang, bang. It announces its purpose repeatedly, signaling the use of this or that argumentative form. "The implicit assertion" is one thing; the "crucial aspect" is another; such and such "is beyond dispute"; "but the axiom is not primarily about" X, "it is about" Y; and "if the axiom . . . merely asserted" Z "there would be no reason to question it." These remarks *about* the argument and its enemies occur in one paragraph on page 10. Right to the last the arguments

4. Fogel, though more sophisticated than most in such matters, is not entirely at ease with the rhetorical analysis to follow, and should not be imagined to agree with all of its conclusions. In correspondence he distinguished between "these pages [of his] and the evidential portions of the book" (Robert Fogel, letter to the author, November 16, 1983), not noticing that the fifty pages analyzed here include the calculation of interregional social saving. He argued modestly that he does "not believe that the introductory chapter [through p. 16: 70% of the passages discussed below come from p. 17ff.] constitutes a proof of anything; it merely attempted to demonstrate that certain widely held views involved implicit magnitudes that had never been measured." Certainly the length of the book attests to Fogel's sincerity in this opinion: if the case was settled by page 16, or even by page 47, there would have been no point in going on to re-engineer hypothetical canals and re-estimate iron output. But the opinion is mistaken if it wishes to separate question raising from question answering. Both contribute to conviction, in similar ways. Distinguishing the "context of discovery" from the "context of justification," we have seen, is a well-worn figure of scientific rhetoric, but is not persuasive.

keep this self-referential character: the calculation is "casual" and "subject to considerable error," a self-deprecating description preparatory to emphasizing nonetheless that "there are grounds for having confidence in the result" (p. 47); the estimates "may be too low," but even if they were raised, they would not amount to much; "indeed"—an argumentative word itself, like "in fact" or "nonetheless"—even an absurdly generous concession to the opposition leaves the estimate low.

The book reeks of the court or debating society. In such places, unlike the laboratory or the corporate boardroom, rhetoric is not disdained, concealed beneath claims of being free from it. It is relished. In such places, and in Fogel's prose, it is the whole point, places where the whole point is not to announce results or to be powerful but simply to have a point.

The subject in Fogel, then, is the argument. He does not write only about the past. He writes as much about the reasonings of history and economics in the 1960s as about how people earned their living in olden days. On page 11, appealing to a common meta-argument in economics, he notes in other historians' arguments a "fallacy of composition"; in the same place he talks about whether proposition X follows from proposition Y, whether one historical argument is implied by another. On page 28—to pick another page at random, for most exhibit it—a remark about the argumentative "importance" of alternatives to the railroad starts the case. A "fact does not, of course, imply" such and such. "What makes this problem interesting" is that so and so "is far from obvious." An event "by no means implies" a certain conclusion. "Consider a hypothetical case." "Clearly, the implication" is thus and such. "Yet" the figure is "much too small . . . to justify" the opponent's case. It is like wrestling with Dan Gable, the great wrestling coach at the University of Iowa, a great wrestler as well, finding him whispering descriptions of his moves as he ties you into knots. Fogel goes on and on and on about the argument, inexhaustibly talking about it while doing it.

The rhetorical contrast with Fishlow's book is sharp. Though also a first-rate professional economist using at bottom the same economic reasoning as Fogel did, Fishlow sought to persuade with a historian's devices, singing sweet songs, evoking scenes in rounded phrases and apt choices of instance, and keeping all the while an ironic distance between the putative facts—or "facts," as any sophisticated historian would wish always to write it—and the tale imposed on the facts. Fishlow's work concerns itself with the history as lived; Fogel's more with the history as written.

The distinction does not damn Fogel, unless it damns many good historians, who spend time arguing about how one should argue about the rise of the English gentry or the economic origins of the American constitution. The issue caused confusion in the immense and ill-tempered controversy over a later book by Fogel, written with Stanley Engerman. It was thought to be a clever remark about *Time on the Cross: The Economics of American Negro Slavery* (1974) to say that it was "static"— a snapshot rather than a moving picture—and that even as a snapshot it was not a rounded portrait of the system. But in his contribution to the history of slavery, as to the history of American railroads, Fogel was not portraying the past in all its life and incident. He was making a point in a scholarly conversation about a portrait, a portrait to be drawn in full later.

The heavily rhetorical rhetoric of the book on railroads inaugurated a new style of economic history, a forensic style that has become important in cliometrics.[5] The book made it fashionable and persuasive in economic history to use the argument *a fortiori* (itself an aggressive rhetorical figure), to which Fogel returns again and again, and to which I shall return presently. But along with this self-consciously methodological innovation came a style more suited to the courtroom than to the study, and widely imitated by younger scholars. Notions of demonstration in the West are permeated by courtroom analogies. These *Essays in Econometric History* became a casebook for young economic attorneys defending the British entrepreneurs of the late nineteenth century or prosecuting the owners of country stores in the postbellum South. It was a book about the rhetoric of economics and history as much as about American railroads.

The Rhetorical Density Explains Its Successes and Its Failures

The personal sources of Fogel's forensic tone are relevant insofar as they illuminate why the rhetoric persuades or does not persuade. Many literary intellectuals share his love of disputation; the

5. Fogel disagrees. He argues in a letter of November 16, 1983, that the forensic rhetoric is confined to cases in which the cliometrician faces a reader whose mind must be pried open in a more or less forceful way. On this interpretation, the cliometrician would appear to judge many minds to be closed.

The Problem of Audience in Historical Economics

horror of disputation among mathematical intellectuals (though Fogel is also one of these) affects their rhetoric, too.[6] Many of the *literati* have the same personal history as Fogel: secondary-school involvement in clubs spent arguing over God, poetry, and politics; university lectures in rhetoric, or a debating society. Fogel was raised in the Bronx and went to Cornell for college, where he studied debate. Fogel's later experience in radical politics gave him still more practice in openly rhetorical argument.

When he finally came to American economic history, he brought to a distinctly right-wing and *goyisch* field the traditions of flamboyantly Talmudic disputation characteristic of New York Jewish intellectuals, especially left-wing intellectuals. The combination of a somewhat heated tone and the methodical treatment of every imaginable point—known anciently as *indignatio, diasyrmus, digestion,* and *diallage*—was not invented by Fogel out of nothing. Marx himself invented it and attached it to self-conscious scientism. It has been one stream of social scientific rhetoric since Marx. In the 1940s one sees it in the cases prepared by labor union intellectuals about such mundanities as the construction of cost-of-living indices.[7] These are pieces of science, but tough, disputatious, lawyerly science. So in Fogel.

Fogel had turned away from Marxist politics when he wrote the book, but the point holds. Being a recent convert to liberal capitalism, he saw deeper into its rhetoric than would someone raised in the faith. The literary critic Kenneth Burke admired Augustine's treatment of the rhetoric of Saint Paul: Paul, like Augustine himself, was "a master of apologetics, and like him one of the twice-born whose sensitiveness to communicative problems was sharpened by the memory of harsh conflicts within, of inner voices at one time opposing each other like rivals in a debate."[8]

The forensic style has consequences for Fogel's persuasiveness. All attempts at persuasion—that is to say, all scholarship—depend in part on what the Aristotelean tradition calls the "ethical appeal." The ethical appeal uses the character *(ethos)* of the speaker as perceived by the audience to encourage the audience to look kindly on the speaker.

6. In his essay on writing mathematics, Paul R. Halmos, a reflective mathematician with a good literary style, admonishes young mathematicians to shun "*ad hominem* remarks and literary frills" (1973, p. 22). The "unrhetorical" style (to be "unrhetorical," it should be clear by now, is an impossibility) was an invention of New Scientists of the seventeenth century.

7. I am indebted to Hugh Rockoff for this point.

8. Burke 1950, p. 75. Augustine was a professor of rhetoric.

The Problem of Audience in Historical Economics

"This interaction between speaker and speech," suggest Perelman and Olbrechts-Tyteca in *The New Rhetoric*, "is perhaps the most characteristic part of argumentation as opposed to demonstration." They continue: "The statement made is in fact not the same coming from one person as from another; its meaning does change. There is not just a simple transfer of values, but a reinterpretation in a new context, which is provided by what one knows of the presumed author. . . .The speaker's life, insofar as it is public, forms a long prelude to his speech" (1958, pp. 317, 318, 320).

Had Einstein's letter to Roosevelt asserting the possibility of a nuclear bomb been written by Harvey Einstein of 3226 Flatbush Avenue, Brooklyn, instead of by Albert Einstein of 112 Mercer Street, Princeton, it would probably have received less attention. Like most other species of argumentation, the ethical appeal is commonly subordinated to *logos*, reason, and its promise of transcendental certainty. Common though it is in the intellectual traditions of the West, the subordination is not obviously correct either as description or as advice. Joseph Wenzel points out that the subordination might well be put the other way around. In the works of Aristotle and of Jürgen Habermas, he argues, "logos may be construed as a subsidiary category of ethos. One exhibits good sense [and therefore good, believable character] by speaking 'truth' " (Wenzel 1983, p. 51).

In any event, the ethical appeal is an important, ancient, and legitimate argument. The most important of the ethical appeals that Fogel, like Muth, wishes to make is to the character of the Scientist. There is no question that Fogel had the appeal in mind. All his methodological papers have promoted what he calls scientific history, though he has recently emphasized the considerable merit in other kinds (cf. Fogel and Elton 1983, pp. 65-70). And the language of his book, like Muth's paper, is filled with scientisms: "the hypothesis can now be stated" (Fogel 1964, p. 19) and "tested" (p. 22); "the objective standard for testing the hypothesis stated above" is X (p. 20); we have, in a properly scientific way, some "estimates" (p. 22 et passim), an "inference" (p. 22), "available evidence" (p. 22), an "order of magnitude" (p. 23), a "method" requiring "the following data" (p. 26), and so forth. The talk of hypothesis-testing uses words appropriate to rolling balls down inclined planes (or, it would seem, claiming to have rolled balls down inclined planes without actually having done so). The appeal is "I am a Scientist: give way."

The form and force of an ethical appeal will depend on the audience addressed. Like all cliometricians Fogel addresses audiences that have two quite different notions of what constitutes good scholarly character, economists and historians. The appeal to the Scientist has some force to both, or to anyone participating in our science-loving civilization. Fogel appeals to historians in particular with his conspicuously displayed mastery of government documents and trade publications relevant to railroads, no trivial bibliographical feat (see his pp. 44–45, nn. 53 and 55). The soothing words of caretaking that he sprinkles around each number are part of an ethical appeal to the character of a historical scholar: "the preceding argument is based on a [merely] hypothetical case" (p. 12); "the calculation is very crude" (p. 23); the estimate is "subject to considerable error" (p. 47). Some historians are deeply suspicious of numbers and are pleased to be told of their frailties. All are impressed by scrutiny of the methods used to construct them, which Fogel delivers in quantity. And the sheer length of the book is an ethical appeal in historical circles, contrary to the ethical appeal of elegance and brevity in less discursive subjects.

But Fogel mainly appeals to economists, presenting the ethos of the Sharp Economist. The necessities of academic politics required it. There were and are no departments of economic history in North America, the field being divided between economics and history. Economic history in 1964 was on the defensive in American departments of economics, dismissed as antique by the new technocrats strutting about the camp in their gleaming armor (they hadn't yet done any fighting in it and hadn't therefore discovered that it didn't cover much). It was essential that young economic historians prove themselves technically able. For this reason the same Albert Fishlow, and Paul David, in the midst of the time they were doing their historical dissertations at Harvard, wrote together a highly technical piece on the general equilibrium theory of second best. Fogel repeatedly displays the brightness of his economic armory. On page 44, for instance, he expresses false doubt (*aporia* in Greek rhetorical terminology) that the value of time lost in winter on waterways can be calculated. Then he shows elegantly and quickly in the next two paragraphs how it in fact can.

Economists have anxieties as well as pride about their scientific rank. Aristotle wrote that "people always think well of speeches adapted to, and reflecting, their own character" (*Rhetoric* 2.13.1390a 25), or, one might better say, reflecting what they wish their character to be. Economists therefore delight in scientific talk, the closer to physics the better. Fogel provides ample delectation. The most delightful case is also the most obviously ornamental in character and probably the most calculated (though least calculable), namely, the proposal to apply to the problem of simulating a counterfactual system of canals "a relatively new mathematical technique—linear programming" (p 26; the technique was some twenty years old at the time). The proposal is made, discussed as a proposal for two pages, then suddenly and permanently dropped, having served its function of establishing the scientific ethos of the writer.

The ethical appeal, then, stands out in Fogel's piece. Yet it did not succeed, except among the most important audience a scholar can convince—young scholars without convictions ready to commit themselves to a novel faith. The annoyance and fear that Fogel inspired in older scholars came from his very mastery of rhetoric. The audience is not being told a story, soothing and uncritical, the refuge of the historian. Nor is it witnessing a cute trick, ironically amused by the magician and by its own reaction, as an audience of economists prefers. Fogel's implied audience listens instead as a jury to an F. Lee Bailey laying out the case for the defense; or, worse prospect, as a team of prosecuting attorneys whom Fogel/Bailey is grinding to bits.

Fogel's relentless progress through each point and his decisive language at each conclusion puts the audience on the defensive, as in a trial. Perelman and Olbrechts-Tyteca write: "The attitude of the speaker can indicate his respect for the audience: discretion, restraint, refusal to pronounce on a point in which he is knowledgeable, and brevity in presentation can all serve as tokens of esteem for his audience" (1958, p. 321). These are decidedly Gallic tokens. In America such taciturnity would more often be given the other possible interpretation, not shy modesty but close-mouthed disdain. The point in any case is that Fogel's fullness of argument, unrelieved as it is by the ironic self-deprecation so important for establishing good character in Britain and North America, overwhelms most audiences, who in defense remain stoutly difficult to persuade.

Some audiences, indeed, do not wish to be persuaded. The doubt that long arguments inspire by their very length; the ignorant suspicion in even very learned minds that rhetoric is after all mere trickery; the belief, nurtured in our society by the lamentable split of fact and values, that most of the important matters are unarguable anyway—all these produce, as Robert Scott remarks, "the feeling that undertaking to persuade others is not quite right."[9] The odd result is that the Announcement, the more bald, unargued, and authoritarian the better, is the favored form of scholarly communication. The authors in *Science* or *Nature*, as I have noted, use a rhetoric of astonishing brevity to an-

9. Robert Scott 1967, p. 9. Impatient with long argument, George Stigler, whose works reflect modernist values uniformly, once wrote in jest that "there are not ten good reasons for anything" (1969, p. 226).

nounce world-shaking results: there it is; take it or leave it. One wonders why unargued cases are accepted more readily than argued ones, even among professional arguers. One would think that in professional writing aimed at a jury of peers the pose of the attorney submitting evidence and argument would be more pleasing to the audience, especially to a mature one, than that of the judge handing down unargued conclusions. But it appears not.[10]

The same is true of history, as Fogel himself notes in a recent discussion of historical method, using, as one might have anticipated, a courtroom analogy:

> The traditional historian [Fogel's term for the alternative to his "scientific" historian, so prone by his own account to controversy and over-elaborate proofs] often comes before his colleagues . . . as an expert witness . . . and his book or paper constitutes his expert testimony. . . .Thus distinguished traditional historians sometimes depart from the monographic pattern of documenting each statement in their study by footnotes. . . . An attack on the credibility of this historian qua witness, and many of the attacks are ad hominem, has the same force as an attack on a witness in court. (Fogel and Elton 1983, p. 54)

That is, even professional historians sometimes prefer history to be presented as the announcement of an Authority, as a statement of how things really were back then, not as some argument in tiresome detail, and most assuredly not as some argument for which there is another side. Fogel reminds the audience repeatedly and annoyingly that history and economics do not fit the epistemology of simple folk who believe that what is, is. His rhetoricity mightily irritates, undermining the ethos he seeks to portray by an excess of enthusiasm in its portrayal.

The point can be put in a dramatistic way, drawing out the metaphor of the audience. If the scholar/actor is talking to himself backstage, the knowledge he claims to have is "belief." If he is talking to an audience

10. Taking the risk of arguments requires a different personality than taking the risk of results. That is one possibility. The other is the external condition under which science operates. It is said that most of the results produced by even very good scientists turn out to be wrong or, more commonly, irrelevant to anything of import. Perhaps the decisiveness with which this weeding out occurs in science makes the emotional investment of explaining why one believes something too large for most people to make. In fields with fewer clear failures—history, for instance, or literature—the investment entailed by close argument is emotionally possible. In science one distances oneself from a result, making it emotionally possible to put it forward, by treating it as just that—a mere "result," no wondrous thing, advanced with seemly diffidence, and probably, after all, explicable by the Fifth Law of Thermodynamics.

onstage, but still from his own point of view, it is "warranted assertability." If he is talking to a sympathetic audience, from the point of view of the audience, it is "persuasiveness." If he is talking to an unsympathetic audience, from the point of view of the audience, it is "compelling argument." Fogel tried for compelling argument; the historians and the older economists would accede only to warranted assertability, or at best a mild and civilized persuasiveness. The book was not successful with them, though strikingly successful with a younger and more mathematical audience that thrilled to his ethical appeal.

Fogel's Book Uses Intensively the Common Topics

Exhibiting the details of Fogel's ethical appeal, then, shows in one way the rhetorical complexity of his case. Another way is to exhibit his use of the arguments themselves. The word is "topics" (Greek *topoi*, or places, as in English "commonplaces" and Latin *loci communes*). These are figures of speech the rhetor can take out from the common storeroom. Fogel's prose gives the impression of using an unusually wide variety of topics, displayed prettily.

One can be more precise by taking two pages or so of Fogel's book and comparing them sentence by sentence with a list of the classical figures of rhetoric. The pages, 10–12, are chosen to match the length of the selection from Muth in the previous chapter, in order later to draw a contrast in their rhetorical richness. They are the two most important pages in the book, arguing for its central point in a preliminary way, before the empirical work to follow. Using the classical names for the devices helps see how the rhetoric works. One can see a house—really see it—only when equipped with the carpenter's vocabulary of pediment and quoin and gable.[11]

Of the classically recognized figures of speech, Fogel uses in these two pages nearly twenty, including the following:

• The whole is *diallage*, the piling up of arguments on one point, the point being that what matters is how good the substitutes for railroads were. Within his diallage he uses these:
 • Repeatedly, he uses *paramologia*, that is, conceding a minor point

11. The list against which Fogel is compared appears in Lanham 1968, sec. 3.11, "Techniques of Argument," and surrounding sections on figures of speech, supplemented a little for omissions (e.g., *reductio ad absurdum, a fortiori,* rhetorical question [*hypophora*]).

the better to achieve a larger: "If the axiom of indispensability merely asserted [X] . . . there would be no reason to question it" (first paragraph). "Although the evidence demonstrating that the eruption of a boom psychology . . . is considerable . . . " (third paragraph). "Even the demonstration that railroads produced effects that were both unique and important . . . " (fourth paragraph). The concession is part of his most characteristic rhetorical figure, in which he says, in effect, "Even if I concede to my opponents such-and-such a point, my argument wins."

• Repeatedly, he draws attention to what he claims is the important aspect of a case. At the end of the first paragraph, the importance of substitution is emphasized by the figure of *anaphora* at the beginning of the next sentence: "The crucial aspect . . . . The crucial aspect." The two alternative expressions of the same idea are repeated for effect: *commoratio.* Each of the two sentences has internally a strongly parallel structure, balancing the phrases in the first sentence (*isocolon*), leaving off phrases in the second (*ellipsis,* as this sentence left off the second occurrence of "sentence"). The beginning of the second paragraph repeats the point again; the second sentence still again: four repetitions of the point in different words (*tautologia*), bordering on *pleonasm.* But it is the main point of the book, and one difficult for much of his implied audience to grasp. If any point warranted emphasis, this one—*a fortiori*—did. The third through the fourth paragraphs draw attention to the central point by attacking its alternatives, that is to say, alternative definitions of what it might mean for railroads to have been "indispensable": the figure is *apophasis,* the orderly rejection of all the alternatives except one.

• Repeatedly, he disparages opposing arguments (*diasyrmus*)—a technique so obviously forensic that historians use it gingerly if at all. Fogel, with other economists, has no such scruples. In the second half of the second paragraph, for instance, he is scandalized by the Lack of Scientific Evidence concerning the allegedly unique contribution of the railroad. One can see the indignation by examining the words that impart it: "almost exclusively"; "systematic"; "virtually"; "questionable"; "rather than on demonstrated fact." In the fourth paragraph (p. 11), again, he adopts an ironic tone to disparage the indispensability of block signals and track walkers, by *reductio ad absurdum.*

• Repeatedly, he notes the absence of decisive evidence. He appeals again to the ideally modernist historian/scientist, who does not carry an umbrella without a scientifically certified prediction of light rain. The "evidence" so often mentioned is quantitative. The figure is therefore a modern one, little used in the nonquantitative civilization that thought most carefully about the means of persuasion.

The Problem of Audience in Historical Economics

• A derivative of the modernist enthusiasm for properly modernist evidence is the figure in the third paragraph (pp. 10f.): "No evidence has been supplied. . . . And it is doubtful such evidence can be supplied" (note the parallel construction). This is one of the common topics of modern intellectual life, carrying conviction among all who pretend to intellectuality. The example at the end of page 11 is simulation (a Fogelian favorite, occurring throughout, as at pp. 23, 24, and 47), one of the special topics in economics and in other quantitative subjects. These carry conviction only among experts.

One can fit the argument of a paper like Muth's much less readily than Fogel's into the classical categories. Muth, with most economists, seems seldom able to carry a rhetorical turn to its conclusion. He says, "It is rather surprising that X is so," but this promising beginning of a good, old-fashioned bout of ironic *thaumasmus* (expression of wonder), which Fogel would have teased out to a paragraph, is immediately abandoned in favor of an appeal to "theoretical reasons." They turn out in the next sentence to be appeals to aesthetic standards, Ockham's razor in particular. And in the next the American Question is asked. The argument is *ad hominem*, that is to say, suitable only for persuading economists, by their very character. But Muth drops quickly even this use of the common topics crucial to his case: he indulges in no fourfold repetition and elaboration, no *commoratio, tautologia,* and *apophasis* here.

So it goes with a rhetorical analysis of the usual technical articles in economics. Unlike Fogel's work, they fit badly into the recognized figures of rhetoric, classically defined, though this does not by any means imply that they are not rhetorical. They are clearly rhetorical, seeking to persuade. That something is thinly and disjointedly argued does not mean it is not argued.

What divides the rhetoric of Fogel from the mainstream of economics is Fogel's heavy use of the standard issue, *common* topics of argument. Using these heavily will inspire a charge of "mere rhetoric," such as Fogel faced for his trouble; by contrast, using mainly the uncommon, *special* topics that appeal mainly to economists or historians will inspire a commendation for eschewing mere rhetoric, the rhetoric disappearing from view behind the mask of the economic or historical Scientist.

By far the most important of Fogel's rich array of common topics was his argument from lower or upper bounds. The book consists of an attempt to find the least upper bound on the benefit from railroads. If the upper bound is small, *a fortiori* the true effect is small. He draws on the argument very frequently (for instance, on pp. 20, 23, 28, 45, and 47), biasing the case against himself. The argument is widely used. Rogue Riderhood in *Our Mutual Friend*, for instance, used it in attempting to frame Gaffer Hexam by perjured affidavit: "He says to me, 'Rogue Riderhood, you are a man in a dozen'—I think he said in a score, but of that I am not positive, so take the lower figure, for precious be the obligation of an Alfred David."[12]

Technically speaking, the argument from upper and lower bounds combines elements of *paramologia* (conceding a smaller point to gain a larger) and the argument *a fortiori*. Consider the following progression from one to the other:

(a) *Paramologia:* Even if I admit as influencing the True magnitude a factor X, which runs against my case, the case that the Truth is small is true.

(b) *Least upper bound:* Even if I take a very large overestimate, call it Erroneous, of the Truth, Erroneous is small, and therefore the Truth is bound to be small.

(c) *A fortiori:* The estimate Erroneous is bound to be larger than the Truth; Erroneous is small; all the more reason to believe (*a fortiori*) that the Truth is small.

In other words, the figure of speech here (*paramologia*) is a version of a much-used mathematical figure; the mathematical figure is a version of a much-used figure of reasoning.

Fogel's use of such figures of speech and reasoning led many graduate students to take up careers of under- and overestimating things. The usual rhetoric of history in such matters (and of economics, though less prominently displayed) demands "accuracy." An estimate of the population of fifth-century Athens must be "accurate"; a description of the American economy as competitive is to be judged for "accuracy." A physicist would attest that the word is meaningless without bounds on the error; and a literary critic would attest that the accuracy necessary to the argument depends on the conversational context. There is no absolute sense of "accuracy," as Oskar Morgenstern once argued to economists in a neglected classic drawing on the rhetoric of applied mathematics, *On the Accuracy of Economic Observations* (1963).

Fogel's method attracted converts because it responded to such remarks. Neither conventional econometrics nor conventional historical method do. The neophyte adopting Fogel's rhetoric could now make estimates that bore on real conversations of scholarship. By recognizing that "accuracy" depends on how much accuracy is needed to persuade,

12. I thank Barry Supple for bringing this piece of evidence to my attention.

he could advance the conversation, building a case on purposely "inaccurate" estimates (for example, small but overstated estimates of something it is desired to prove small).

The puzzlement with which the ploy was greeted in historical circles can be explained by its melding of two rhetorical traditions quite foreign to history. "Least upper bound" is in fact a term from mathematical analysis. The aggressive use of arguments *a fortiori* characterizes left-wing politics (or right-wing politics: in any case the wings, not a center unable to argue from a radical stance). A recent convert from active political life in his first year of graduate school in economics, refreshing his knowledge of mathematical analysis remembered from a college year as an engineering student—all of which describes Fogel in 1958— would see that the mathematical and political rhetorics were in fact identical. Science and politics meet in their forms of argument.

The Book Also Uses the Special Topics of Economics

Fogel's contribution to economic method, then, is classically rhetorical, drawing on the common topics. But of course, like any economist—indeed, partly in order to make the ethical appeal that he *was* like any other economist—Fogel used also the special topics of economic discourse. Special topics are potted thoughts for specialists, ready in the storeroom marked "Economists Only" to be used prettily for some argumentative purpose.[13] Alongside appeals to symmetry, which is a common topic, mathematicians used the special topic of "for every episilon greater than zero there exists a delta greater than zero such that X. . . . " Alongside appeals to the good story, which is a common topic, history uses the special topic of "the facts here are derived from primary sources that I have personally examined." The common topic appeals to reasons that most people can appreciate; the special topic to reasons that only specialist can. Though special topics are often called "jargon" and sometimes merely are, they often serve a legitimate function. Not every argument can be made attractive to one's mother.

The test of the specialness of the topics is how they affect noneconomists. Noneconomists either will not react to them at all, viewing them as mere unintelligible knots in the prose, or will misunderstand them, giving them more or less weight than they warrant. If you are not familiar with the history of a conversation, you will misunderstand the

---

13. I offer the Greek words, *idioi topoi*, to anyone who wishes to make use of them.

remarks made in it, and if you are bold, you will make remarks of your own that do not bear on the subject at issue. Fogel speaks for example on page 11 of the "opportunity to profit from unexpected changes in the value of land" consequent on an improvement in transportation. A historian reading this, unless a genius of untutored perspicacity like Frederick Maitland or Marc Bloch, is unlikely to realize that profits in the sense of capital gains must be unexpected if they are to exist. Few without training in economics will realize that if a rise in land values is widely expected it is no longer an opportunity for profit, because the value of the land will have risen immediately. The force of the word "unexpected" escapes the noneconomist entirely. Here Fogel is speaking to his economist colleagues, as though in an aside.

Again, he speaks on page 10 of the "incremental contribution over the next best alternative." To an economist the phrase is familiar poetry, bringing to mind an apparatus of thought in handsome graphs. He accedes to the metaphor. The noneconomist, on the other hand, does not understand why the "next best alternative" would be especially relevant. Even if he understands it, to believe it he needs to believe that people do things for good reasons. But the noneconomist believes he knows they often do not: he can easily believe they would sometimes pick walking, or carts, rather than the relatively more efficient canals if deprived of their beloved railroads. And "incremental" is equally foreign to a noneconomist's way of thinking, which sees the railroad as immense and lumpy, no "increment" at all. The special topics evoke special responses in the economist. They are quick little arguments. But of course they leave noneconomists cold.

The ringing declaration on the bottom of page 12 that "the issue can only be settled empirically" will strike the historian as simply absurd. He does not know any other way to settle disputes about the way things are. The associated remark that "large equity effects do not necessarily imply large changes in the productive efficiency of the economy" will strike him as absurd in another way. The notion that all that matters is the net effect will please economists but not many other people. Talk that belittles the so-called equity effects strikes them as odd, even immoral. (Truth to tell, based as it is on the hypothetical compensation never actually forthcoming, as I mentioned earlier, it probably is.)

So the special topics can hardly be expected to persuade noneconomists. Regrettably, they repel them. The opportunity cost of enchanting one's fellow economists is alienating noneconomists. There is no such thing as a free argument. But the thing needed to be done if Fogel was to convince his closest colleagues—though it should be noted that at Rochester, Chicago, and Harvard he was a professor of history too.

The Problem of Audience in Historical Economics

A desire to speak to economists explains the sudden turn of the argument at the top of page 13, a pretty pirouette. He speaks to historians when patiently explaining just before the turn why manipulations of rates by railroads did not necessarily cause a loss of income to the whole nation. The economist asks, But what if the manipulation leads to monopoly? Another economist shoots back (dropping Schumpeter's name: *commemoratio*), Monopoly can be good for you. Speculation is met with counterspeculation. It's the scholar's way of saying, So's your uncle.

The discussion of the special topic of adding a constraint is another instance of conversing with economists, this time more extensively. Fogel argues on page 20 that forcing traffic to take the route suitable to a railroad when the railroad has been imagined out of existence will lead to expensive transportation. The advantage of the railroad will appear to be all the greater, giving all the more reason, *a fortiori*, to think its advantage small if the calculation does in fact prove small. Economists know the topic in other applications: at its most abstract, a maximizing system is hurt by the addition of a constraint. Fogel spends a good deal of time on it, more time, for example, than on the topic next door to this one in the row of arguments, the "next best alternative." All of page 20 talks of it, and it is mentioned elsewhere. The elaborate footnote 10 attached to the argument, the longest in the book, takes the form of dividing up the possible indexes and discussing each, the figure *diaeresis*, for which Fogel's teacher at Johns Hopkins, Fritz Machlup, was famous.

Some of the special topics are so special that they are not topics. That is, they are not intelligible even to most economists on first reading. If repeated enough in a scholarly conversation they would take on a topical character. Fogel anticipates criticism and wards it off with many such cryptic little arguments (the figure is *procatalepsis*). A comparatively lengthy example is the talk without evidence in paragraph 16 about the marginal cost of canals. Canals have to be able to take easily the extra burden imposed on them in Fogel's counterfactual world without railroads. "The available data" is supposed to imply that they could take it easily. The "data" turns out to be unelaborated common knowledge, but seeing the implications of the common knowledge in this case is not easy even for an economist.

Another argument forestalling criticism is embodied in a dependent clause on page 12: "given the historical stability of the aggregate saving and capital-output ratio." Like the argument about the marginal cost of canals, it later grew into a substantial literature. Both have to do with the three-line proof of the small social saving of railroads. The alleged fact of stability in the savings rate was announced by Fogel's mentor, Simon Kuznets. Fogel claims implicitly here that if true (it is not if human capital is included), it parries a possible thrust. The thrust was delivered some years later by Jeffrey Williamson, who argued that the railroad caused a big rise in savings rates. Williamson's argument fails if during the coming of railroads the savings rates did not in fact rise.

Fogel crams a good deal of economics into each page, more than is usual even in densely argued theoretical works. Page for page it is good stuff, a point not lost on the committee that elected this historian to one of the first economics memberships in the National Academy of Sciences. Fogel plays the economic audience well; and no blame attaches. That is what special topics are for.

The Test Invented an Audience

The talk of special and general topics presupposes a division in the audience between specialist and generalist. Above all, rhetoric emphasizes the audience. It rejects a view of speaking that imagines politicians and poets and even economists speaking into a void, or to themselves. We must all choose an audience for our productions. The teacher of composition emphasizes that a writer does not have the choice to abstain from the choice, yet most students try anyway, or fail to try. Whether consciously or not, further, the writer does more than merely choose an audience from the existing population: in his mind's eye, or his writing's tone, the readers become not merely his choice but his creation.

The idea is that of Kenneth Burke, Walker Gibson, Wayne Booth, Louise Rosenblatt, and other exponents of rhetorical criticism (Burke 1950; Gibson 1950; Booth 1961, p. 138; Booth 1974b; Booth 1979, pp. 268ff.; Rosenblatt 1978). The author of *Emma*, to take Booth's favorite example, creates an authorial persona, an "implied author," who speaks to another of her creations, the "implied reader." The actual reader must adopt the role of the implied reader if he is to enjoy or believe the book (see Figure 2). The author's domain is everything within the lines.[14] The reader comes along for the ride: the actual readers "assume,

14. Which is how this notion differs from other strands in reader-response criticism. Among the Barthes-Fish tribe the reader is ruler. The author is no authority. He merely produces a text, which the fanciful reader uses at will. In the United States the two approaches dwell to some degree in different academic departments, the rhetorical one in Communications and Theatre Arts (or Rhetoric), the deconstructionist one in English (or Comparative Literature).

The Problem of Audience in Historical Economics

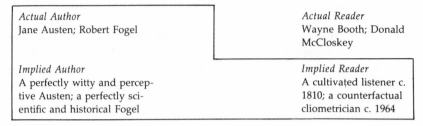

Actual Author	Actual Reader
Jane Austen; Robert Fogel	Wayne Booth; Donald McCloskey
Implied Author	Implied Reader
A perfectly witty and perceptive Austen; a perfectly scientific and historical Fogel	A cultivated listener c. 1810; a counterfactual cliometrician c. 1964

Figure 2. The Author Creates an Implied Reader and an Implied Author

for the sake of the experience, that set of attitudes and qualities which the language asks us to assume." "A bad book," continues Walker Gibson, "is a book in whose mock reader we discover a person we refuse to become, a mask we refuse to put on, a role we will not play" (Gibson 1950, pp. 1, 5). The implied author in this little drama, of course, has the floor. He delivers an oration to the implied reader. That is why it is a matter of rhetoric.

Fogel would seem to require two implied readers, both close to contradictions in terms, the historically interested economist and the economically sophisticated historian. Fields under dispute between two methods, as American economic history was during the 1960s, cannot have one reader. Yet much writing, Fogel's included, presupposes one alone, able to appreciate every nuanced remark about fixed capital-output ratios or the wisdom of the Joint Traffic Association, *Proceedings of the Board of Managers,* 1896. At the time Fogel wrote there were few actual readers who could take on the role of his ideal implied reader.

But the excellence of his work, and the work of other pioneers, created in time actual ideal readers for Fogel's books, the cliometric movement. Fogel was an orator setting up his soapbox in Hyde Park, gathering after a while a crowd capable of appreciating his speech. This is how scholarly discourse changes: the crowd gathers bit by bit around a different orator with a different implied audience. The audience is not so much selected as trained, trained by repeated attempts to imagine itself as the implied reader. Something of the sort appears to have occurred in modern mathematics. Hilbert's program of formal rigor has been pushed so far that some present-day mathematicians only understand formal rigor of a Hilbertian sort. An audience of such mathematicians is merely puzzled, even confused, by attempts to give physical or other motivation to mathematical argument. An audience deaf to certain forms of talk has been assembled.

Fogel created an implied reader more definite than merely a generalized historical economist. His reader is an earnest fellow, much impressed by science, in love with figures and the bottom line, a little stubborn in his convictions but open to argument and patient with its details. Such an implied reader is less attractive than the more common one in successful academic prose. Albert Fishlow's book, by contrast, creates an implied reader more distant and disengaged, one sensitive to ironies, amused by verbal rotundities, impatient with closely argued economics but very patient indeed with narrative indirection. It is something like the implied reader of the best history.

The implied reader of the best economics shuttles gracefully amongst algebraic, geometric, and literary arguments. Fogel, though perfectly capable in all three, sticks to prose. The economical reader, even if a socialist, needs no factual proof of the efficacy of markets. The belief impelled socialist economists in the 1930s to invent an oxymoronic theory of "market socialism." Fogel, though well educated in such mysteries, spends much of his book amassing evidence that markets do in fact work—an inquiry that, in part by his example, became a leading *topos* of cliometrics. Above all the economical reader delights in the simplest argument available. Economists shave dangerously close with Ockham's razor. If some apparently complex behavior can be reduced to a slogan or a three-line proof the economist can be relied upon to seize it. Fogel, though well aware that to the right audience his point could be made in three lines, felt it necessary to write nine thousand more.

The three-line proof draws on all the peculiarities of the implied reader of modern economics. It translates a literary remark about the indispensability of railroads into algebra, then draws on the logic of markets to make the simplest available inference. To the implied reader that economists invite their actual readers to become, the proof is persuasive. Fogel gives it on page 11, repeating it in a slightly different form on pages 23 (where he states the opposite case the better to knock it down: *exadversio*) and 24. But it could not persuade the reader Fogel wished to create, and whom by his eloquence he did in time create.

Fogel, then, accomplished a good deal with his rhetoric. Style, the genre, the audience, are not "mere matters of form." Hayden White remarks that "the link between a given historian and his potential public is forged on the pretheoretical, and specifically linguistic, level of consciousness" (1973, p. 429). Amelie Oksenberg Rorty again said it well. In economic scholarship, as in philosophical scholarship, it is a good part (not all) of the substance:

> Conviction is often carried by a charismatic, authoritative
> style: its clarity and condensation, the rhythms of its sentences,

The Problem of Audience in Historical Economics

and its explosive imagery. But often the form of a work assures its legitimation: a dedication indicating continuity of descent, a *nihil obstat*, the laying on of hands by footnotes acknowledging the advice of established authorities, the imprimatur of publication by a major university press. The apparatus of footnotes, appendixes, graphs, diagrams, formulas, used with measure and discretion, indicate a proper sobriety. . . . Sobriety, attention to detail, care without obsession, the right balance of generality and attention, an easy rather than a relentless use of imagery and metaphor—these are integral to philosophical legitimation. (1983, p. 546)

Fogel, however, was doing more than working within an existing scholarly genre and existing audiences. He made up new ones. Thomas Kuhn's notion of revolutions of thinking in physics as shifts in paradigms has been of course grossly overworked, applied mindlessly to shifts far from revolutionary in fields far from physics. The case of Fogel and cliometrics, however, does make the point that the shifts are not only or even largely shifts in explanatory models, but in ways of talking. Fogel changed the subject of the conversation and changed its rules.

Conversation is the best metaphor of scholarship. John Gardner (1984, p. 97) described good fiction as a "vivid and continuous dream" and pointed to the failures in the writer's technique and the writer's personality that disturb the dream, waking the reader "as if a playwright were to run up on the stage, interrupting his characters, to remind us that he has written all this." Good scholarship is not so solipsistic; it is a lucid and sustained conversation. Bad scholars commit the vices of bad conversationalists: monologue, meanness of tone, dullness, and, above all, irrelevance.

The metaphor of scholarship as a conversation is more capacious even than that of speechmaking. It allows the audience a role, letting it heckle or, better, voice sober objections to some Socrates. A successful speech in scholarship and in other appeals to reason is not a monologue. It asks the audience to participate in a lucid conversation (albeit a guided one), not the vivid dream of novelists and other rabble rousers. It is true in the law, as William Robinson remarked long ago, in *Forensic Oratory: A Manual for Advocates* (1893, p. 29): "Every oration is in reality a dialogue, in which the doubts and objections of the auditor are so many silent interrogatories to which the orator audibly replies." And it is true in successful scholarship, such as Fogel's.

Conversations, of course, use language. It is impossible to have a language of one's own, untouched by tradition or by the rest of the conversationalists. The mutual persuasion known as knowledge in history or in economics, as in physics or literature, is a social event, like a coronation in London or a day in the wheat pit on the Chicago Board of Trade. It is sometimes a new style of conversation, a new way of speaking. Fogel (to use a distinction drawn by Roland Barthes) was an author rather than a writer, a creator of a new genre, a Max Planck or a Gerard Manley Hopkins, an author of a new way of conversing rather than a user of a preexisting genre. Even the science of the counting house and the railroad station, cold-spirited as it is, draws on the gilded rhetoric of poets and mathematicians.

8 THE UNEXAMINED

RHETORIC OF ECONOMIC

QUANTIFICATION

It is perhaps clear by now that economists use rhetorical means to achieve their ends. I here extend the assertion to what one might think would be the least rhetorical part of economics, its statistics. Even in the most narrowly technical matters economists have shared convictions about what makes an argument strong, convictions which they have not examined, which they can communicate to graduate students only tacitly, and which contain many elements embarrassing to the official rhetoric. The convictions can be exposed by literary criticism.

But why does it matter that economists are givers of orations? Why does it matter that economics is a branch of literature, open to the techniques of literary study? Will economics be improved? The fullest answer is provided here: rhetorical criticism can strengthen quantitative argument in economics. Self-consciousness about the rhetoric of his statistics can raise the standard of the most technical arguments the economist uses.

Consider the typical procedure in econometrics. From economic theory, politics, and the workings of the economist's psyche, all of which are in the rhetorical sense unexamined, come "hypotheses" about some bit of the economy. The hypotheses are then specified as straight lines, linear models being those most easily manipulated. The straight lines are fitted to someone else's collection of facts. This far the official and workaday rhetoric correspond, and the one might with justice be called a guide to the other.

Presently, however, they diverge. If the results of the fitting to the data are "reasonable," on grounds that are not themselves subject to examination, the article is sent off to a journal for publication, and added to the résumé of the economist. If the results are unreasonable, the hypothesis is consigned to do a loop, as they say at the computation center: the economic scientist returns to the hypotheses or the specifications, altering them until a publishable article emerges. The product may or may not have value, but it does not acquire its value from its adherence to the official rhetoric. It violates the official rhetoric blatantly.

But official rhetorics are seldom much help. Even at the level of tests of statistical significance the workaday rhetoric violates the philosopher's law. But so what? It is a cliché of cynicism in economics and related statistical fields on that an apparently "significant" result does not have the significance it claims if the hypothesis has been manipulated to fit the data. That only significant results get published has long been a scandal among statistical purists: they fear with some reason that at the 5 percent level of significance something like 5 percent of the computer runs will be successful. But the intellectual scandal is not the failure to achieve modernist standards of scientific purity. The scandal is the failure to think about why one might want to ignore them.

It would be arrogant to suppose that one knew better than thousands of intelligent and honest economic scholars what the proper form of argument was. The Received View is arrogant in this way, laying down legislation for science on the basis of epistemological convictions held with a vehemence inversely proportional to the amount of evidence that they work. Better to look hard at what is in fact done. In an important book that is an exception to the general neglect of rhetorical considerations in econometrics Edward Leamer asks what purpose the workaday procedures in econometrics may be serving (Leamer 1978; esp. p. 17). Instead of comparing them with an obsolete doctrine in the philosophy on science, he compares them with reasons that ought to persuade a reasonable person, with what really warrants assent, with, in short, the actual rhetoric of econometrics. As Christopher Sims points out in a review,

There is a myth that there are only two categories of knowledge about the world—'the' model, given to us by 'economic theory', without uncertainty, and the parameters, about which we know nothing except what the data, via objectively specified econometric methods, tells us. . . . The sooner Leamer's cogent writings can lead us to abandon this myth, to recognize that nearly all applied work is shot through with applications of uncertain, subjective knowledge, and to make the role of such knowledge more explicit and more effective, the better. (Sims 1978, p. 567)

The Unexamined Rhetoric of Economic Quantification

Yes. The very title of Leamer's book is an outline of rhetoric in econometrics: *Specification Searches: Ad Hoc Inference with Nonexperimental Data.*

Examples of the search abound. In seminars in economics it is common for the speaker to present a statistical result, apparently irrefutable by the rules of positive economics, yet to be met by choruses of "I can't believe it" or "It doesn't make sense." Milton Friedman's own Money Workshop at Chicago in the late 1960s and the early 1970s was a case in point.

Put in statistical language, the rhetorical context that creates such scepticism can be called a priori beliefs and can be analyzed in Bayesian terms: ask explicitly how the probability an economist assigns to a hypothesis is changed by the evidence. That the rhetorical community in economics might reject apparently solid results and accept apparently flimsy ones shows the strength of prior beliefs. Some economists, for example, reject the statistically solid result that oil prices appear in a regression explaining inflation, while accepting the flimsy result that money alone causes inflation. Others do the reverse, believing oil prices to be flimsy and money solid. Both groups justify their beliefs by claiming that *they* look at the evidence. The Bayesian point, however, is that the way you look at the evidence is affected by the beliefs you bring to the looking. Yet for all the Bayesian talk in economics, economists do not take seriously a responsibility to be candid about their prior beliefs.

To cut the discussion off at declarations of prior beliefs, however, is to perpetuate the fact-value split of modernism. It leaves most of what matters in science to squeals of pleasure or pain. "I am a monetarist: you must present me with overwhelming evidence against the importance of money to get me to budge." Or, "I am an ecclectic Keynesian: dammit, we *know* that relative prices of oil affect the level of other prices."

Bald declarations of what the economist *is* or what he *knows* leave too much unargued. What is required is an examination of the workaday rhetoric that leads to the prior beliefs. It is not enough, as Cooley and LeRoy do in their recent, penetrating paper, "Identification and Estimation of Money Demand" (1981), merely to stand appalled at the infection of econometric conclusions by prior beliefs. If econometric argument does not persuade, it is because the field of argument is too narrow, not because the impulse towards thoughtfulness and explicitness which it embodies is wrong. The arguments need to be broadened, and prior convictions argued, not merely dismissed.

Rhetorical Standards Are Necessary to Measure the Integration of Markets

The rhetoric of quantification, in other words, is a leading case for study. A man who wishes to convince his modernist neighbor will show him numbers. Numbers are believed to tell. Numbers are believed to be objective, intersubjective, conclusive. Most people, and even most economists, believe that once you have reduced a question to numbers, you have taken it out of human hands.

The best quantitative scientists know that this is naive. The critical point, a rhetorical one, is that a number is high or low relative only to some standard, and the only relevant standard is provided by the human conversation. Ten degrees below zero is paralyzing cold by the standard of Virginia, a normal day by the standard of Saskatoon in January, and a heat wave by the standard of most interstellar gas. Everyone knows this. The *New Yorker* cartoon shows faucets labeled "Hot: A Relative Concept" and "Cold: A Relative Concept." A thing is not large in itself. It is large (or yellow, rich, cold, stable, well-integrated, selfish, free, rising, monopolistic) relative to something else, and the something has to be specified. The question "But how large is large?" applies to any scholarly paper whatever. It is a seminar standby, like "How do you construe 'knowing'?" or, in a statistical mode, "Have you examined your residuals?" The how-large-is-large question inherits some of its sturdy excellence from its father in thought, the terrifying, mind-stunning "So what?" (and from its Jewish mother, "So what else is new?"). Few better questions can be asked, because most inadequate scholarship work errs more in relevance than in execution.

What is most remarkable about this obvious question is how often it is not asked. The question of how large is large causes great embarrassment, for example, when economists and other social scientists pretend to advise. On the issue of how much better black children do in nonsegregated schools, for example, Robert Crain of the Johns Hopkins Center for Social Organization of Schools remarks that "there is a great deal of debate about when improvement is a big deal and when it isn't a big deal." Complaining that social scientists have been trained to think in terms of merely statistical significance, he notes (1984, p. 12) that they "have never arrived at a consensus on how big a number is big." The same point can be made about the collateral controversy over race and I.Q., now blessedly stilled if not resolved. The technical issue was whether or not the averages of white and and black I.Q.'s were different statistically. I.Q. is a questionable notion to begin with and hard to measure free of cultural bias. The crucial point, however, is that the distributions of black and white I.Q.'s largely overlap. An alleged difference in averages, however real by the standard of merely statistical significance, would *not* therefore be a Big Deal. It has no practical use. On the basis of a statistically significant difference between the races in average I.Q., for instance, one would hardly propose to use race as a criterion for excluding certain children from certain schools: under such a policy, even accepting its repulsive moral base, most of the students would be placed in the wrong school. Statistically significant or not, the difference is too small to matter.

The point comes up repeatedly in statistical thinking about society. Asking the pragmatic questions—"So what?" "How large is large?" "What does it matter for the intellectual or political or moral issue at hand?"—would embarrass many disputes.

Economists do no worse than most in failing to answer the questions. Much of economics turns on quarrels of characterization: Is America monopolistic? Were medieval peasants selfish? Is the market for goods worldwide? Is capitalism stable? These are quantitative questions, all depending on answers to the question "How large is large?" That the quarrels of characterization go on, and on, passing from one century to the next unamended, that Mommsen had most of the story of Roman monetary history right and that List had most of the arguments for protection, though they are wrong, suggest that the rhetoric has failed.

Of course, it may be that some of the how-large-is-large questions cannot be resolved on this side of the Last Judgment. Even good rhetoric does not guarantee certitude. But the rhetoric in the disputes does not appear to engage the disputants. The customs of scholarly disputation appear on the surface to be legal or logical, settling disputes by appeal to a court or to a proof. Something, however, is amiss: law cases end with the judgment, mathematical proofs with Q.E.D. But quantitative arguments in history and economics that draw habitually on the metaphors of case and proof often possess little of their closure. The right characterization of the degree to which purchasing power parity holds in the modern world or of the amount of competition in America or of the amount of selfishness in the Middle Ages eludes pursuit down the decades. The reason is that no one answers the question "How large is large?" Everyone knows it, but no one answers it.

"No one" is a little too strong. Whenever a quantitative argument is felt to have persuasive force, its author has impressed his audience, by that very fact. The author has impressed the audience that railroads mattered only a little for American economic growth or that entrepreneurship mattered only a little for British economic decline (quantitative economic historians, from whom these conclusions are drawn,

The Unexamined Rhetoric of Economic Quantification

specialize in belittling). On some internal psychological scale pondered together by reader and writer the calculated matter is felt to have small weight.

For reasons that are not clear, however, scholars are notably reluctant to exhibit their scales for public test and adjustment. It should be alarming that the crucial last step in assessing a quantitative argument is private. The point of counting is to lay out the steps in an argument for inspection by those who care to look. Counting grew up with experiment, in the sixteenth and seventeenth centuries: Hooke of England held his experiments in the public rooms of his college, the first laboratory being therefore quintessentially public. In like fashion, calculation was to be be exhibited, not concealed for purposes of witchcraft or theosophy. Yet the last step of most calculations in economics or history is sleight of hand, the more convincing because the magician performs it so absentmindedly: "The coefficient in a regression of domestic prices on foreign prices is statistically insignificantly different from 1.00, and *therefore* purchasing power parity is true." "The number of formal whippings of slaves was less than 0.7 [or perhaps 1.2] a year, and *therefore* the lash was insignificant [or perhaps significant]."[1]

Many more cases could be supplied from quantitative economics. The canonical case is the integration of markets. For some fifty years certain economists have been measuring the correlation between two parts of a market and concluding triumphantly that the market was indeed integrated. The trouble is that other economists, often using the same statistics, have concluded gloatingly that it was not.

Historical economists have more often seen the need for a standard, if only the standard that, yes, the integration of markets did increase as better ships were built for sea lanes cleared of pirates and as postroads, semaphores, and finally telegraph poles tied prices together. Knowing that from 1400 to 1760 the spread of prices of grain in Europe fell steadily (as one may see in the grand diagrams accompanying Braudel and Spooner's contribution to the *Cambridge Economic History of Europe*, 4:470) is at least better than knowing merely that around 1600 the ratio of the wheat price in Venice to the price in Warsaw was five to one.

From the bare, lone number one can infer nothing, because no standard is provided for saying whether the number is large or small. One says a market is "integrated" when judging the differential to be small, but the word means only what we together have agreed for the moment

---

1. This should not be taken as personal apostasy from the quantitative faith. In nonquantitative arguments the sleight of hand is still there, though it comes earlier.

The Unexamined Rhetoric of Economic Quantification

to let it mean, namely, a "small" differential. In a particular conversation about the wheat market we implicitly take the words "a small differential" to mean whatever the character of wheat trading was in some standard time and place, say Europe in 1900. Like Humpty Dumpty, we pay the words of characterization—the market is "integrated" or "competitive" or "black"—and quite properly therefore feel free to order them about. But to talk as though the lone number for 1600 shorn of linguistic convention says anything about market integration in 1600 is to play a less reasonable one of Humpty's games. "Why," he asked, "is a mouse when it spins?" and answered, "The higher the fewer."

One cannot decide, then, whether the market in wheat was integrated without agreeing, consciously or not, to the rules of a language game in which "integrated" means something. A statistic of integration means something by having a certain value in another standard situation in which we already agree it means "well-integrated." If we all agree that the market for wheat in 1900 was "well-integrated," for instance, then we have a standard for talking meaningfully about the value of some statistic relevant to integration in another time, such as 1600.

Suppose, for example, that the average correlation of prices of wheat in cities a hundred miles apart in Europe was .95 in 1900 (expressing prices in the same currency, taking the correlations over decades, using weekly data, and so forth). Suppose, too, that we agree "for purposes of argument" (as the sensible phrase goes) that the European wheat market in 1900 was what we mean by well-integrated. We have then a standard by which to judge the degree of integration of the wheat market in Europe in 1600, or of China in 1900, or of the Western Mediterranean in the fifth century B.C. The particular standard is not very helpful, of course, because by the standard of 1900 none of these markets were "well-integrated." But at least we know that. (It is "we" who know it: the matter is social.) To know merely that the correlation of grain prices between Shanghai and Peking in A.D. 1900 was .85 or between Athens and Syracuse in 430 B.C. was .70 is by itself to know nothing at all.

One needs a standard, then. The point is obvious in the case of official measurements in units of Winchester heaped bushels or light years or meters. It is obvious that a certain platinum-iridium bar at the International Bureau of Standards outside Paris is "the meter" (or was: they do such things atomically nowadays). No one would propose to call a race a "10,000" with the units left off, leaving it to the internal scales of the runners to decide whether it was 10,000 meters or 10,000 inches (or tons or Greek mercenaries, for that matter: the higher the fewer). The official meter bar, a socially agreed-upon way of speaking for the sake of argument, gives the 10,000 its meaning or, as we say, its units. Race numbers or correlations get their units and their significance from people, not from God.

The standard, or units, for measures of market integration must come from some time or country that is worth comparing with the case at hand. One cannot decide if Britain and America were in the same market for purposes of thinking about their money supplies without some relevant standard. The so-called Genberg-Zecher criterion is one, the standard of sameness in markets *within* the two countries. We speak of Britain's money supply as something needing special consideration in our theories, as Midlothian's money supply or Cornwall's does not. We speak of America's money supply as though "America" were a significant aggregate for some purpose, but we do not speak of California's money supply or Vermont's. Behind the speaking, then, must lie an implicit standard. The standard is that a market area in bricks, saws, and sweaters defined to contain without comment both California and Vermont is apparently not disparate enough to require a separate money supply. The degree to which the prices of bricks, saws, and sweaters move parallel in California and Vermont, therefore, provides a criterion (the very Genberg-Zecher one) for measuring the degree of integration between America as a whole and Britain. If the degree of parallelism is no larger between America and Britain than it is between California and Vermont, then—for purposes of argument—one might as well include Britain as California in America's money supply. The borders of countries will in this conversation lack point.

It is easy to become muddled on the matter of comparative standards of market integration. For many years, under the baleful influence of Karl Polanyi (Michael's brother), some students of the classical world have been trying to show that it was not integrated economically (Finley 1973). In the absence of self-consciousness about standards the discussion has become muddled. Members of the Polanyi school have usually taken some condition they believe characteristic of integrated markets in general, such as the existence of centralized places for selling or of specialized traders, and have argued that Mesopotamia in the second millennium B.C. or Rome under the republic did not have it. In effect they have ruminated on the phrases "integrated markets" or "capitalism," or whatever, in the abstract and have attempted to arrive at their essences (studying economics in a haphazard way, but that is another story). Then they have turned to the historical evidence (taking it in peculiar ways, but that is still another story) to see if they can smell an essence. Essences, though, do not provide usable standards, espe-

The Unexamined Rhetoric of Economic Quantification

cially quantitative standards. The absence of one among many *sufficient* conditions for market integration (central markets and specialized dealers, to be sure, but also computerized billing, cheap diesel trucks, the interstate highway system, and the telephone) does not imply the absence of market integration. The Polanyi procedure is a fallacy of negating the antecedent. That telephones imply integrated markets (and by some standards they do) does not imply that economies without telephones do not have integrated markets.

A better way to advance the conversation would be to examine the characteristics of actual economies already known—in other words, agreed—to be integrated. Few would deny that the North Atlantic in the eighteenth century, for example, was an integrated market in grain, timber, and gold. Fewer still would deny that the characteristics of integration in the North Atlantic in the eighteenth century are a relevant standard to hold up to the classical world. Gibbon held up such a standard; Smith did too. Their theatres of language are still ours. A conversation exists in which the eighteenth century is the background. The characteristics of integration actually present in the eighteenth century, therefore, are relevant standards of integratedness to apply elsewhere. To be sure, square-rigged ships and sextants will show up in the list of characteristics. This will not lead one to conclude that integration of the Roman and Sicilian market in wheat was therefore impossible. The job will be to select the characteristics—such as a correlation of prices of .90 or large flows in response to price differentials—that allow one to judge whether the Roman trade was integrated or not integrated relative to the North Atlantic.

The reasoning applies to other cases of market integration. A battle of books is now going on among American colonial historians over whether or not Americans in the eighteenth century participated in a market economy. Another heats up from time to time over whether and when the British labor market became integrated in the nineteenth century. And still another has raged since World War I, fought out by each generation of economists since Taussig and Wicksell, over whether nations participate fully in a world market for goods in the twentieth century. The outcomes matter. The smaller stakes are whether or not simple economic models of supply and demand can be applied to whole nations or whole worlds. It would be nice to avoid having separate models for each isolated New England farm or modern nation. But there are stakes beyond neatness, or at least so the scholars fighting and dying at the fronts believe. The very use of economic models in classical economic history, the dating of capitalism in America's infancy, the causes of British growth during the nineteenth century, the rationality (if any) of the efforts since Keynes to understand and govern economies at the merely national level all depend on the largeness of some measure of integration. The discussions do not face up to the question of "How large is large?" It is no wonder that they are inconclusive and ill-tempered, scholarly Chickamaugas with much slaughter on both sides.

The quarrels about market integration are not the only important economic discussions that fail to confront the Overwhelming Question. Attempts to measure the largeness of birthrates in the eighteenth century, of social and geographical mobility in the nineteenth century, of entrepreneurial failure in Britain, and of the influence of Federal Reserve policy in America, to mention a few, must all conclude with an answer to "How large is large?" They seldom do. The answer to the question has to be framed comparatively, speaking of some other time or place in which we agree the birthrate was low, mobility high, entrepreneurship trivial, or monetary policy strong. Comparison gives social statistics their meaning.[2]

In Like Fashion, Rhetorical Standards Are Necessary in Linguistics to Measure the Similarity of Languages

Comparative linguistics provides a useful parallel. The question whether Danish or Norwegian are to be accounted separate languages is parallel to the question whether Copenhagen and Oslo are to be accounted separate markets for labor. The two issues in fact

2. Historians will wonder what all this has to do with comparative history, as identified by the great French historian Marc Bloch. His "Contribution towards a Comparative History of European Societies" (1928) enumerated the virtues of comparison in seeing the very data to be explained by history, in discerning the mutual influences between regions, and above all in discovering the "real causes" of the similarities and differences among nations by setting them side by side. In this way one may learn more about early economic growth in the Lowlands or the role of banking in the early stages of industrialization. But Bloch was not making the same point as that made here. In essence he was commending the virtues of experiment, controlled as well as history can; in the vocabulary of statistical disciplines, he was telling historians to fit lines, to do regression analysis. Go to the library or the computer center and assemble a number of cases in which modern wives facing the job market or medieval peasants cultivating open fields make their choices under differing circumstances. From what changes and stays the same in response to the differences you will be able to infer an effect of, say, the husband's income on the wife's market work or the king's peace on the peasant's open fields. The point here, however, is that once a comparison or a regression is finished it must be interpreted, given some meaning in the scholarly conversation.

The Unexamined Rhetoric of Economic Quantification

influence each other. Wider politics affects both, since it matters whether one language or wage level is treated as standard relative to the other. If Danish were the tongue of influence in a Dano-Norwegian kingdom (as it once was, producing the *Riksmaal*, or realm-speech), Norwegian would be treated as a provincial dialect (*Landsmaal*, or country-talk), the way Lowland Scots is treated as a provincial dialect relative to South-eastern English. If wages in Copenhagen were taken as the standard in the kingdom for subsidy payments or for setting the salaries of government workers, then the labor markets of far Oslo would be treated as a provincial branch of the central market in Denmark. The distinctions between languages are manmade, not written in the heavens.

The concern here is with the habits of linguistic scholars on such questions. The point is that they face the same puzzle that economists face: How large is large? How large do the differences between dialects of Dano-Norwegian have to be before one accounts Danish and Norwegian separate languages? The linguists sometimes use "mutual intelligibility" as a standard for defining a language, but like the correlation of prices, it immediately demands a higher-order standard. The assertion that a correlation of .80 between prices of grain in Glasgow and London may be said to be "high" demands, as I have said, a social context. So does the assertion that the phrase "days of auld lang syne" may be said to be "mutually intelligible" to a Glaswegian and a Cockney. How intelligible? When speaking slowly with an attempt to approach the standard dialect? In the newspaper? At a pub sing-song? How large is large?

The vagueness of dialects sharpens the matter. L. R. Palmer worried in the early pages of his standard treatment of *The Latin Language* (1954) about whether Oscan, Umbrian, Sabellian, and Volscian should be taken as languages separate from Latin or together with Latin as mere dialects of a common "Italic." He remarks that "this is largely a dispute about terms that have no precise scientific definition" (p. 6), by which he appears to mean, as people do when they talk this way, no definition that would end argument forever. His definition of language ("a system of vocal signals used by a given community") reduces to mutual intelligibility. His standard of intelligibility, to which he appends a condition of social "solidarity" in order to allow for such cases as the political divisions of Scandinavian, is whether native speakers feel they are speaking the same language. He uses, too, a definition by questionnaire—asking the native speakers. This is of course reasonable, though for a dead language with very limited early remains, he is in practice driven back to more objective but less persuasive standards: for the case of Umbrian, "it has been calculated that 60–70 percent of the words contained in the Iguvinian Tables are different from Latin, whereas for Greek only 10–15 percent of the words occurring in the Cretan Gortynian Laws are not found in Attic" (p. 7). Note in this the explicitly comparative standard. When Palmer wants to persuade a reader that Latin and Umbrian are to be accounted different languages, he places the two on a scale defined by dialects of Greek.

A definition of markets limits by questionnaire might be helpful to economists, though they would have to recover from their addiction to modernism first. If their epistemology permitted it, they could *ask* a worker whether she felt herself to be in the same market for labor as people in the next county. In any event economists are in the same fix as are linguists, who find themselves saying of Osco-Umbrian compared with Latin, "The degree of unintelligibility is far greater ... than between Italian and Spanish" (Palmer 1954, p. 8). The familiar case provides an argumentative standard.

The study of language and the study of economies, to recall an earlier distinction, have a diachronic as well as a synchronic aspect. Since linguists are interested in how languages came to be what they are as well as how they work at a particular time, they have available another, developmental definition to set beside the puzzles of such static definitions: namely, genealogy. If Italic begat both Osco-Umbrian and Latin, then the latter are sister tongues and that is that. In the simple case of one language developing without external influences the genealogical definition supplies its own standards. Latin developed into Italian and Rumanian. But the case of "Italic" developing into Latin and Osco-Umbrian, it happens, is more cloudy.

One might well apply the genealogical definition to the problem of markets. If two allegedly distinct markets had common ancestors —or, what would be more useful, common descendants—then one might agree to call them one. Such a definition would not be very persuasive, though perhaps interesting for some other purpose. Institutionalists in economics—who include anthropologists and geographers interested in economic affairs but not trained in modern, static, synchronic, neoclassical economics—take an interest in such matters. They wish to know who the grandfathers of the present traders were, where the market "came from," "how it was financed," and other things, none of which is of any use to a static study of markets. The static study demands a definition free of historical context. (One may say, so much the worse for the static study.) It demands not a story but a rule. And the rigor of a scholarly rule depends on which scholars one is talking to.

The linguistic analogy applies to the problem of markets even in details of technique. Linguists, for instance, draw maps of "isoglosses," similar to isoquants in production theory or isobars in meteorology, which show where dialect words are the same. The words "bag" (as for groceries) and "sack," "purse" and "pocketbook," "brook" and "rill," can be plotted on a map and their boundaries discerned. If the isoglosses appear to pile up on top of each other, then one is looking at a line between distinct dialects or languages. One could do the same with correlations of prices, mapping the rings of isocorrelation around marketing centers, for instance, or plotting the frequency distribution of correlations for products ranging from the tradeable to the strictly local. In either case some standard is needed, a standard depending on how much it took to persuade other scholars in view of what conversations among them had already taken place.

Linguists, like economists, come often to the verge of standards without crossing over into articulating them. Saussure remarks that "a dialect is defined, roughly speaking, by a *sufficient* accumulation of such concordances [of isoglosses]" (1915, p. 203; italics added). But how sufficient is sufficient? In his *Descriptive and Comparative Linguistics: A Critical Introduction* (1972), Palmer treats dialectology most lucidly, but stops the search for standards on page 278: dialectical boundaries are places where "within such a bundle of isoglosses there is a *palpable degree of uniformity*" (italics added). The point is that palpability lies in the fingers of the toucher. In *Defining a Linguistic Area: South Asia* (1976), Colin Masica, speaking of the clustering of isoglosses, says, "Opinions may, of course, differ on what constitutes a significant degree of clustering, even though *mathematical procedures would appear to offer a way of deciding*" (p. 6; italics added). Would that it were so. Quantification raises in a usefully clear form the question of how large is large; but quantification without a rhetoric of the scholarly conversation does not answer it.

That Is, the Speech Acts of Scholars Are Social Actions

Everything said so far about quantitative assertions in history or economics or linguistics is probably true of assertions generally. One can always ask "So what?" And the answer will always depend on one's audience and the human purposes involved. Most assertions are made for purposes of persuading some audience. This is not a shameful fact: it is charming that human beings are cuddly, preferring to cling together against the indifferent cold. Their sociability leads them to make remarks they hope others will believe and use.

The Unexamined Rhetoric of Economic Quantification

Even scholars are human beings. When they come to interpret a "plain fact," such as the extent of the American market or the degree of similarity among Italic languages, the economic and historical and linguistic scholars must be appealing to other human beings. The assertion of a plain fact derives its force—which J. L. Austin called its "performative" character, as contrasted with its "constative" or merely declarative character—from the conventions of conversation in which it takes place: "We must consider the total situation in which the utterance is issued—the total speech-act" (Austin 1975, p. 52). The functioning of the American capital market, it is said, became significantly better in the closing years of the nineteenth century (Davis 1965). A rise in the American money supply, it is said, will cause a significant amount of inflation, albeit with a long and variable lag. The "significance" here must be relative to some experience in conversation that American economic historians and economists have had. Otherwise the assertions do not do their work.

Especially the assertions are not just true or false in themselves. In his *How to Do Things with Words*, Austin wrote

> Suppose that we confront "France is hexagonical" with the facts, in this case, I suppose, with France, is it true or false? Well, *if you like* up to a point. . . . it is true *for certain intents and purposes*. It is good enough *for a general, perhaps, but not for a geographer*. . . . But then someone says, . . ."it has to be true or false—it's a statement, isn't it?" How can one answer? . . . It is just rough, and that is the right and final answer. . . . It is a rough description; it is not a true or false one. . . . "true" and "false" . . . do not stand for anything simple at all; but only for a general dimension of being a *right or proper thing to say . . . in these circumstances, to this audience, for these purposes and with these intentions.* (Austin 1975, pp. 143, 145; italics added)

In commenting on this passage Stanley Fish makes most elegantly the point here about quantitative thinking in economics:

> All assertions are . . . produced and understood within the assumption of some socially conceived and understood dimension of assessment. . . . the one thing you can never say about France is what it is *really* like, if by "really" you mean France as it exists independently of any dimension of assessment whatever. The France you are talking about will always be the product of the talk about it, and will *never* be independently available. . . . What the example of France shows is that all facts are discourse

The Unexamined Rhetoric of Economic Quantification

specific . . . and that therefore no one can claim for any language a special relationship to the facts as they "simply are," unmediated by social or conventional assumptions.

It may help in swallowing such a pill to note that not only ordinary-language philosophers and modern literary critics talk this way. Modern physicists say similar things about the realest of realities. And Beltrami's proof in 1868 that Lobachevskian geometry can have no possible self-contradictions *if* Euclidean geometry has none has been taken as the model of how to go about such tasks in mathematics. There are no proofs of consistency available for every mathematical system (as was later proved by Gödel with perfect generality), only proofs for some that attach one part of mathematical discourse to another.

The better sugar coating of the pill is simply to note that the social and persuasive character of the act of assertion is, after all, routinely sensible, something on which we act daily. We look naturally for external standards with which to make judgments, quantitative or not. Does your son have big feet? Well, how many fourteen-year-olds *do* have size thirteen shoes? Reporting "size thirteen" without some conversational context would not advance the discussion. Is "Ode on a Grecian Urn" a good poem? Well, compare and contrast it with one hundred randomly selected poems. Decisions such as these cannot be made independent of the conversations of humankind. *We* decide what are big feet, good poems, and large statistics of market integration. The criteria are social, not solipsistic. They are written in the literary conversations of scholars, not in the stars or in statistical tables of the levels of significance of Student's *t*.

The social character of scientific knowledge does not make it arbitrary, touchie-feelie, mob-governed, or anything else likely to bring it into disrepute. It is still, for instance, "objective," if that is a worry. In vulgar usage the objective/subjective distinction beloved of Western philosophy since Descartes means discussable/undiscussable. But even in a sophisticated sense "objectivity" has a necessarily social definition: we know that the yield of corn in the Middle Ages was objectively low because we converse with people who agree with our evidence and our calculations and our standard of comparison validating the word "low."

Nor are such human standards peculiar to the human sciences. The mathematician Armand Borel notes that "something becomes objective . . . as soon as we are convinced that it exists in the minds of others in the same form that it does in ours, and that we can think about it and discuss it together" (1983, p. 13). A scale of particle durations, star sizes, or electrical activity of the brain depends on being able to "discuss it together." The scale, to repeat, is of man, not of God.

The Unexamined Rhetoric of Economic Quantification

The standards for quantitative statements, then, have to be conversational. It is only because a conversation about nuclear particles or market integration has arrived at a certain point that calculations of rates of decay or of correlations of prices are to the point. The rhetoric of conversation, not the logic of inquiry, provides the standards for science.

9   THE RHETORIC OF

SIGNIFICANCE TESTS

The Discussion of Purchasing Power Parity Is Rhetorically Muddled

A good example of how the official rhetoric can lead a substantial literature in economics astray is the rhetoric on purchasing power parity. When examined in light of the rhetoric of economic quantification, the example leads to a larger matter: the use of statistical significance.

The economic question at stake in the quarrel over purchasing power parity is again the question of whether markets are integrated. Is the world's economy like the economy of the Midwest, in which Iowa City and Madison and Champaign all face given prices for goods? Or is it more like the solar system, in which each planet's economy is properly thought of in isolation? If the Iowa City view is correct, then the prices of all goods will move together everywhere, allowing for exchange rates between currencies. If the Martian view is correct, they will move differently. If the Iowa City view is correct, then all economic models closed to the rest of the world, whether Keynesian or monetarist or rationally expecting, are wrong; if the Martian view is correct, then economists can (as they do) go on testing macroeconomic faiths against merely American experience since the 1940s.

The question of whether prices are closely connected internationally, then, is important. The official rhetoric does not leave much doubt as to what is required to answer it: collect facts on prices in, say, the United States and Canada and then . . . well . . . *test* the hypothesis (derived in orthodox fashion from a higher-order hypothesis; using objective data; looking only at observable facts; controlling the experiment as much as possible; and so forth, according to the Received View). A large number of economists have done this. Half of them conclude that purchasing power parity works; the other half conclude that it fails.

The conclusions diverge not because the economists are stupid or because economics is arbitrary but because the disputants have not considered their rhetoric. In particular they have not considered their standards for conclusions. A misleading but nonetheless superb paper by Irving Kravis and Robert Lipsey on the subject, for instance, concludes that purchasing power parity fails, in terms that are worth repeating: "We think it *unlikely* that the *high* degree of national and international commodity arbitrage that many versions of the monetarist theory of the balance of payments contemplate is *typical* of the real world. This is not to deny that the price structures of the advanced industrial countries *are linked* together, but it is to suggest that the links are *loose* rather than *rigid*" (1978, p. 243; italics added). Every italicized word involves a comparison against some standard of what constitutes unlikelihood or highness or typicality or being linked or looseness or rigidity. Yet here, and elsewhere in the tortured literature of purchasing power parity, no standard is proposed.

The narrowest test of purchasing power parity, and the one that springs most readily to a mind trained in the official rhetoric, is to plot the price in the United States (of steel or of goods in general, in levels or in differences) against the corresponding price abroad, allowing for the exchange rate. If the slope of the line thus fitted is 1.00, the hypothesis of purchasing power parity is said to be confirmed; if not, not.

Kravis and Lipsey perform such a test. Being good economists they are evidently made a little uncomfortable by the rhetoric involved. They admit that "each analyst will have to decide in the light of his purposes whether the purchasing power parity relationships fall close enough to 1.00 to satisfy the theories" (p. 214). Precisely. In the next sentence, though, they lose sight of the need for an explicit standard if their argument is to be cogent: "As a matter of general judgment we express our opinion that the results do not support the notion of a tightly integrated international price structure." They do not say what a "general judgment" is or how one might recognize it. The purpose of an explicit economic rhetoric would be to provide guidance.

The guidance Kravis and Lipsey provide for evaluating their general judgment is a footnote (p. 214) reporting the general judgments of Houthakker, Haberler, and Johnson that deviations from parity of anything under 10 or 20 percent are acceptable to the hypothesis. (It happens, incidentally, that the bulk of the evidence offered by Kravis and Lipsey passes rather than fails such a test, belying their conclusions.) But accepting or rejecting one unargued standard by comparing it with another unargued standard does not much advance the art of argument in economics.

Kravis and Lipsey, to be quite fair, are unusually sensitive to the desirability of having some standard, more sensitive than are most economists working the field. They return repeatedly to the question of a standard, though without resolving it. They reject in one unpersuasive sentence on page 204 the only standard proposed in the literature so far, the Genberg-Zecher criterion described earlier. They draw a distinction on pages 204–5, on page 235, and again on page 242 between the statistical and the economic significance of their results. So frequently do they make the point that it must be counted one of the major points in the paper. Even small differences between domestic and export prices, they say on page 205, can make a big difference to the incentive to export: "This is a case in which statistical significance [that is, a correlation of the two prices near 1.0, which one might mistakenly suppose to imply that they were insignificantly different] does not necessarily connote economic significance." Yet they do not turn the sword on themselves. No wonder: without a rhetoric of *economic* significance, and in the face of a modernist rhetoric of statistical significance with the prestige of alleged science behind it, they are not aware they are wielding the sword.

The abuse of the word "significant" in connection with statistical arguments in economics is universal. Statistical significance seems to give a criterion by which to judge whether a hypothesis is true or false. The criterion seems to be independent of any tiresome consideration of how true a hypothesis must be to be true enough.

But the world does not serve up free intellectual lunches. Tables of significant tests cannot properly nourish a science. The point in the present case is that the "failure" of purchasing power parity in a regression of the usual type is not measured against a standard. How close does the slope have to be to the ideal of 1.00 to say that purchasing power parity succeeds? The literature is silent. The standard used is the irrelevant one of statistical significance, that is, how likely it is that the result might arise from the chances of the sample, in view of how large the sample is. By such a rhetorical device a sample size of a million yielding a tight estimate that the slope was .9999—if "significantly" different from 1.00000—could be produced as evidence that purchasing power parity had "failed," at least if the logic of the usual method were to be followed consistently. Common sense, presumably, would rescue the scholar from asserting that an estimate of .9999 with a standard error of .0000001 was significantly different from unity in a significant meaning of significance. Such common sense should be applied to findings of slopes of .90 or 1.20. It is not.

An example is J. D. Richardson's paper "Some Empirical Evidence on Commodity Arbitrage and the Law of One Price" (1978). He regresses Canadian prices on American prices multiplied by the exchange rate for a number of industries and concludes: "It is notable that the 'law of one price' fails uniformly. The hypothesis of *perfect* commodity arbitrage is rejected with 95 percent confidence for every commodity group" (p. 347; italics added). The question is, Why in an imperfect world would it matter that *perfect* arbitrage is rejected?

The irrelevance of the merely statistical criterion undermines the literature, whether favorable or unfavorable towards purchasing power parity. For instance, towards the end of a fine article favorable to purchasing power parity, Paul Krugman writes: "There are several ways in which we might try to evaluate purchasing power parity as a theory. We can ask how much it explains [that is, R-square]; we can ask how large the deviations from purchasing power parity are in some absolute sense; and we can ask whether the deviations from purchasing power parity are in some sense systematic" (1978, p. 405). The defensive usage "in some absolute sense" and "in some sense" betrays his unease, which is in the event justified. There is no "absolute sense" in which a description is good or bad. The sense must be comparative to a standard, and the standard must be argued.

Similarly, Jacob Frenkel, an enthusiast for purchasing power parity as such things go among economists but momentarily bewitched by the ceremony of statistical line-fitting, says that "if the market is efficient and if the forward exchange rate is an unbiased forecast of the future spot exchange rate, the constant [in a fit of the spot rate today on the future rate for today quoted yesterday] . . . should not differ *significantly* from unity" (1978, p. 175; italics added). In a footnote on the next page, speaking of the standard errors of the estimates for such an equation in the 1920s, he argues that "while these results indicate that markets were efficient and that on average forward rates were unbiased forecasts of future spot rates, the 2–8 percent errors were *significant*" (italics added). He evidently has forgotten his usage of "significant" in another signification. What he appears to mean is that he judges errors of 2–8 percent to be large in some unspecified economic sense, perhaps as offering significant profits for lucky guessers of the correct spot rate. In any event, it is unclear what his results imply about their subject, purchasing power parity, because significance in statistics, however useful it sometimes might be, is not the same thing as economic significance.

The argument is not that levels of significance are arbitrary. Of course they are. The argument is that it is not known whether the range picked out by the level of significance affirms or denies the hypothesis. Nor is it that economists often should use intervals rather than points for their null hypotheses. True as it is, the interval would still have to be chosen, by recourse to the rhetoric of the economic issue at hand. Tables of significance do not make the choice.

The Rhetoric of Significance Tests

Nor certainly is the argument that econometric tests are to be disdained. Quite the contrary. The argument is that the econometric tests have not followed their own rhetoric of hypothesis testing. Nowhere in the literature of tests of purchasing power parity does there appear a loss function. We do not know how much it will cost in policy wrecked or analysis misapplied or reputation ruined if purchasing power parity is said to be true when by the measure of the slope coefficient it is only, say, 85 percent true.

The notion of the loss function, due to the economist and statistician Abraham Wald, for a time undergirded modern econometrics. In present econometric practice it has been set aside in favor of a merely statistical standard, and an irrelevant one related to sampling error at that. We are told how improbable it is that a slope coefficient of .90 came from a distribution centered on 1.00 in view of the one kind of error we claim we know about (unbiased sampling error with finite variance). But we are not told whether it matters to the truth of purchasing power parity where such limits of confidence are placed.

Silence on the matter is not confined to the literature of purchasing power parity. Most texts on econometrics do not mention that the goodness or badness of a hypothesis is not ascertainable on merely statistical grounds. Statisticians themselves are more self-conscious, although the transition from principle to practice is sometimes awkward. A practical difficulty in the way of using the Wald theory in pure form, A. F. Mood and F. A. Graybill complain, is that "the loss function is not known at all or else it is not known accurately enough to warrant its use. If the loss function is not known, it seems that a decision function that in some sense minimizes the error probabilities will be a reasonable procedure" (1963, p. 278). The phrase "in some sense" appears to be a marker of unexplored rhetoric among the intellectually honest. In any event, the procedure they suggest might be reasonable for a general statistician, who makes no claim to know what is a good or bad approximation to truth in fields outside statistics. It is not reasonable for a specialist in international trade or macroeconomics. If the loss function is not known, it should be discovered. And that will entail a study of the question's rhetoric, productive of standards.

A standard of economic significance in questions of parity is the degree to which the customary regressions between countries resembles similar regressions within a single country. The standard is by now familiar. We agree, for purposes of argument, that the United States is to be treated as a single point in space. It is to be treated as one economy across which distances are said not to matter for the purposes of talking about inflation or the balance of payments. Having done so we have a standard: is Canada, economically speaking, just as closely integrated with the United States as is California with Massachusetts? Is the Atlantic economy as closely integrated as the American economy? The Genberg-Zecher criterion (after its inventors Genberg 1976; McCloskey and Zecher 1976) brings the conversation going on out in the hall explicitly into the seminar room: "How large is large?" asks someone. "Well, it is large relative to something else you just admitted is large." This is how scientific conversation progresses; it does not progress by piling up numbers without their context.

Scientific conversations are richer than the scientists understand. The Genberg-Zecher criterion is not the only conceivable standard. The degree of market integration in some golden age (1880–1913 perhaps, or 1950–70) might be one; the profits from arbitrage above normal profits might be another; the extent to which an X percentage deviation from purchasing power parity does or does not disturb some assertion about the causes of inflation might be still another. The point is to have standards of argument, to go beyond the inconclusive rhetoric provided by the pseudoscientific ceremony of hypothesize-fit-test-publish in most of modern economics.

The Test of Statistical Significance Is a Poor Rhetoric of Economic Argument

Standards of argument will answer the question, How large is large? The usual criterion for answering it in economics, which is the statistical test of significance, does not answer it. The criterion is a poor one. It would be good to abandon it. Because it appears to provide a way of processing "how large is large" questions on a scale limited only by the computer budget of the investigator, it has crowded out the sounder rhetoric of quantification. In the dear dead days of mechanical calculators, when the inversion of a 5-by-5 matrix was a feat and the inversion of a 10-by-10 not worth risking one's marriage to achieve, economists and other social scientists with quantitative tastes had to know exactly why they were calculating each statistic. They had to think. Giants walked the earth then, chained to a Freiden mechanical calculator and their copies of statistical handbooks by Fox and Snedecor. Or so they say. In any event they were unable to pollute the air with trivial significance tests.

The inadequacies of significance tests as a rhetoric for quantification can be summarized either by the narrowness of what they do or by the breadth of what they do not do. What they do is tell the intrepid

The Rhetoric of Significance Tests

investigator what the probability is that *because of the small sample he faces* he will make a mistake of excessive gullibility in accepting a false statistical proposition, conventionally taken to be the proposition that some number is zero (or some other single interesting alternative). That is all. The procedure keeps one from being made to look a certain, narrow kind of fool. There is no protection against other kinds of foolishness, such as using entirely the wrong variables in one's regression equation; or even using a single wrong variable, which is sometimes enough to make one look very foolish indeed. One is protected from the narrow foolishness in talking about a narrowly defined hypothesis for a narrow sort of error, namely, the error that comes from having too small a random sample—not a *non*random sample, understand (for that there is no protection), just a too-small but perfectly random one.

Economists use the mathematics of sampling daily, yet rarely in fact take samples. The mathematics applies most naturally to situations in which the statistician literally draws a sample, such as a sample of glebe terriers from English villages to be used to determine the geography of scattered holdings of land. Such "active" sampling entails no metaphysics about unobservable error terms. The statistician knows the error term to be independently and identically distributed because he has used a table of random numbers having such qualities to choose the sample. He could select the entire universe if he wanted, but chooses instead to select the 11th, the 356th, the 7,864th, the 5,645th, and so forth out of the 10,000 villages in order to make his task manageable. There is still an element of luck about it, but the provenance of the luck is known: remarks about its provenance is what statistical theory is about.

What might be called by contrast "passive" sampling involves some metaphysics but in some situations not too much. If the sample is given, not taken, literal *data* instead of *capta*, then the statistician must wave a magic wand over the sample and declare it to be random. He has not arranged by *taking* the sample for it to be random (in the sense of having errors to which sampling theory can apply: to repeat, independently and identically distributed about zero). But if the sample is anyway a selection from a definite universe, such as a selection of annual reports from the universe of all corporations or a selection of countries having adequate statistics on gold flows from the universe of all countries, the stretch is not large. Supposing there is no reason to believe that the company reports near at hand or the countries with adequate statistics on gold flows are unrepresentative, one can—and everyone does—go ahead with some confidence to calculate significance levels.

It ought to be more widely recognized by economists, however, that it involves a great deal more metaphysics to apply such mathematics to time series. The attending metaphysicians are usually the very ones who claim to scorn a metaphysics of morality or psychology. The metaphysical argument is that the actual course of, say, American national income since the late 1940s is a sample out of the universe of all possible processions of American national income since the war. Income might have grown in such and such a way; or thus and such; but in fact the fates chose the way it actually did grow. Therefore, the fates have selected a random sample suitable for statistical treatment.

The naive observer of this intellectual leap might infer that the sample must therefore contain only one observation, namely, the one realization of the possible worlds. A sample of size one does not leave much room for significance tests. To such an argument the econometrician answers with some irritation, "No, no: each *year* is a separate observation."

Salviati: But how then do you know the annual observations are independently and identically distributed?
Econometricus: I assume they are.
Salviati: What did you say?
Econometricus: I *assume* they are. It's the usual procedure. The journals are filled with it.
Salviati: But surely annual observations are likely to be highly autocorrelated. [Salviati may be naive but he is not uneducated.]
Econometricus: Yes, true: often they would be. But I have sophisticated sorts of first differencing to get rid of the autocorrelation. Here, let me show you my Cochrane-Orcutt. . . .
Salviati: Perhaps some other time. Let me see if I understand the basic point, though. Roughly speaking, you take the annual *change* in the variable instead of taking merely its level. You think you know that *this* produces a properly random error term.
Econometricus: Yes, roughly speaking. And sometimes not so roughly.
Salviati: And how do you know that *that* error term, the one in first differences, has the classical properties?
Econometricus: Well . . . uh . . . I *assume* it does.
Salviati: Hmm, yes. Of course. I thought as much. Tell me, do you read Kant or Heidegger?
Econometricus: [who also is educated]: Heavens no! Those are metaphysicians.

The Rhetoric of Significance Tests

Salviati: And what are you?
Econometricus: Me? Why, no metaphysician, I assure you. I deal strictly in meaningful hypotheses.

Few economists appreciate the narrowness of what tests of significance can do. Again Edward Leamer is useful. In his recent paper "Let's Take the Con out of Econometrics" (1983) he points out, to speak technically, that the specification error from omitting an important variable—and what student of society imagines he has kept in mind every important variable?—leaves a term in the expression for the sample covariance that does *not* go to zero as the sample size increases. The term does not change at all, because it is not caused by sampling error; it is caused (as I just said) by specification error. The precision of the statistical estimates therefore does *not* increase much with sample size.

Further, the specification error leaves no trace of its evil presence. The methods of statistics deal, quite properly, with sampling errors alone, and cannot be expected to help with others. When these others are serious, as we all believe they usually are, there is no point in continuing to talk relatively much about the (relatively small) sampling error. To do so, as economists and other quantifiers do nowadays on a massive scale, is to imitate the drunk who looks for his wallet under the lamp post because the light is better there.

Leamer's solution to the problem will please historians, anthropologists, geologists, and other scholars who have more patience with facts than economists have. Go back into the dark and look for other kinds of evidence, not more evidence of the same kind (the sampling problem oversolved again), but evidence of different kinds, whose biases are distributed independently of the biases in the first kind. Including these will cut the error in half. Including a third kind will cut it to a third. Leamer's argument amounts to a formalization of the workaday method of the historian: look at *all* the evidence (vain hope), or at least a sample of all the various different kinds, triangulating the historical object instead of trying to measure its distance directly with the one tiny ruler at hand.

It is clear, then, that the breadth of what tests of significance do not do is great. They do not answer the question, How large is large? How large the number of whippings of American slaves had to be to be considered important is a difficult question, on which various sorts of comparative evidence will bear. (Were free workers subject to corporal punishment? What did the slaves consider to be an excessive number of beatings? How much were slaves beaten in other slave societies?) The merely statistical significance of one or another estimate of the number, however, should interest no one very much.

Yet the test of significance is routinely used to decide all manner of economic questions, and economists are drunk with it. The brightness of the light under the lamp post is the problem. The wattage has been increased by a fall in the price of computation. The cost of a regression coefficient in 1960 was probably not much below $10; nowadays it is probably well below 10 cents. And there is no further obstacle to taking up a position hard by the lamp post. The elements of regression analysis (or of axiom manipulation) are easy to learn, and suit the temper of the bright twenty-two-year-old with some mathematical ability. As a political scientist remarked, viewing the decay of argument in his field, "There are enough tricks important in regression to make graduate education necessary, but they are not so many or so difficult as to restrict its practice further than that" (Nelson 1983, p. 219).

Graduate students in the social sciences view courses in econometrics, sociometrics, or psychometrics as courses in how to become applied economists, sociologists, or psychologists. Their teachers know better, though the flattery of the young can turn even their heads. The delusion is nourished by democracy, which partly explains its special prevalence in America. Anyone of normal intelligence can after such a course decipher the output of the Statistical Package for Social Sciences. No elite culture is necessary, no long subordination to Doktor Herr Professor, no knowledge accumulated through middle age. This emancipation of the young is no trivial advantage of modernist methodism. True, there is a cost in self-satisfied ignorance. It is a fine thing nonetheless that a thorough reading of Takayama's *Mathematical Economics* or Dhrymes' *Econometrics*—or, in other intellectual cultures, the New Testament or the first volume of *Capital*—can give a young person a weapon. The young have few enough weapons against the power of the old.

Economists young and old act as though they believe that in regressions the number of standard errors that a coefficient lies distant from zero tells whether the variable is worthwhile—worth keeping in the regression, worth keeping in mind, worth using for public policy, worth keeping in one's theory. They cannot do it. The decisions are too important to be left to chance. Whether or not a coefficient is significantly different from zero is not a statistical question. The distance from zero that some number has to be in order to be large must be answered by comparison with the results of parallel conversations. Statistical significance deserves a place in the economist's box of tools, but a minor one. It cannot take over the job of defining economic significance.

That it has taken over the decisions about significance cannot be blamed entirely on statisticians. The best of them are sometimes amazed to see their modest little arguments marching and countermarching on foreign fields in impossible campaigns. William Kruskal, past president of the American Statistical Association, exclaimed that "surely such fundamental points as the distinction between statistical and substantive significance must be elementary to econometricians who readily handle five-stage maximum likelihood estimation and utility functions with values in Banach spaces" (letter to the author, April 26, 1982). The warnings in his article on significance tests in the *International Encyclopedia of Statistics* (1968) are commonplaces among statisticians, but unknown by most users of statistics.

It would be good, I have been arguing, if econometricians and other quantitative observers of society would recognize explicitly that in the end their quantitative judgments are part of the public rhetoric of their field, not something they can entrust to a statistical handbook or rituals with the local canned regression program. This is to say that they should stop looking under the lamp post.

The Rhetorical History of Statistics Is the Source of the Difficulty

The overuse of statistical significance, then, arises from its ease of use. But it arises also from the rhetoric in its name. Surely we serious scientists, it insinuates, should be interested first of all in "significant" coefficients: we the great and good would not wish to waste our time on trivialities. The British statistical tradition was dominated in its childhood by Karl Pearson and in its adolescence by R. A. Fisher. Both, and especially Fisher, had a gift for naming their ideas. As William Kruskal has argued,

> Suppose that Sir R. A. Fisher—a master of public relations—had not taken over from ordinary English such evocative words as "sufficient," "efficient," and "consistent" and made them into precisely defined terms of statistical theory. He might, after all, have used utterly dull terms for those properties of estimators, calling them characteristics *A*, *B*, and *C*. . . . Would his work have had the same smashing influence that it did? I think not, or at least not as rapidly. . . . Or turn to Fisher's wonderful phrase "analysis of variance". . . . Is it too cynical to think that the lovely term—half-mystery, half-promise—and the orderly tables helped to win acceptance, quite aside from the underlying theory? (Kruskal 1978, p. 98)

The Rhetoric of Significance Tests

"Significance" is a still older coinage. The idea, though not the corresponding word, dates to Laplace's famous memoir of 1773 on the distribution of the orbits of twelve comets: he was able to reject the hypothesis that they were in the same plane as the planets and was able therefore to affirm that they originated outside the solar system (Scott 1953, p. 202). Lancelot Hogben identifies the first statistical use of the word as John Venn's, in 1888, speaking of differences expressed in units of probable error: "They inform us which of the differences in the above tables are permanent and significant, in the sense that we may be tolerably confident that if we took another similar batch we should find a similar difference; and which are merely transient and insignificant, in the sense that another similar batch is about as likely as not to reverse the conclusion we have obtained" (Venn, quoted in Hogben [1968], p. 325). The argument is reasonable: when properly applied to a literal sample, significance *does* entail permanence in the statistical sense he described. But a difference—for instance between $\beta = .999$ and $\beta = 1.000$—could be permanent (not likely to be an accident of the sample) without being "significant" in any other meaning.

This is the mischief. By the 1910s and 1920s the usage was becoming common among sophisticated research workers (Pearson 1911; Yule and Greenwood 1915; Fisher 1925, p. 43), and as it spread to the less sophisticated, the task of undoing the rhetorical damage commenced. The first of many works making the same point as is made here was written as early as 1919 (Boring 1919). Argument against the mechanical use of significance became early on a commonplace in statistical education. By 1939, for example, a *Statistical Dictionary of Terms and Symbols* of no great intellectual pretensions was putting the point utterly plainly: "A significant difference is not necessarily large, since, in large samples, even a small difference may prove to be a significant difference. Further, the existence of a significant difference may or may not be of practical significance" (Kurtz and Edgerton 1939, s.v. "Significant Difference"). Kendall and Stuart's *Advanced Theory of Statistics* explicitly recognized the mischief in the rhetoric, recommending the colorless phrase "size of the test" in preference to "significance level."[1]

The notion that statistical significance is a machine for important scientific inferences can be attributed to the work in the 1920s of R. A. Fisher, whose opposition to more rational machinery was robust and sufficient. In the 1930s Jerzy Neyman and E. S. Pearson, and then more

1. Kendall and Stuart 1951, p. 163n. Compare Morrison and Henkel 1969, who proposed the even less colorful phrase "sample error decision procedure" to replace "significance test" (p. 198).

The Rhetoric of Significance Tests

explicitly Abraham Wald, argued that actual statistical decisions should depend on substantive, not merely statistical, significance. In 1933 Neyman and Pearson wrote (of type I and type II errors):

Is it more serious to convict an innocent man or to acquit a guilty? That will depend on the consequences of the error; is the punishment death or fine; what is the danger to the community of released criminals; what are the current ethical views on punishment? From the point of view of mathematical theory all that we can do is to show how the risk of the errors may be controlled and minimised. The use of these statistical tools in any given case, in determining just how the balance should be struck, must be left to the investigator. (Neyman and Pearson 1933, p. 296)

Wald went further: "The question as to how the form of the weight [i.e., loss] function W (θ, ω) should be determined, is not a mathematical or statistical one. The statistician who wants to test certain hypotheses must first determine the relative importance of all possible errors, which will entirely depend on the special purposes of his investigation" (1939, p. 302).

These notions of bringing cost and benefit into the scientific decision are of course attractive to economists (and no wonder, for Wald was one, having studied with Karl Menger in Vienna in the 1920s). But his suggestions have been largely ignored by economists, in favor of conventions about publishable levels of significance. Most textbooks in econometrics do not mention that the goodness or badness of a hypothesis cannot be decided on merely statistical grounds.

Statisticians are more aware of the intellectual foundations of their discipline, but at the last even they hesitate to take a stand. Recall the unease of Mood and Graybill, for instance, and their conclusion that "if the loss function is not known, it seems that a decision function that in some sense minimizes the error probabilities will be a reasonable procedure" (1963, p. 278). Note the "it seems," and "in some sense . . . reasonable." It is not made clear in what sense one could reasonably decide that it seems reasonable without a loss function.

When after the Second World War the various -metrics associated with positivism in philosophy and social engineering in politics became normal in social science, the test of significance became a universal reflex. A few sociologists and psychologists in the late 1950s and 1960s protested. Their protest is known as the Significance Test Controversy, summarized most conveniently in a reader edited by Denton E. Morrison and Ramon E. Henkel (1970; see also Lieberman 1971). Economists are accustomed to supposing that they are ahead of other social scientists in statistical sophistication. In this matter, with a few exceptions (Arrow 1959; Griliches 1976), they are not.

Morrison and Henkel, for instance, noted in 1969 that "significance tests . . . are not legitimately used for any purpose other than that of assessing the sampling error of a statistic designed to describe a particular population on the basis of a probability sample" (Morrison and Henkel 1970, p. 186). The point is elementary. The mathematics depends, of course, on the aptness of a metaphor, the urn model of chance. In their elementary book *Statistics*, David Freedman, Robert Pisani, and Roger Purves (1978) repeatedly make the point that without an urn model (they call it a "box") the tests of significance make no sense:

> Statistical inference can be justified only in terms of an explicit chance model for the data. No box, no inference. (p. 407)

> The square root law applies only to draws from a box. (p. 408)

> Every legitimate test of significance involves a box model. (p. 440)

> If an investigator makes a test of significance when he has data for the whole population, watch out. (p. 490)

> Unless there is a clearly defined chance model, a test of significance makes no sense. (p. 497)

> Be very suspicious of P-values [chi-square tests of significance in cross-classifications] computed from samples of convenience. (p. 499)

Economists do not heed these elementary warnings. Commonly, as we have seen, they deal with "samples" that are not samples at all, but entire populations. The national income and electricity consumption of OECD countries in 1970 is not a sample of anything, and therefore the calculation of the "significance" of the relation between the two variables lacks point: the relation is what it is. There is no problem of inferring the characteristics of the population from the "sample." The characteristics *are* the characteristics of the population.

> *Econometricus* [lecturing to Sagredo, with Salviati looking on]: I have calculated from the census of the slave population of Trinidad in 1813 certain regressions of demographic models, complete with tests of significance. The results are highly significant.

Sagredo: Gee, that's impressive. How big was your sample?
Econometricus: 17,000: there were 17,000 slaves in Trinidad.
Sagredo: Wow! That's even more impressive.
Salviati [restraining himself no longer]: No, Sagredo, less so. If the
urn model could be imagined, the results would be *less* impressive: sample size is not an additional virtue, additional to
significance. A large sample *causes* significance. "The rejection of
the null hypothesis when the number of cases is small speaks
for a more dramatic effect in the population" [Bakan 1966, p.
154]. But in any event the urn model cannot be imagined. This
is not a sample from a universe, but a universe itself. We have
the contents of the urn spilled out before us: there is no problem
of inference.
Econometricus: What nonsense you speak, Salviati, misleading our
good friend Sagredo here! Don't you know that all this was settled long ago? The particular 17,000 are . . . uh . . . is a realization
of all possible such populations.
Salviati: Then what is your sample size?
Econometricus: Why, 17,000, you dunce.
Salviati: I should think it would be one: in sampling all possible
configurations of slave populations on Trinidad you have so far
found one.
Econometricus: One! My Lord! He says "one"!
Salviati: I suggest that you increase your sample size, which seems
at present small. Perhaps you can go into the second of your
hypothetical worlds and get the second observation; and into
the third and get the third; and into the fourth. . . .
Econometricus: Really, Salviati, you are quite mad. My procedure is
purest routine, the custom of our field.
Salviati: Doubtless, but what is the urn model that justifies the
routine? From what urn is the 17,000 a sample?
Econometricus: As I said, all possible worlds. Or the world of Trinidad observed with error. Or the world of slaves in 1813.
Salviati: You deal in too many hypotheticals for a poor simple man
like me. You propose, then, to make inferences from your data
on Trinidad to the slaves of, say, Sweden? And the urn, by
merest chance, is located in Port of Spain? I must say, "on what
basis this assumption is warranted except on the desire of the
researcher to apply the statistical inference model is not clear"
[Morrison and Henkel 1969, p. 190].
Econometricus: You are an incorrigible purist, Salviati. We must be
practical. Sagredo, if you value your tenure, pay no heed to this

madman. Come, have a look at my new program, PUBPER ("publish or perish"), which searches and researches the data until it finds statistically significant results.[2]

The Unexamined Rhetoric Damages the Practice of Economists

It is not easy, then, to justify the use of probabilistic models to answer nonprobabilistic questions. One might retort that economists, or at least good ones, do not make such mistakes. But they do, as may be seen from their best practice, in the *American Economic Review*. Of the 159 full-length papers published in the four regular issues per year during 1981, 1982, and 1983, 50 used regression analysis and tests of significance. From this sample of convenience I have taken a probability sample of ten for preliminary scrutiny:

A. Wallace E. Huffman, "Black-White Human Capital Differences: Impact on Agricultural Productivity in the U.S. South" (Mar. 1981).

B. Eugene F. Fama, "Stock Returns, Real Activity, Inflation, and Money" (Sept. 1981).

C. Lars Jonung, "Perceived and Expected Rates of Inflation in Sweden" (Dec. 1981).

D. John Cogan, "The Decline of Black Teenage Employment: 1950–70" (Sept. 1982).

E. John M. McDowell, "Obsolescence of Knowledge and Career Publication Patterns" (Sept. 1982).

F. Mark R. Rosenzweig and T. Paul Schultz, "Market Opportunities, Genetic Endowment, and Intrafamily Resource Distribution: Child Survival in Rural India" (Sept. 1982).

G. Joe Peek, "Interest Rates, Income Taxes, and Anticipated Inflation" (Dec. 1982).

H. Ben S. Bernanke, "Nonmonetary Effects of the Financial Crisis in the Propagation of the Great Depression" (June 1983).

2. PUBPER exists: see the hostile comment on it by Freedman, Pisani, and Purves 1978, p. A-23. Compare the dialogue in Margaret Jarman Hagood, *Statistics for Sociologists* (1941), reprinted in Morrison and Henkel 1970, which early on treated the notion of sampling from all possible worlds favorably (though more thoughtfully than has become customary since).

The Rhetoric of Significance Tests

I. Ronald S. Warren, Jr., "Labor Market Contracts, Unanticipated Wages, and Employment Growth" (June 1983).
J. Robert Moffitt, "An Economic Model of Welfare Stigma" (Dec. 1983).

No unfavorable comparison with the forty others is implied in the sample. These are in most ways remarkably fine papers: one cannot examine the pick of the crop in economics without being impressed by the intelligence and industry that the field has attracted. Since the purpose here is to criticize a socially sanctioned practice, not to embarrass individual writers, I shall adopt a seemly veil of letters, and will not document the practice in more detail than necessary.

Of the ten papers, only two do not admit to experimenting with the regressions, sometimes with hundreds of different specifications. None propose to alter their levels of significance to allow for the experimentation. When admitting to experimentation the papers will often mention in extenuation a test of "robustness" (e.g., G, p. 985). They do not cite the literature in which the theory of robustness is articulated (e.g., Mosteller and Tukey 1977, pp. 16, 203, 327, 404, and throughout; Leamer 1978, chap. 6 and throughout).

The procedures that gave rise to the final equation are not usually mentioned (though B appears to give all the equations fitted, from which one might infer—perhaps by a regression study—how the favored specifications were chosen). In only one of the ten is the simplest procedure of selection described candidly: "If the direct estimate of β_i ... was not significantly different from zero, then coefficients to be estimated that contained β_i as one part of a product were set equal to zero" (A, p. 103). Mechanical dropping of insignificant variables, though widely practiced, has little warrant in statistical theory. Four of the ten papers experiment extensively. In these the experiment in finding significant coefficients seems to be the main point. But as a psychologist wrote some years ago, "If enough data are gathered, the [null] hypothesis will generally be rejected. If rejection of the null hypothesis were the real intention in psychological experiments, there usually would be no need to gather data (J. Nunnally, quoted in Bakan 1966, p. 150). By this he means that all null hypotheses are rejectable if the sample is large enough, for the parameter in the universe will never (well, hardly ever) be exactly 0 or 1.000. All simple null hypotheses (and alternative hypotheses, for that matter) are wrong a priori. For all the modernist rhetoric of falsification, searching for wrong ones cannot be the point.

Only two of the ten do not use a sign test in conjunction with a significance test: the variable has a statistically significant coefficient *and the right (or expected) sign.* Little statistical theory seems to lie behind the practice, although it seems sensible enough—a beginning, indeed, to looking beyond statistical significance to the size of the coefficient. Only one of the ten (paper A) uses a sample of convenience so convenient that it looks like a universe: all counties in Alabama, Mississippi, North Carolina, and South Carolina. Four of the ten use true samples: the opinions of 6,000 Swedes on the current and expected rate of inflation; the vital statistics of 1,331 rural households in India; the employment statistics of 565 female family heads from the over-mined Michigan Panel; and the career patterns of an indefinite number of academics collected from professional handbooks. The only doubt here is the disproportion of effort in dealing with sampling errors when other errors are probably more serious. At $N = 6,000$ we can surely dismiss Student and attend to bias. As Leamer remarked, "When the sampling uncertainty . . . gets small compared to the misspecification uncertainty . . . , it is time to look for other forms of evidence, experiments or nonexperiments" (1983, p. 33). The other five papers use time series. One can only ask quietly and pass on, From what universe is a time series a random sample, and if there is one, is it one we wish to know about?

The most important question is whether the economists in the sample mix up statistical and substantive significance. Even on purely statistical grounds the news is not good: none of the papers mention the word "power," though all mention "significance." That is, all neglect to follow the letter of the statistician's advice: "When . . . power is at least moderately large for alternatives interestingly different from the null hypothesis, one is in a satisfactory position. . . . what is in fact reasonable depends strongly on context. To examine reasonableness it is necessary to inspect, at least roughly, the entire power function. Many misuses of significance testing spring from complete disregard of power" (Kruskal 1968). Some follow the spirit, avoiding the excessive gullibility of the type II error by treating the machinery of hypothesis-testing with a certain reserve. Most do not. Only three of the ten do not jump with abandon from statistical to substantive significance. The very language, though mostly formulaic, sometimes exposes the underlying attitude. Paper F says, "The coefficients on the education variable are negative in sign, consistent with their representing wealth, but are not statistically *important*" (p. 813; italics added).

Seven of the papers, then, let statistical significance do the work of substantive significance.[3] Paper I, for example, commits a routine falla-

3. It is a relief to report that there were no significant patterns of ideology or nonstatistical methodology. For a large size of the test (the sample is small) one could reject the hypothesis that monetarism or Keynesianism or Chicagoism or Minnesotaism led to special clumsiness in the handling of tests of significance.

The Rhetoric of Significance Tests

cy of equivocation in its use of the word "significant." It contrasts the Keynesian model, which assigns "to exogenous variations in the volume of labor market contacts a *significant* role in determining the time path of employment," to the neoclassical model, which assigns the role to "the effects of deviations of actual from expected real wages" (p. 393; italics added). The next paragraph notes that "the empirical results suggested that changes in the number of vacancy contacts rather than wage misperceptions *significantly* affected employment growth" (italics added). The only evidence for the latter is statistical significance. There is no attempt to show how large the two effects are, or whether the statistical tests of the difference between them are powerful, or what standard of largeness one should use.

At the end of paper G, again, after running dozens of specifications through the screen of statistical significance, the author experiences a twinge of guilt: "Now that the existence of statistically significant income tax effects in the Fisher equation has been established, one might be interested in the degree to which these effects are also quantitatively significant" (p. 989). Indeed one might, though the hour is late. In four of the seven papers with significant errors in the use of significance, there is some discussion of how large a coefficient would need to be to be large, but even these let statistical significance do most of the work. And even in the three papers that recognize the distinction and apply it consistently, there is flirtation with intellectual disaster. Paper H, for instance, speaks of an equation showing "an effect of price shocks on output that is statistically and economically significant" (p. 268) but on the next page appears to take the mere presence of the right sign as the measure of "economically significant," leaving statistical significance in charge of the science.

Even the best economists, in short, overuse the statistical test of significance.

If economists do not wish to leave science to chance, they should rethink the rhetoric of statistical significance. Something should be done. It might be done in econometrics courses, which could teach the relevant decision theory. Judging from results, they do not teach it now. It would help if the standard computer packages did not generate *t*-statistics in such profusion. The Durbin-Watson statistic is similar, generated by the packages regardless of whether or not the data are the time series that make the statistic meaningful. Because it is there, available to demonstrate painlessly his technical competence, the young economist itches to find some use for the statistic even in a cross-section. It would be charitable to warn students off such decisive demonstrations of their incompetence by a printed question in the package: "Do you really have a time series?"

The packages might likewise ask in large type: "Do you really have a probability sample?" "Have you considered power?" and, above all, "By what standard would you judge a fitted coefficient large or small?" They might ask at the beginning, "Do you really want to look under the lamp post?" Or perhaps they could merely ask, printed in bold capitals beside each *t*-statistic, "So what else is new?"

10 THE GOOD OF RHETORIC

IN ECONOMICS

The question is, as usual, why it matters. Suppose that modernism is dead, that economics is rhetorical, and that the rhetoric of quantification needs reexamination. So what?

One thing is clear: the absorption of rhetorical thinking in economics will not precipitate any revolution in the substance of economics. Rhetoric does not claim to provide a new methodology, and therefore does not provide formulas for scientific advance. It does not believe that science advances by formula. It believes that science advances by healthy conversation, not adherence to a methodology. To claim that rhetorical sophistication is a formula for advances in economics would be self-contradictory. Life is not so easy that an economist can be made much better at what he does merely by reading a book.

Economics at present is, in fact, moderately well off. It may be sleep-walking in its rhetoric, but it seems to know in any case approximately where to step. The criticisms of economics for being "too mathematical" or "too static" or "too bourgeois" are not very persuasive, though articulated often enough. They are of the form "you can't know the Truth using those wretched mathematical/static/bourgeois methodologies." The criticisms come down to methodological faiths, which neglect to demonstrate the practical force of their complaints. By what rhetorical standard "can't" you understand an economy using a static model? The critics do not say.

The other "failures" of economics are commonly overstated. Economists disagree; but so do mathematicians. Economics does not predict the future well; but predicting the future is not possible anyway, as economics itself shows. Yet economists—like paleontologists and historians, who also disagree and also predict poorly—can tell quite brilliant stories about the past, stories on which they often agree. The neoclassical economist tells a brilliant story about productivity change over the past two centuries; the Marxist economist tells one about the struggle for control of the workplace in the nineteenth century; the Austrian economist tells one about the spontaneous order in the supply of money before state intervention. The main achievement of economics is not the prediction and control assigned to it by modernist social engineering, but the making of sense out of economic experience. Considering the lack of self-awareness, as, for instance, in statistical procedures, it is notable that economics does achieve as much as it does.

I do not venture any extravagant claim, then, that rhetoric can revolutionize economics. But some good can come of it. Economics has a neurosis, the neurosis of modernism, which a rhetoric of economic inquiry can expose to rational scrutiny. A rhetorical criticism, like a course of psychoanalysis, might make economists more self-aware, modest, and tolerant, better in person and profession. Consider the ways of relieving the burdens on their goodness.

Rhetoric Can Improve Economic Prose

First of all, economics is badly written, written by a formula for scientific prose. The situation is not so bad as it is in, say, psychology, where papers that do not conform to the accepted formula (Introduction, Survey of Literature, Experiment, Discussion, and so forth) are in some journals not accepted. The *Publication Manual of the American Psychologial Association*, for instance, is fully 208 pages of modernist methodology. It is clearly meant to be a joke. A jolly good one it is, too, giving for instance page upon page of advice on style couched in the most miserable style the editors could manage, and fully ten hilarious pages on the official formula for a scientific paper. Economists, too, though lacking the ready wit of psychologists, have stumbled without much self-awareness towards conventions of prose that are bad for clarity and honesty, as some of their number have said from time to time (Salant 1969; Galbraith 1978; McCloskey 1985b). The study of rhetoric, it must be admitted, does not guarantee the student a good English style. But at least it makes him blush at the disdain for the reader that some economics exhibits.

The economist's English contains a message, as we have seen, usually, "Look at how very scientific I am." Sometimes the message is more genial: Zvi Griliches' irony says, "Do not make a fetish out of these methods I am expounding: they are mere human artifices." Milton Friedman's style, so careful and clear, has to an exceptional degree the character of the Inquirer. Economics will not raise up a race of Dennis Robertsons, Robert Solows, or George Stiglers by becoming more sensitive to the real messages in scientific procedure and prose. But maybe it can stunt the growth of the other kind.

Rhetorical thinking might free economics from its enslavement to the deductivist style of mathematical papers and the inductivist style of physical papers. Close observers of these last have for many years been attacking their fraudulence. As I have noted, the biologist Peter Medawar (1964) asked once "Is the Scientific Paper Fraudulent?"—by which he meant merely to question its notable lack of candor. The scientist, after struggling with a piece of work for many months, will lay out the results in the form of axiom-proof or experiment-result as though there was nothing to it, really. In the rhetoric of the Scientific Paper (invented in the late seventeenth century, before which time scientists communicated in blank verse and dialogues) the scientist buries the substance, the reason this line of argument was chosen rather than another, the mistake to be avoided, the trick to be relished. Economic literature exhibits maladies identical to these, diagnosed by Imre Lakatos in mathematics and physics: "The problem-situation, the conjecture which the experiment had to test, is hidden away. The author boasts of an empty, virgin mind. . . . Inductivist style, just like its deductivist twin . . . , while claiming objectivity, in fact fosters a private guild-language, atomises science, suffocates criticism, makes science authoritarian" (1976, p. 143n).

The attitude of economists towards style exhibits prettily what they might learn from a rhetoric of inquiry. Many economists, and many other people, believe that style and substance are separable, that style, like "mere rhetoric," is a superficial appeal to the emotions to be added later when doing the "polishing." The custom of separating "research" and "results" from "writing them up" permeates the scholarly culture, and economists are merely following the custom. Yet anyone who has written much can testify that one does not learn about the details of an argument until writing it up in detail, and in writing up the details one often discovers flaws in the fundamentals.

People who write self-critically, trying to say what they mean, find often that what seemed a truth when floating vaguely in the mind looks like an error when moored to the page. In economics as in other fields, writing self-critically will uncover good reasonings. If I write about seeking profit in a sentence in which I have searched conscientiously for the right words, I will commonly enrich my thinking: is it, to be exact, "profit" or "gain" or "maximum wealth" or "satisfaction" or "success"? Is it "seeking" or "finding" or "having" or "uncovering" or "inventing" or "bumping into"? If I write about supply and demand in a sentence that I have balanced properly, I will often see new symmetries in the world. If I force myself to explain my equation in words, I will understand it in another way. Writing resembles mathematics: if mathematics is a language, an instrument of communication, so too is language a mathematics, an instrument of thought.

Many economists, and many other people, believe that good style is God-given, which justifies their amateurish attitude towards its revision. Economists do not mind criticism of their economics or their mathematics or their statistics, because they have been professionally trained to take it and give it. The criticism spills into self-criticism and raises standards all round. Criticism of their writing is quite another matter. Graduate programs do not teach economists to take and give criticism of writing with anything approaching good grace. Economists regard criticism of their writing style the way people unfamiliar with ideas regard criticism of their ideas: with considerable annoyance. The man in the street cherishes his erroneous ideas about free trade because they are, says he, "just matters of opinion," which he is "entitled to believe" because "this is a free country, isn't it?" He regards his ideas as part of his character, like his personality or his body type, and takes very unkindly indeed to critical remarks about them. Likewise the amateur economic writer (unhappily common in a field that writes much) regards his attachment to his impenetrable acronyms or his "not only . . . but also" or his "However" at the beginning of a sentence as part of his character:

> *Linus:* What's this?
> *Lucy:* This is something to help you be a better person next
> year. . . . This is a list I made up of *all* your faults. [Exit]
> *Linus* [reading, increasingly indignant]: Faults? You call these
> *faults?* These aren't faults! These are *character traits!*

Now of course matters of style in writing are not "just matters of opinion." The figure of speech "it's just a matter of opinion" is commonly used to end the conversation about a rhetorical matter: if it's "just opinion" (and not "fact" or "Science"), then it can't be worth conversation, can it? Yet all we have is conversation; that is, just opinions about the earth's orbit, the law of the excluded middle, the Law of Demand, and the use of the passive voice in modern English prose.

There are "scientific" rules of good style, having to do with the psychology of perception (cf. Hirsch 1977), but these would be incomplete advice for improvement. There is much tacit knowledge, too, and powerful social customs. A writer signals to his audience what sort of writer he is by his ability to emulate George Orwell or James Thurber. They set the standard because in so many ways they wrote well, which is to say that in so many ways they played skillfully a game of language. The standard is perfectly "objective," as most matters of taste can be made to be. One merely asks.

Good writing and good science are correlated in economics as elsewhere. Good writing does not assure scientific success: that would be "bad" rhetoric, "mere" style. But it is notable that Solow, Stigler, Fogel, and Schultz, among other actual and prospective Nobel laureates in the field, write with clarity and vigor.

Rhetoric Can Improve Teaching

A second burden is that economics is badly taught, not because its teachers are stupid, but because they often do not recognize the tacitness of economic knowledge, and therefore teach by axiom and proof instead of by problem-solving and practice. To quote Polanyi yet again: "The transmission of knowledge from one generation to the other must be predominately tacit. . . . The pupil must assume that a teaching which appears meaningless to start with has in fact a meaning that can be discovered by hitting on the same kind of indwelling [a favorite Polanyi expression] as the teacher is practicing" (1966, p. 61). It is frustrating for students to be told that economics is not primarily a matter of memorizing formulas, but a matter of feeling the applicability of arguments, of seeing analogies between one application and a superficially different one, of knowing when to reason verbally and when mathematically, and of what implicit characterization of the world is most useful for correct economics. Life is hard. As a blind man uses his stick as an extension of his body, so whenever we use a theory "we incorporate it in our body—or extend our body to include it—so that we come to dwell in it" (Polanyi 1966). Problem-solving in economics is the tacit knowledge of the sort Polanyi describes. We know the economics, but cannot say it, in the same way a musician knows the note he plays without consciously recalling the technique for executing it. A singer is a prime example, for there is no set of mechanical instructions one can give to a singer on how to hit a high C. The economist Arnold Harberger often speaks of so-and-so being able to make an economic argument "sing." Like the directions to Carnegie Hall, the answer to the question "How do you get to the Council of Economic Advisors?" is "Practice, practice."

Modernism and methodology have intruded into the classroom. The modernist routine is easy to teach, which is one reason it is taught so widely. This is a pity, because the way we teach becomes the way we think. The groundless claim that economic knowledge is axiomatic permits the teacher to spend the term developing the axioms, with an occasional theorem. It is easier to start with axioms of choice or definitions of unbiasedness than to defend the rhetoric from which they derive. It is hardest of all to teach how to argue like an economist, that is, how to enter the conversation of the field. Students come to think of the formal economics as being the economics; when they come to teach others, they teach by theorem and "observable implication" rather than by argument and figure of speech. Modernism breeds modernism.

Economists reveal their modernist impulses in the way they think about teaching too. The journals of economic education, like those of economic scholarship, are jammed with modernist exercises in deriving the obvious. They do not tell how to teach, but whether multiple choice quizzes lead to better scores on multiple choice examinations than do essays. Only evidence that is falsifiable, quantifiable, objective is permitted into the discussion, with the result that what good teachers know about teaching is not transmitted to bad teachers. As it has a tendency to do, epistemology has taken over common sense in economic education. There are good teachers in economics, but a lack of self-consciousness about the rhetoric of the field keeps them from competing with the rest.

Rhetoric Can Improve Relations with Other Disciplines

Another burden placed on economics by its modernist methodology and its unselfconsciousness about rhetoric is that economics is misunderstood and, when regarded at all, disliked by humanists, scientists, and other outsiders. The humanists dislike it for its baggage of antihumanist methodology. The scientists dislike it because it does not in reality attain the rigor (supposing rigor to be the main virtue) that its methodology claims to achieve. The bad foreign relations have many costs. For instance, as was noted above, economics has recently become imperialistic. There is now an economics of history, of sociology, of law, of anthropology, of politics, of political philosophy, of ethics. The flabby methodology of modernist economics simply makes the colonization more difficult, raising irrelevant methodological doubts in the minds of the colonized folk.

Arjo Klamer speaks of rhetoric creating "space" for conversations, among economists (Klamer 1983) and between economists and other people. The discovery about a century ago that parts of economics could be expressed in mathematics, especially in the mathematics of nineteenth-century physics, allowed conversation to commence between economists and other quantitative intellectuals. They suddenly had in common little jokes about first-order conditions and massaging the data. To recur to an earlier example, an economist, without understanding much of the detail, does not feel out of place in a seminar of astronomers discussing the theory that the sun has a companion star that every so often shakes a hail of comets down upon unsuspecting dinosaurs. He feels a thrill of recognition ("Joke number 35": "Ha, ha, ha") when a particle physicist, equally ignorant of the detail but equally at home in this type of conversation, inquires into the stability of the interaction between the sun and its companion: stability is necessary, you see, for the notion to work as an explanation of a *regular* series of mass extinctions. In like fashion the realization that economists are speaking prose can create space for conversations with literary intellectuals. Economists and students of literature can suddenly share little jokes about dead metaphors and authorial intentions. Economics is both literary and mathematical. An unreflective narrowing of its conversations to one or the other does not serve the science well. It leaves economics less influential in civilization at large than its brilliance warrants.

The rhetoric of argument among economists themselves differs from the rhetoric they use when speaking to outsiders. It is well known that outsiders, with such defective taste, do not like many of the figures of speech used by economists. Nothing delights economists more, for instance, than the display of apparent paradox: that large saving (a private virtue) leads unintentionally to unemployment (a public vice); or that selfishness, the bane of private life, leads unintentionally to public riches. Other social scientists enjoy this sort of thing, too. Unintended consequences are reckoned beautiful in any piece of argument in the social sciences, betraying perhaps a Calvinist origin for these studies. The paradox justifies the claim of expertise: "You, layman, see only the surface; I see deeper currents." When economists exhibit their paradoxes to the layman, however, they are surprised by how coldly they are received.

A professional layman is the journalist. As a spinner of words himself he recognizes the rhetorical character of economics, at least outside the rhetoric of mathematics and statistics. Yet he swallows to some degree the claim to objectivity—which is to say, a claim to an impossible "lack of rhetoric." Influenced by the economist's pretension to scientific status, though properly suspicious of it, the journalist has an uneasy time with economists, quite unlike his relation to a space scientist or historian or other newsworthy scholar. The economist for his part is uneasy too, and inclined to tactical maneuver: "The reporter for *Time* or CBS News will listen to a complicated paragraph which specifies assumptions with care and admits the statistical evidence has some weaknesses, and will reduce it to one unqualified, wrong sentence. That being so, there is a powerful temptation for the economist to skip the complicated paragraph and replace it by one declarative sentence. It may not do justice to the issue, but at least it will be one's own" (Solow 1981, p. 17). An appreciation of the rhetoric of economic discourse would lighten the burden on both sides.

Rhetoric Can Improve Economic Argument

A fourth burden is that economists pointlessly limit themselves to "objective" facts. The modernist notion is that common sense is nonsense, that knowledge must somehow be objective, not *verstehen* or introspection. But, to repeat, we have much at our disposal about ourselves as economic molecules, if we would examine the grounds for assent.

The curious status of survey research in modern economics is a case in point. Unlike other social scientists, economists are extremely hostile towards questionnaires and other self-descriptions. Second-hand knowledge of a famous debate among economists in the late 1930s is part of every economist's education. The debate concerned a study asking businessmen directly whether or not they conformed to economic laws. It is revealing that the failure of such a study—never mind whether that was indeed the study—is supposed to convince economists to abandon all self-testimony. One can get an audience of economists to laugh out loud by proposing ironically to send out a questionnaire on some disputed economic point.

Economists are so impressed by the confusions that might possibly result from questionnaires that they have turned away from them entirely, and prefer the confusions resulting from external observation. They are unthinkingly committed to the notion that only the externally observable behavior of economic actors is admissible evidence in arguments concerning economics. But self-testimony is not useless, even for the purpose of resolving the marginal cost–average cost debate of the 1930s. One could have asked, "Has your profit margin always been the same?" "What do you think when you find sales lagging?" (Lower profit margin? Wait it out?) Foolish inquiries into motives and foolish use of human informants will produce nonsense. But this is true of foolish use of any evidence.

Economics, with political science and psychology and some others, appears to be ready to graduate from the elementary school of positivism, with its little rules against self-testimony and requiring the teacher's permission to introspect. The narrowing of inquiry was supposed to bring learning. The lessons, though, were too simple for adults in science. The realization that elementary school is not enough for a scientific life should be a maturing experience.

It is true, for instance, that no proposition about economic behavior has yet been overturned by econometrics, at any rate not to the standard that the hypothetico-deductive model of science would demand. One would worry about this, however, only if one believed the elementary-school version of econometrics. Econometrics for adults claims merely to tell us how complicated life is, how few are the scientific matters that can be settled by the look-see of the crucial experiment, how we must look behind the appearances of the data.

Modernism was not a bad idea, no more than going to elementary school was a bad idea. In their time even the fanatical and intolerant versions of positivism and modernism and scientism served purposes, sometimes good, such as killing airy speculation about word roots in linguistics; or defending Darwin and Pasteur from the damaging if correct charge that they started with theories and made the facts fit the theories; or limiting the range of economics enough to make the reception of mathematics possible. The mischief comes from supposing that modernism and the rest are more than tactics during a moment in the political history of a science. Clinging with a childlike faith to the slogan that modernism constitutes an Epistemology forever true merely leads, like other cases of arrested psychological development, to scholarly neurosis. The slogans of epistemology arise from an absence of self-awareness. Know thyself, lest thou convince thyself without thought that only neoclassical or Austrian or Marxist evidence is worthwhile.

Literary criticism, especially rhetorical criticism, provides a model of self-consciousness for economics. An economic criticism in the style of literary criticism would not be criticism in the naive sense of second-guessing Shakespeare or Samuelson, telling where they miss or where exceed the mark. The American Question applies: if you're so smart, oh critic, why ain't you the poet of words or of ideas? In *Anatomy of Criticism* Northrop Frye attacks "the odious comparisons of greatness" as "pseudo-dialectics, or false rhetoric," as "an anxiety neurosis prompted by a moral censor" which has "made the word critic a synonym for an educated shrew" (1957, pp. 24–27). He goes on, as many have, to construct a criticism more—one hesitates to use the word—positive than normative in its intent.

Without apportioning stars or giving thumbs-up signs for good behavior, then, an economic criticism would have many uses, chiefly to see what economists were doing—really doing. It can reveal the machinery of economic inquiry, as has the "criticism" (in this sense) of Samuelson, Becker, Solow, Muth, Fogel, and the rest.

An economic criticism would make use of the history of economic thought, and be of some use to it in turn. But it would not be the same study. It would be the synchronic match to the diachrony of intellectual history, as literary criticism is to literary history, and economic theory to economic history. The technique of research used by the macroeconomic theorist Axel Leijonhufvud supplies a case in point. He views the history of economic thought as a decision tree, beginning with, say, Adam Smith, who made such and such a theoretical choice on thus and such a question; continuing through Ricardo and Mill and Marshall, who made others; and so forth down to the present state of economic science. At each branch is a road not taken. When economics reaches a dead end—as it has by common consent, for instance, in thinking about the real side of foreign trade—one can either strike out blindly through the yellow wood or, better, return to the previous branching and take the other road. The technique is "criticism" of science, in the sophisticated sense of an aid to understanding, for the purpose of helping the science to progress.

Ignorant of the history of economic thought, and misled by an attachment to an unenlightening account of how economic science operates, the modern economist spends a good deal of time wandering in the wood. Returning to the previous branching takes advantage of the useful past of economics.

In any case, the rewards to economic criticism would be better economic thinking, though by no methodological route. One does not legislate for scientific progress. One can at most make mild and modest suggestions by showing how it is done and how it was. But mainly one merely shows how the poet does the trick, the better to see it plain.

And Improve the Temper of Economists

A fifth and final burden of an unexamined rhetoric is that scientific debate among economists is too often long-lasting and ill-tempered. For all their agreement, their journals contain much bitter controversy about equilibrium and unemployment, droning on from one century to the next. No wonder. Economists do not have an official rhetoric that persuasively describes what they find persuasive. The mathematical and statistical tools that gave promise in the bright dawn of ending economic dispute have not succeeded, not because they were

The Good of Rhetoric in Economics

wrong but because too much has been asked of them. Believing, mistakenly, that operationalism and objectivity and statistical significance are enough to end all dispute, the economist assumes that his opponent is dishonest when he does not concede the point at issue, or that he is motivated by some ideological passion and by self-interest, or that he is simply stupid. It fits the modernist split of fact and value to attribute all disagreements to political differences, since facts are alleged to be, unlike values, impossible to dispute.

The typical economist, alas, is harshly if unreflectively dogmatic, demanding that students or colleagues be members in good standing of this or that church. Sales people for university textbooks in the United States complain that an economics professor simply will not look at a text that does not come from the right church: he asks, shamefully, is the book monetarist or neoclassical or Marxist or Keynesian? Simple-mindedness accentuates the dogmatism. The categories are notably crude, often borrowed from the crudities of journalists: bloody red papist or black Protestant; don't trouble me with the details.

The extent of real disagreement among economists, as I have argued several times, is in fact exaggerated. The extent of their agreement, however, makes the more puzzling the venom they bring to minor disputes. The assaults on Milton Friedman or on J. K. Galbraith have a bitterness beyond reason. The unreason, though, has its reason. If one cannot reason about values, and if most of what matters is placed in the value half of the fact-value split, then it follows that one will embrace unreason when talking about things that matter. The claims of an overblown methodology of science serve merely to spoil the conversation.[1]

Economists, without thinking much, have metaphors about the economy; and they have also, without thinking much, metaphors for their scholarly conversation. It would be good for them to become aware of their metaphors and improve them in shared discourse. The metaphors of trial by jury or of stating the findings of a chemical assay or of diplomatic debate at the United Nations are better selected than fallen into headlong.

A rhetorical cure for these mental disabilities would reject philosophy as a guide to science. At the least it would reject a philosophy that

---

1. Listen to an economist's economist, the late Harry Johnson: "The methodology of positive economics was an ideal methodology for justifying work that produced apparently surprising results without feeling obliged to explain why they occurred" (Johnson 1971, p. 13). I do not need to think about the evidence for widespread monopolistic competition because my methodology tells me the evidence is irrelevant.

pretended to legislate the knowable. The persuasive cure is literary and rhetorical. The cure would not throw away the illuminating regression, the crucial experiment, the unexpected implication unexpectedly falsified. These too persuade reasonable scholars. Nonargument is the alternative to narrow argument only according to the dichotomies of modernism. The cure would restore the health of economics, disguised now under the neuroses of an artificial methodology of science.

WORKS CITED

INDEX

WORKS CITED

This is a list of works cited in the text, not a bibliography of the subject or a list of works consulted. Works are listed here and cited in the text by date of original publication. Page references, however, are always to the latest edition, reprint, or translation given.

Akerlof, George A., and Dickens, W. T. 1982. "The Economic Consequences of Cognitive Dissonance." *American Economic Review* 72 (June): 307–19.

Alchian, Armen. 1950. "Uncertainty, Evolution, and Economic Theory." *Journal of Political Economy* 58 (June): 211–21.

Ames, Edward, and Reiter, Stanley. 1961. "Distributions of Correlation Coefficients in Economic Times Series." *Journal of the American Statistical Association* 56 (September): 637–56.

Aristotle. *Rhetoric*. Trans. W. Rhys Roberts. In *Aristotle: Rhetoric and Poetics*. New York: Random House, Modern Library, 1954.

Arrow, Kenneth. 1959. "Decision Theory and the Choice of a Level of Significance for the *t*-Test." In Ingram Olkin and others, eds., *Contributions to Probability and Statistics: Essays in Honor of Harold Hotelling.* Stanford: Stanford University Press.

Austin, J. L. 1975. *How to Do Things with Words.* 2d ed. Cambridge: Harvard University Press. (Revision of 1962 ed.; from the William James Lectures of 1955).

Aydelotte, William O. 1981. "The Search for Idea in Historical Investigation." *Social Science History* 5 (Fall): 371–92.

Bakan, David. 1966. "The Test of Significance in Psychological Research." *Psychological Bulletin* 66 (December): 423–37. Reprinted in Bernhardt Lieberman, ed., *Contemporary Problems in Statistics: A Book of Readings for the Behavioral Sciences.* New York: Oxford University Press, 1971.

Barfield, Owen. 1947. "Poetic Diction and Legal Fiction." Reprinted in Max Black, ed., *The Importance of Language*, pp. 51–71. Englewood Cliffs, N.J.: Prentice Hall, 1962.

Barthes, Roland. 1960. "Authors and Writers," in his *Critical Essays* (trans. 1972). Reprinted in S. Sontag, ed., *A Barthes Reader.* New York: Hill and Wang, 1982.

Battaglio, Raymond C., and others. 1981. "Commodity Choice Behavior with Pigeons as Subjects." *Journal of Political Economy* 84 (February): 116–51.

Bazerman, Charles. 1981. "What Written Knowledge Does: Three Examples of Academic Discourse." *Philosophy of the Social Sciences* 11 (September): 361–87.

Works Cited

Bazerman, Charles. 1983. "Scientific Writing as a Social Act: A Review of the Literature of the Sociology of Science." In Paul Anderson and John Brockmann, eds., *New Essays in Scientific and Technical Communications: Theory, Research, and Practice.* Farmingdale, N.Y.: Baywood.

Bazerman, Charles. Forthcoming. "The Modern Evolution of the Experimental Report in Physics: Spectroscopic Articles in *Physical Review,* 1893–1980." *Social Studies of Science.*

Bazerman, Charles. n.d. "Early Development in Argumentation in Physics." Unpublished MS, Department of English, Baruch College, New York.

Beardsley, Monroe C. 1967. "Metaphor." In *The Encyclopedia of Philosophy.* New York: Macmillan and Free Press.

Becker, Gary S., and Stigler, George J. 1977. "De Gustibus Non Est Disputandum." *American Economic Review* 67 (March): 76–90.

Bentham, Jeremy. 1824. *The Book of Fallacies, from Unfinished Papers.* London: Hunt.

Black, Max. 1962. *Models and Metaphors: Studies in Language and Philosophy.* Ithaca: Cornell University Press.

Blaug, Mark. 1980. *The Methodology of Economics; or, How Economists Explain.* Cambridge: Cambridge University Press.

Bloch, Marc. 1928. "A Contribution towards a Comparative History of European Societies." In J. E. Anderson, trans., *Land and Work in Medieval Europe: Selected Papers by Marc Bloch.* New York: Harper and Row, 1969.

Boland, Lawrence A. 1979. "A Critique of Friedman's Critics." *Journal of Economic Literature* 17 (June): 503–22.

Boland, Lawrence A. 1982. *The Foundations of Economic Method.* London: Allen and Unwin.

Booth, Wayne C. 1961. *The Rhetoric of Fiction.* Chicago: University of Chicago Press.

Booth, Wayne C. 1967. "The Revival of Rhetoric." In Martin Steinmann, Jr., *New Rhetorics.* New York: Scribner's.

Booth, Wayne C. 1974a. *Modern Dogma and the Rhetoric of Assent.* Chicago: University of Chicago Press.

Booth, Wayne C. 1974b. *A Rhetoric of Irony.* Chicago: University of Chicago Press.

Booth, Wayne C. 1979. *Critical Understanding: The Powers and Limits of Pluralism.* Chicago: University of Chicago Press.

Borel, Armand. 1983. "Mathematics: Art and Science." *Mathematical Intelligencer* 5, no. 4: 9–17.

Boring, Edwin G. 1919. "Mathematical versus Scientific Significance." *Psychological Bulletin* 16 (October): 335–38.

Boulding, Kenneth. 1975. *Ecodynamics: A New Theory of Societal Evolution.* Beverly Hills: Sage.

Braudel, Fernand, and Spooner, Frank. 1967. "Prices in Europe from 1450 to 1750." In E. A. Rich and C. H. Wilson, eds., *The Cambridge Economic History of Europe,* vol. 4. Cambridge: Cambridge University Press.

Bronowski, Jacob. 1965. *Science and Human Values*. Rev. ed. New York: Harper and Row.
Brooks, Cleanth, and Warren, Robert Penn. 1949. *Modern Rhetoric*. 2d ed. New York: Harcourt, Brace.
Burke, Kenneth. 1945. *A Grammar of Motives*. Berkeley: University of California Press, 1969.
Burke, Kenneth. 1950. *A Rhetoric of Motives*. Berkeley: University of California Press, 1969.
Burke, Kenneth. 1961. *The Rhetoric of Religion: Studies in Logology*. Berkeley: University of California Press, 1970.
Burke, Kenneth. 1968. "Interaction: Dramatism." In *The International Encyclopedia of the Social Sciences*. New York: Macmillan.
Caldwell, Bruce. 1982. *Beyond Positivism: Economic Methodology in the Twentieth Century*. London and Boston: Allen and Unwin.
Campbell, John Angus. 1984. "Charles Darwin: Rhetorician of Science." Paper presented at the Iowa Symposium on the Rhetoric of the Human Sciences, Iowa City, March.
Carlston, Donal E. 1984. "Turning Psychology on Itself." Paper presented at the Iowa Symposium on the Rhetoric of the Human Sciences, Iowa City, March.
Cicero, Marcus Tullius. *De Oratore*. Trans. E. W. Sutton. Vol. 1. Cambridge: Harvard University Press, 1942.
Coase, Ronald. 1982. "How Should Economists Choose?" The G. Warren Nutter Lectures in Political Economy, Washington, D.C.: American Enterprise Institute.
Cohen, Kalman, and Cyert, Richard. 1975. *Theory of the Firm*. 2d ed. Englewood Cliffs, N.J.: Prentice-Hall.
Collins, Harry M., and Pinch, T. H. 1982. *Frames of Meaning: The Social Construction of Extraordinary Science*. London: Routledge and Kegan Paul.
Commager, Steele. 1965. "Notes on Some Poems of Catullus." *Harvard Studies in Classical Philology* 70: 83–110.
Cooley, T. F., and LeRoy, S. F. 1981. "Identification and Estimation of Money Demand." *American Economic Review* 71 (December): 825–44.
Copi, Irving. 1978. *Introduction to Logic*. 5th ed. New York: Macmillan.
Crain, Robert. 1984. Quoted in Ellen K. Coughlin, "Social Scientists' Research on School Desegregation: Mountains of Data, But Nothing That Everybody Agrees On." *Chronicle of Higher Education*, May 16, p. 12.
Crosman, Richard. 1980. "Do Readers Make Meaning?" In Susan R. Suleiman and Inge Crosman, eds., *The Reader in the Text: Essays on Audience and Interpretation*, pp. 149–64. Princeton: Princeton University Press.
Davis, Lance. 1965. "The Investment Market, 1870–1914: The Evolution of a National Market." *Journal of Economic History* 25 (September): 355–99.
Davis, Philip J., and Hersh, Reuben. 1981. *The Mathematical Experience*. Boston: Houghton Mifflin.
Davis, Philip J., and Hersh, Reuben. 1984. "Mathematics and Rhetoric." Paper presented at the Iowa Symposium on the Rhetoric of the Human Sciences, Iowa City, March.

Works Cited

Denton, Frank. 1983. "Econometric Data Mining as an Industry." Unpublished MS, Department of Economics, McMaster University, October (forthcoming in the *Review of Economics and Statistics*).

Dettmer, Helena. 1983. *Horace: A Study in Structure*. Altertumswissenschaftliche Texte und Studien, Bd. 12. Hildensheim, West Germany: Olms.

Dettmer, Helena. 1984a. "The Design of the Catullan Corpus." Unpublished MS, Department of Classics, University of Iowa.

Dettmer, Helena. 1984b. "A Fresh Look at Catullus 1–9." *Liverpool Classical Monthly* 9 (May).

Dewey, John. 1916. *Essays in Experimental Logic*. New York: Dover.

Dewey, John. 1929. *The Quest for Certainty: A Study of the Relation of Knowledge and Action*. New York: Putnam, 1960.

Duhem, Pierre. 1906. *The Aim and Structure of Physical Theory*. Princeton: Princeton University Press, 1954.

Eagleton, Terry. 1983. *Literary Theory: An Introduction*. Minneapolis: University of Minnesota Press.

Einstein, Albert. 1953. "Aphorisms for Leo Baeck." Reprinted in *Ideas and Opinions*. New York: Dell, 1973.

Elster, Jon. 1979. *Ulysses and the Sirens: Studies in Rationality and Irrationality*. Cambridge: Cambridge University Press.

Farley, John, and Geison, Gerald L. 1974. "Science, Politics, and Spontaneous Generation in Nineteenth-Century France: The Pasteur-Pouchet Debate." *Bulletin of the History of Medicine* 48:161–98.

Feige, Edgar. 1975. "The Consequences of Journal Editorial Policies and a Suggestion for Revision." *Journal of Political Economy* 83 (December): 1291–96.

Feyerabend, Paul. 1975. *Against Method: Outline of an Anarchistic Theory of Knowledge*. London: Verso, 1978.

Feyerabend, Paul. 1978. *Science in a Free Society*. London: New Left Books.

Finley, M. I. 1973. *The Ancient Economy*. London: Chatto and Windus.

Fischer, David Hackett. 1970. *Historians' Fallacies*. New York: Harper and Row.

Fish, Stanley. 1980. *Is There a Text in This Class? The Authority of Interpretive Communities*. Cambridge: Harvard University Press.

Fisher, R. A. 1925. *Statistical Methods for Research Workers*. Edinburgh: Oliver and Boyd.

Fishlow, Albert. 1965. *American Railroads and the Transformation of the Antebellum Economy*. Cambridge: Harvard University Press.

Flory, Marleen Boudreau. 1983. "Semantics and Symbioses: How to Write an Article to Impress Your Peers." *Chronicle of Higher Education*, January 26.

Fogel, Robert W. 1960. *The Union Pacific Railroad: A Case of Premature Enterprise*. Baltimore: Johns Hopkins University Press.

Fogel, Robert W. 1962. "A Quantitative Approach to the Study of Railroads in American Economic Growth: A Report of Some Preliminary Findings." *Journal of Economic History* 22 (June): 163–97.

Fogel, Robert W. 1964. *Railroads and American Economic Growth: Essays in Econometric History*. Baltimore: Johns Hopkins University Press.

Fogel, Robert W. 1979. "Notes on the Social Saving Controversy." *Journal of Economic History* 39 (March): 1–54.

Fogel, Robert W., and Elton, G. R. 1983. *Which Road to the Past? Two Views of History.* New Haven: Yale University Press.

Fogel, Robert W., and Engerman, Stanley. 1974. *Time on the Cross: The Economics of American Negro Slavery.* Boston: Little, Brown.

Freedman, David; Pisani, Robert; and Purves, Roger. 1978. *Statistics.* New York: Norton.

Frenkel, Jacob. 1978. "Purchasing Power Parity: Doctrinal Perspectives and Evidence from the 1920s," *Journal of International Economics* 8 (May): 169–91.

Frey, Bruno S.; Pommerehne, Werner W.; Schneider, Friedrich; and Gilbert, Guy. 1984. "Consensus and Dissension among Economists: An Empirical Inquiry." *American Economic Review* 74 (December): 986–94.

Friedman, Milton. 1953. "The Methodology of Positive Economics." In his *Essays in Positive Economics.* Chicago: University of Chicago Press.

Friedman, Milton. 1975. *An Economist's Protest.* 2d ed. Glen Ridge, N.J.: Thomas Horton and Daughters.

Friedman, Milton. 1984. "Comment [on McCloskey and Zecher 1984]." In Michael D. Bordo and Anna J. Schwartz, eds., *A Retrospective on the Classical Gold Standard, 1821–1931.* Chicago: University of Chicago Press and National Bureau of Economic Research.

Friedman, Milton, and Schwartz, Anna J. 1963. *A Monetary History of the United States, 1867–1960.* Princeton: Princeton University Press.

Frye, Northrop. 1957. *An Anatomy of Criticism.* New York: Atheneum, 1967.

Galbraith, John Kenneth. 1978. "Writing, Typing, and Economics." *Atlantic* 241 (March): 102–5.

Gardner, John. 1978. *On Moral Fiction.* New York: Basic Books.

Gardner, John. 1984. *The Art of Fiction: Notes on Craft for Young Writers.* New York: Knopf.

Geertz, Clifford. 1983. "Anti-Anti-Relativism." Unpublished MS, Institute for Advanced Study, Princeton, N.J.

Geison, Gerald. Forthcoming. *The Private Science of Louis Pasteur.* New York: Oxford University Press.

Genberg, A. Hans. 1976. "Aspects of the Monetary Approach to the Balance-of-Payments Theory: An Empirical Study of Sweden." In Jacob A. Frenkel and Harry G. Johnson, eds., *The Monetary Approach to the Balance of Payments.* London: Allen and Unwin.

Georgescu-Roegen, Nicholas. 1975. *Entropy, Law, and the Economic Process.* Cambridge: Harvard University Press.

Gibson, Walker. 1950. "Authors, Speakers, Readers, and Mock Readers." *College English* 11 (February): 265–69. Reprinted in Jane P. Thompkins, ed., *Reader-Response Criticism: From Formalism to Post-Structuralism.* Baltimore: Johns Hopkins University Press, 1980.

Goodman, Nelson. 1954. *Fact, Fiction, and Forecast.* Cambridge: Harvard University Press.

Works Cited

Goodman, Nelson. 1978. *Ways of Worldmaking.* Indianapolis: Hackett.

Goodman, Nelson. 1983. "Notes on the Well-Made World." *Erkenntnis* 19: 99–107.

Gould, Stephen Jay. 1977. *Ever Since Darwin.* New York: Norton.

Gould, Stephen Jay. 1981. *The Mismeasure of Man.* New York: Norton.

Graff, Gerald. 1983. "The Pseudo-Politics of Interpretation." *Critical Inquiry* 9 (March): 597–610.

Griffith, John G. 1968. "A Taxonomic Study of the Manuscript Tradition of Juvenal." *Museum Helveticum* 25 (April): 101–38.

Griliches, Zvi. 1976. "Automobile Prices Revisited: Extensions of the Hedonic Hypothesis." In N. E. Terleckyj, ed., *Household Production and Consumption.* Studies in Income and Wealth, vol. 40. New York: National Bureau of Economics Research.

Habermas, Jürgen. 1973. *Legitimation Crisis.* Trans. T. McCarthy. Boston: Beacon Press, 1975.

Hagood, Margaret Jarman. 1941. *Statistics for Sociologists.* New York: Holt, Rinehart.

Halmos, Paul R. 1973. "How to Write Mathematics." In Norman E. Steenrod and others, *How to Write Mathematics*, pp. 19–48. Providence: American Mathematical Society.

Harberger, A. C. 1971. "Three Basic Postulates of Applied Welfare Economics." *Journal of Economic Literature* 9 (September): 785–97.

Hausman, Daniel. 1981. *Capital, Profits, and Prices: An Essay in the Philosophy of Economics.* New York: Columbia University Press.

Hawke, Gary. 1970. *Railways and Economic Growth in England and Wales, 1840–1870.* Oxford: Oxford University Press.

Heiner, Ronald. 1983. "The Origin of Predictable Behavior." *American Economic Review* 73 (September): 560–95.

Heinzelmann, Kurt. 1980. *The Economics of the Imagination.* Amherst: University of Massachusetts Press.

Henderson, Willie. 1982. "Metaphor in Economics." *Economics,* Winter, pp. 147–53.

Hexter, J. H. 1971. "The Rhetoric of History." In his *Doing History.* Bloomington: Indiana University Press.

Hirsch, Abraham, and Marchi, Neil de. 1985. "The Methodology of Positive Economics." Unpublished MS, Department of Economics, Brooklyn College, City University of New York.

Hirsch, Eric D. 1977. *The Philosophy of Composition.* Chicago: University of Chicago Press.

Hirschman, Albert. 1970. *Exit, Voice, and Loyalty.* Cambridge: Harvard University Press.

Hirschman, Albert. 1984. "Against Parsimony: Three Easy Ways of Complicating Some Categories of Economic Discourse." *American Economic Review* 74 (May): 89–96.

Hogben, Lancelot. [1968]. *Statistical Theory: The Relationship of Probability, Credibility, and Error.* New York: Norton.

Horsburgh, H.J.N. 1958. "Philosophers against Metaphor." *Philosophical Quarterly* 8 (July): 231–45.

Housman, A. E. 1922. "The Application of Thought to Textual Criticism." In J. Diggle and F. R. D. Goodyear, eds., *The Classical Papers of A. E. Housman*, 3:1058–69. Cambridge: Cambridge University Press, 1961.

Houthakker, Hendrick, and Taylor, Lance. 1970. *Consumer Demand in the United States: Analysis and Projections, with Applications to Other Countries.* 2d ed. Cambridge: Harvard University Press.

Hume, David. 1748. *An Enquiry Concerning Human Understanding.* Oxford: Oxford University Press, 1975.

Hutchison, Terence. 1938. *The Significance and Basic Postulates of Economic Theory.* 2d ed. New York: Kelley, 1960.

James, William. 1907. "Pragmatism's Conception of Truth." In Alburey Castell, ed., *Essays in Pragmatism by William James*, pp. 159–76. New York: Hafner, 1948.

Johnson, Harry G. 1971. "The Keynesian Revolution and the Monetarist Counterrevolution," *American Economic Review* 61 (May): 1–14.

Jones, G. T. 1933. *Increasing Returns.* Cambridge: Cambridge University Press.

Kearl, J. R.; Pope, Clayne; Whiting, Gordon; and Wimmer, Larry. 1979. "A Confusion of Economists?" *American Economic Review* 69 (May): 28–37.

Kelvin, William Thompson, Lord. 1883. "Electrical Units of Measurement." In his *Popular Lectures and Addresses*, vol. 1. London, 1888–89.

Kendall, M. G., and Stuart, A. 1951. *The Advanced Theory of Statistics.* 3rd ed. Vol. 2. London: Griffin.

Klamer, Arjo. 1984. *Conversations with Economists: New Classical Economists and Opponents Speak Out on the Current Controversy in Macroeconomics.* Totowa, N.J.: Rowman and Allanheld.

Kline, Morris. 1980. *Mathematics: The Loss of Certainty.* New York: Oxford University Press.

Knight, Frank. 1940. " 'What is Truth' in Economics?" [Review of Hutchison 1938.] *Journal of Political Economy* 48 (February): 1–32. Reprinted in his *On the History and Method of Economics: Selected Essays.* Chicago: University of Chicago Press, 1963.

Kornai, Janos. 1983. "The Health of Nations: Reflections on the Analogy between Medical Science and Economics." *Kyklos* 36:191–212.

Kravis, I. B., and Lipsey, R. E. 1978. "Price Behavior in the Light of Balance-of-Payments Theories." *Journal of International Economics* 8 (May): 193–246.

Krugman, P. R. 1978. "Purchasing Power Parity and Exchange Rates: Another Look at the Evidence." *Journal of International Economics* 8 (August): 397–407.

Kruskal, William. 1968 (updated 1978). "Significance, Tests of." In *International Encyclopedia of Statistics.* New York: Macmillan.

Kruskal, William. 1978. "Formulas, Numbers, Words: Statistics in Prose." *The American Scholar* 47 (Spring): 223–29. Reprinted in D. Fiske, ed., *New Directions for Methodology in Social and Behavioral Sciences.* San Francisco: Jossey-Bass, 1981.

196

Works Cited

Kuhn, Thomas. 1970. *The Structure of Scientific Revolutions*. 2d ed. Chicago: University of Chicago Press.

Kuhn, Thomas. 1977. *The Essential Tension: Selected Studies in Scientific Tradition and Change*. Chicago: University of Chicago Press.

Kurtz, A. K., and Edgerton, H. A., eds. 1939. *Statistical Dictionary of Terms and Symbols*. New York: Wiley.

Lakatos, Imre. 1976. *Proofs and Refutations: The Logic of Mathematical Discovery*. Vol. 1. Cambridge: Cambridge University Press.

Lakatos, Imre. 1978. *The Methodology of Scientific Research Programmes*. Cambridge: Cambridge University Press.

Lakatos, Imre, and Musgrave, Alan, eds. 1970. *Criticism and the Growth of Knowledge*. Cambridge: Cambridge University Press.

Landau, Misia. 1984. "Paradise Lost: The Theme of Terrestiality in Human Evolution." Paper presented at the Iowa Symposium on the Rhetoric of the Human Sciences, Iowa City, March.

Langland, William. *The Vision of Piers Plowman: A Complete Edition of the B-Text*. Ed. A.V.C. Schmidt. New York: Dutton, 1978.

Lanham, Richard A. 1968. *A Handlist of Rhetorical Terms: A Guide for Students of English Literature*. Berkeley and Los Angeles: University of California Press.

Latour, Bruno, and Woolgar, S. 1979. *Laboratory Life: The Social Construction of Scientific Facts*. Beverly Hills: Sage.

Leamer, Edward. 1978. *Specification Searches: Ad Hoc Inferences with Nonexperimental Data*. New York: Wiley.

Leamer, Edward. 1983. "Let's Take the Con out of Econometrics." *American Economic Review* 73 (March): 31–43.

Leary, David E. 1984. "Telling Likely Stories: The Rhetoric of the New Psychology, 1880–1920." Paper presented at the Iowa Symposium on the Rhetoric of the Human Sciences, Iowa City, March.

Lepienes, Wolf. 1983. Unpublished MS on the history of sociology. Institute for Advanced Study, Princeton, N.J.

Levi, Edward. 1948. *An Introduction to Legal Reasoning*. Chicago: University of Chicago Press, 1967.

Lewis, C. S. 1939. "Buspels and Flansferes: A Semantic Nightmare," in his *Rehabilitations and Other Essays*. Reprinted in Max Black, ed., *The Importance of Language*. Englewood Cliffs, N.J.: Prentice Hall, 1962.

Lieberman, Bernhardt. 1971. *Contemporary Problems in Statistics: A Book of Readings for the Behavioral Sciences*. New York: Oxford University Press.

Lovell, Michael C. 1983. "Data Mining." *Review of Economics and Statistics* 45 (February): 1–12.

Lucas, Robert E., Jr., and Sargent, Thomas J., eds. 1981. *Rational Expectations and Econometric Practice*. Vol. 1. Minneapolis: University of Minnesota Press.

McCaleb, Thomas. n.d. "Capsule Contributions of Nobel Prize Winners in Economics." Unpublished MS, Department of Economics, University of Florida.

McClelland, Peter. 1975. *Causal Explanation and Model Building in History, Economics, and the New Economic History.* Ithaca: Cornell University Press.

McCloskey, D. N. 1970. "The Loss to Britain from Foreign Industrialization." Reprinted in his *Enterprise and Trade in Victorian Britain.* London: Allen and Unwin, 1981.

McCloskey, D. N. 1985a. *The Applied Theory of Price.* 2d ed. New York: Macmillan.

McCloskey, D. N. 1985b. "Economical Writing." *Economic Inquiry,* April.

McCloskey, D. N., and Zecher, J. Richard. 1976. "How the Gold Standard Worked, 1880–1913." In Jacob A. Frenkel and Harry G. Johnson, eds., *The Monetary Approach to the Balance of Payments.* London: Allen and Unwin.

McCloskey, D. N., and Zecher, J. Richard. 1984. "The Success of Purchasing Power Parity." In Michael D. Bordo, and Anna J. Schwartz, eds., *A Retrospective on the Classical Gold Standard, 1821–1931.* Chicago: University of Chicago Press and National Bureau of Economic Research.

McCrea, W. H. 1983. Review of Allaby and Lovelock, *The Great Extinction. Times Literary Supplement,* July 19.

Machlup, Fritz. 1955. "The Problem of Verification in Economics." *Southern Economic Journal* 22 (July): 1–21.

Mackie, J. L. 1967. "Fallacies." In *The Encyclopedia of Philosophy.* New York: Macmillan and Free Press.

Masica, Colin. 1976. *Defining a Linguistic Area: South Asia.* Chicago: University of Chicago Press.

Mayer, Thomas. 1975. "Selecting Economic Hypotheses by Goodness of Fit." *Economic Journal* 85 (December): 877–83.

Mayer, Thomas. 1980. "Economics as a Hard Science: Realistic Goal or Wishful Thinking?" *Economic Inquiry* 18 (April): 165–78.

Mechling, Elizabeth Walker, and Mechling, Jay. 1983. "Sweet Talk: The Moral Rhetoric against Sugar." *Central States Speech Journal* 34 (Spring): 19–32.

Medawar, Peter. 1964. "Is the Scientific Paper Fraudulent?" *Saturday Review,* August 1, pp. 42–43.

Millis, Harry A. 1934. "The Union in Industry: Some Observations on the Theory of Collective Bargaining." *American Economic Review* 25 (March 1935): 1–13.

Mood, A. F., and Graybill, F. A. 1963. *Introduction to the Theory of Statistics.* 2d ed. New York: McGraw-Hill.

Morgenstern, Oskar. 1963. *On the Accuracy of Economic Observations.* 2d ed. Princeton: Princeton University Press.

Morrison, Denton E., and Henkel, Ramon E. 1969. "Significance Tests Reconsidered." *American Sociologist* 4 (May): 131–40. Reprinted in Morrison and Henkel 1970.

Morrison, Denton E., and Henkel, Ramon E. 1970. *The Significance Test Controversy: A Reader.* Chicago: Aldine.

Mosteller, Frederick, and Tukey, John W. 1977. *Data Analysis and Regression.* Reading, Mass.: Addison-Wesley.

Works Cited

Muth, John F. 1961. "Rational Expectations and the Theory of Price Movements." *Econometrica* 29 (July): 315–35.

Nelson, John. 1983. "Models, Statistics, and Other Tropes of Politics; or, Whatever Happened to Argument in Political Science?" In D. Zarefsky, M. O. Sillars, and J. Rhodes, eds., *Argument in Transition: Proceedings of the Third Summer Conference on Argumentation*. Annandale, Va.: Speech Communication Association.

Nelson, John; Megill, Allan; and McCloskey, D. N., eds. Forthcoming. *The Rhetoric of the Human Sciences: Papers and Proceedings of the Iowa Conference on Rhetoric, Scholarship, and Public Affairs, March, 1984*.

Newman, John Henry, Cardinal. 1870. *An Essay in Aid of a Grammar of Assent*. New York: Image, 1955.

Neyman, Jerzy, and Pearson, E. S. 1933. "On the Problem of the Most Efficient Tests of Statistical Hypotheses." *Philosophical Transactions of the Royal Society*, ser. A, 231:289–337.

Novick, Peter. 1984. "The 'Objectivity' Question and the Professional Culture of American Historiography." Paper presented at the Iowa Symposium on the Rhetoric of the Human Sciences, Iowa City, March.

Oakeshott, Michael. 1933. "Poetry as a Voice in the Conversation of Mankind," in his *Experience and Its Modes*. Reprinted in his *Rationalism in Politics*. New York: Basic Books, 1962.

O'Brien, Patrick. 1977. *The New Economic History of Railroads*. London: Croom, Helm.

Ortony, Andrew, ed. 1979. *Metaphor and Thought*. Cambridge: Cambridge University Press.

Palmer, Leonard R. 1954. *The Latin Language*. London: Faber and Faber.

Palmer, Leonard R. 1972. *Descriptive and Comparative Linguistics: A Critical Introduction*. New York: Crane, Russak.

Passmore, John. 1961. *Philosophical Reasoning*. 2d ed. London: Duckworth, 1970.

Passmore, John. 1966. *A Hundred Years of Philosophy*. 2d ed. London: Penguin.

Passmore, John. 1967. "Logical Positivism." In *The Encyclopedia of Philosophy*. New York: Macmillan and Free Press.

Pearson, Karl. 1911. "Probability That Two Independent Distributions of Frequency Are Really Samples from the Same Population." *Biometrika*, vol. 8.

Peirce, Charles. 1877. "The Fixation of Belief." Reprinted in *Values in a Universe of Chance: Selected Writings of Charles S. Peirce*. Ed. P. P. Wiener. Garden City, N.Y.: Doubleday, 1958.

Perelman, Chaim, and Olbrechts-Tyteca, L. 1958. *The New Rhetoric: A Treatise on Argumentation*. Trans. John Wilkinson and Purcell Weaver. Notre Dame: University of Notre Dame Press, 1969.

Perlman, Mark. 1978. Review of Hutchison's *Knowledge and Ignorance in Economics*. *Journal of Economic Literature* 16 (June): 582–85.

Plato. "Phaedrus." in E. Hamilton and H. Cairns, eds., *The Collected Dialogues of Plato*, trans. R. Hackforth. Princeton: Princeton University Press, 1961.

Polanyi, Michael. 1962. *Personal Knowledge: Towards a Post-Critical Philosophy.* Chicago: University of Chicago Press.

Polanyi, Michael. 1966. *The Tacit Dimension.* Garden City, N.Y.: Doubleday.

Polya, George. 1954. *Induction and Analogy in Mathematics.* Vol. 1 of *Mathematics and Plausible Reasoning.* Princeton: Princeton University Press.

Popper, Karl. 1934. *The Logic of Scientific Discovery.* English trans. New York: Harper, 1968.

Popper, Karl. 1945. *The Open Society and Its Enemies.* London: Routledge.

Popper, Karl. 1976. *Unended Quest: An Intellectual Autobiography.* London: Collins.

Quine, Willard. 1948. "On What There Is." *Review of Metaphysics* 2 (September): 21–38. Reprinted in his *From a Logical Point of View.* 2d ed. Cambridge: Harvard University Press, 1961.

Quine, Willard. 1951. "Two Dogmas of Empiricism." *Philosophical Review* 51 (January): 20–43. Reprinted in his *From a Logical Point of View* (see above).

Quintilian, Marcus F. *Institutio Oratoria.* Trans. H. E. Butler. Cambridge: Harvard University Press, 1920.

Reder, Melvin. 1982. "Chicago Economics: Permanence and Change." *Journal of Economic Literature* 20 (March): 1–38.

Reynolds, L. D., and Wilson, N. G. 1974. *Scribes and Scholars: A Guide to the Transmission of Greek and Latin Literature.* 2d ed. Oxford: Oxford University Press.

Richards, I. A. [1925]. *Principles of Literary Criticism.* New York: Harcourt Brace Jovanovich.

Richards, I. A. 1936. *The Philosophy of Rhetoric.* New York: Oxford University Press.

Richardson, J. D. 1978. "Some Empirical Evidence on Commodity Arbitrage and the Law of One Price," *Journal of International Economics* 8 (May): 341–51.

Robinson, William. 1893. *Forensic Oratory: A Manual for Advocates.* Boston: Little, Brown.

Roll, Richard, and Ross, Stephen. 1980. "An Empirical Investigation of the Arbitrage Pricing Theory." *Journal of Finance* 35 (December): 1073–1103.

Root-Bernstein, Robert. 1983. "Mendel and Methodology." *History of Science* 21 (September): 275–95.

Rorty, Amelie Oksenberg. 1983. "Experiments in Philosophic Genre: Descartes' *Meditations.*" *Critical Inquiry* 9 (March): 545–65.

Rorty, Richard. 1979. *Philosophy and the Mirror of Nature.* Princeton: Princeton University Press.

Rorty, Richard. 1982. *The Consequences of Pragmatism: Essays.* Minneapolis: University of Minnesota Press.

Rorty, Richard. 1984a. "Relativism." Unpublished MS, University of Virginia.

Rorty, Richard. 1984b. "Science as Solidarity." Paper presented at the Iowa Symposium on the Rhetoric of the Human Sciences, Iowa City, March.

Rosen, Stanley. 1980. *The Limits of Analysis.* New York: Basic Books.

Works Cited

Rosenberg, Alexander. 1976. *Microeconomic Laws: A Philosophical Analysis.* Pittsburgh: Pittsburgh University Press.

Rosenblatt, Louise M. 1978. *The Reader, the Text, the Poem: The Transactional Theory of the Literary Work.* Carbondale: Southern Illinois University Press.

Salant, Walter. 1969. "Writing and Reading in Economics." *Journal of Political Economy* 77 (July–August): 545–58.

Samuelson, Paul A. 1947. *The Foundations of Economic Analysis.* Cambridge: Harvard University Press.

Sarkar, Husain. 1983. *A Theory of Method.* Berkeley and Los Angeles: University of California Press.

Saussure, Ferdinand de. 1915. *Course in General Linguistics.* Trans. Wade Baskin. New York: McGraw-Hill, 1959.

Schuster, J. A. 1983. "The Developmental and Structural Demystification of Descartes' Method: A Case Study in the Construction of Scientific Discourse." Unpublished MS, University of Wollongong, N.S.W., Australia.

Scitovsky, Tibor. 1976. *The Joyless Economy.* New York: Oxford University Press.

Scott, Elizabeth. 1953. "Testing Hypotheses." In R. J. Trumpler and H. F. Weaver, eds., *Statistical Astronomy.* New York: Dover, 1963.

Scott, Robert. 1967. "On Viewing Rhetoric as Epistemic." *Central States Speech Journal* 18 (February): 9–17.

Searle, John. 1969. *Speech Acts: An Essay in the Philosophy of Language.* Cambridge: Cambridge University Press.

Sharpe, William. 1970. *Portfolio Theory and Capital Markets.* New York: McGraw-Hill.

* Shell, Marc. 1978. *The Economy of Literature.* Baltimore: Johns Hopkins University Press.

Sims, Christopher. 1978. "Review of Leamer's *Specification Searches.*" *Journal of Economic Literature* 16 (June).

Sims, Christopher. 1982. "Scientific Standards in Econometric Modeling." Unpublished paper for the twenty-fifth anniversary of the Rotterdam Econometrics Institute, April.

Solow, Robert. 1957. "Technical Change and the Aggregate Production Function." *Review of Economics and Statistics* 39 (August): 312–20.

Solow, Robert. 1981. "Does Economics Make Progress?" *Bulletin of the American Academy of Arts and Sciences* 36 (December).

Stebbing, L. Susan. 1943. *A Modern Elementary Logic.* 5th ed. Revised by C. W. K. Mundle. London: Methuen, 1965.

Steiner, George. 1975. *After Babel: Aspects of Language and Translation.* London: Oxford University Press.

Steiner, Mark. 1975. *Mathematical Knowledge.* Ithaca: Cornell University Press.

Steiner, Mark. 1978. "Mathematical Explanation." *Philosophical Studies* 34 (August): 135–51.

Stigler, George J. 1966. *The Theory of Price.* 3d ed. New York: Macmillan.

Stigler, George J. 1969. "Does Economics Have a Useful Past?" *History of Political Economy* 1 (Fall): 217–30.

Works Cited

Stigler, George J. 1977. "The Conference Handbook." *Journal of Political Economy* 85 (April): 441–43.

Stigler, Stephen. 1978. "Francis Ysidro Edgeworth, Statistician." *Journal of the Royal Statistical Society*, ser. A, 141:187–313.

Stone, Lawrence. 1984. Letter. *Harper's*, June.

Supple, Barry. 1971. "Can the New Economic History Become an Import Substitute?" In D. N. McCloskey, ed., *Essays on a Mature Economy: Britain after 1840*, pp. 423–30. London: Methuen.

Syme, Ronald, 1956. "Piso and Veranius in Catullus." *Classica and Mediaevalia* 17:129–34.

Toulmin, Stephen. 1958. *The Uses of Argument*. Cambridge: Cambridge University Press.

Toulmin, Stephen. 1982. "The Construal of Reality: Criticism in Modern and Postmodern Science," *Critical Inquiry* 9 (Autumn): 93–110.

Tufte, Edward R. 1983. *The Visual Display of Quantitative Information*. Cheshire, Conn.: Graphics Press.

Tullock, Gordon. 1959. "Publication Decisions and Tests of Significance: A Comment." *Journal of the American Statistical Association* 54 (September): 593 only.

van Heijenoort, John. 1967. "Godel's Theorem." in *The Encyclopedia of Philosophy*. New York: Macmillan and Free Press.

von Mises, Ludwig. 1949. *Human Action*. New Haven: Yale University Press.

Wald, Abraham. 1939. "Contributions to the Theory of Statistical Estimation and Testing Hypotheses." *Annals of Mathematical Statistics* 10 (December): 299–326.

Ward, Benjamin. 1972. *What's Wrong with Economics?* New York: Basic Books.

Webster, Glenn; Jacox, Ida; and Baldwin, Beverly. 1981. "Nursing Theory and the Ghost of the Received View." In Joanne McCloskey and Helen Grace, eds., *Current Issues in Nursing*, pp. 16–35. Boston: Blackwell Scientific.

Weinberg, Steven. 1983. "Beautiful Theories." Revision of the Second Annual Gordon Mills Lecture on Science and the Humanities, University of Texas, April 5, 1983.

Wenzel, Joseph W. 1983. "Ethical Proof: A Re-examination of Aristotelian Theory." In D. Zarefsky, M. O. Sillars, and J. Rhodes, eds., *Argument in Transition: Proceedings of the Third Summer Conference on Argumentation*, pp. 43–53. Annandale, Va.: Speech Communication Association.

Whately, Richard. 1846. *Elements of Rhetoric*. 7th ed. Carbondale: University of Illinois Press, 1963.

White, Hayden. 1973. *Metahistory: The Historical Imagination in Nineteenth-Century Europe*. Baltimore: Johns Hopkins University Press.

Williams, Gordon, ed. 1969. *The Third Book of Horace's Odes*. Oxford: Oxford University Press.

Williamson, Jeffrey. 1974. *Late Nineteenth-Century American Development: A General Equilibrium History*. Cambridge: Cambridge University Press.

Willis, James. 1972. *Latin Textual Criticism*. Urbana: University of Illinois Press.

Works Cited

Yule, G. U., and Greenwood, M. 1915. "The Statistics of Anti-Typhoid and Anti-Cholera Inoculation and the Interpretation of Such Statistics in General." *Proceedings of the Royal Society of Medicine*, vol. 8.

Zeckhauser, Richard and Stokey, Edith. 1978. *A Primer for Policy Analysis*. New York: Norton.

Zellner, Arnold. 1968. *Readings in Economic Statistics and Econometrics*. Boston: Little, Brown.

INDEX

Alchian, Armen, 15
Allegory, 78, 79
American Economic Review, 3, 4
Analogy, 41, 60, 61, 72, 78, 79, 83, 108, 125
Anaphora, 127
Anarchy, 29, 39–40
Antimodernism, 10, 11, 50–51
Apophasis, 127, 128
Appeal: to authority, 71, 72, 85; ethical, 121–22, 123, 124, 126, 130; to historian, 123, 127; to scientist, 122–23, 127
Argument, 119, 121–22, 126; *ad hominem*, 59, 103, 128; *a fortiori*, xx, 115, 120, 127, 128–29, 120, 132; to/from authority, 12–13, 49, 60, 71, 72, 85; economic, 72–73, 104; indubitable, 30; persuasive, 38–39, 44–45, 47, 57–58; probable, 30; rationality in, 36; standards for, 155–59; from symmetry, 103; theoretical, 103; types of 49; from upper and lower bounds, 115, 128–29, 130
Aristotle, 27, 29, 71, 122, 123; on persuasion, 100; on power of rhetoric, 38
Arrow, Kenneth, 73
Art, and science, 55–56
Assertions, 150–53
Audience, xvii; cliometrician's, 122–23; Fogel's, 116, 117, 122–23, 124, 126, 127, 131–32, 134–35; implied, 133, 134–35; persuaded, 124; rhetoric and, 133–37; speaker and, 124
Augustine, 121
Austin, J. L. 13, 57, 151
Author, implied, 133, 134
Authority, 12–13, 49, 60, 71, 72, 85

Bacon, Francis, 97
Bakan, David, 168, 170
Baldwin, Beverly, 7
Barfield, Owen, 78
Barthes, Roland, 137

Battaglio, Raymond C., 58
Bayes, Rev. Thomas, 30; theorem of, 140
Bazerman, Charles, 57
Becker, Gary, 8, 76, 77–79
Bentham, Jeremy, 48
Bernanke, Ben S., 169
Black, Max, 76, 77; on metaphors, 82, 83
Blaug, Mark, 21, 36
Bloch, Marc, 131, 147*n*2
Boland, Lawrence, 13, 26
Booth, Wayne, 6, 59, 67, 86, 133; defines rhetoric, 29; on falsifiability, 56; on legal reasoning, 72; on modernism, 5, 99
Borel, Armand, 152
Boring, Edwin G., 165
Braudel, Fernand, 143
Bronowski, Jacob, 75, 100
Burke, Kenneth, 30, 55, 57, 58, 65, 66, 67, 69, 85, 86, 99, 105, 121, 133; on tropes, 84

Caldwell, Bruce, 26
Cameron, Rondo, 114
Campbell, John, 97
Capital, human, 77–78
Carnap, Rudolf, 30, 34
Cato the Elder, definition of orator, 37
Catullus, 109
Chicago school of economics, 8–9
Chronicle of Higher Education, 102
Cicero, 27, 29, 37, 50, 105
Cliometrics, 114–15, 120, 122–23, 135
Coase, Ronald, 19
Cobweb theorem, 94–95, 107
Cogan, John, 169
Cohen, Kalman, 9
Commager, Steele, 110
Commoratio, 127, 128
Comte, Auguste, 12
Conversation, xvii, xviii–xix, 3, 5, 27–28, 137, 177; as metaphor of scholarship, 136; norms of, 24–25; and

Conversation *(continued)*
quantification, 150–53; rhetoric
examines, 28, 29; space for, 179–80;
standards of, 29
Cooley, T. F., 140
Copi, Irving, 49
Crain, Robert, 141
Craver, Earlene, 39
Criticism: economic, 69, 174–75, 182–83;
literary, 55, 56, 65, 66, 182
Crosman, Richard, 40
Cyert, Richard, 9

Darwin, Charles, 15, 97
David, Paul, 123
Davis, Lance, 114, 151
Davis, Philip J., 33, 34
Demand, law of, 58–62
Demarcation: of economics and other
disciplines, 58–59; by methodology, 8,
26; positivism on, 42; problem, 26, 39,
41; of science and art, 55–56; of science
and non-science, 42–43; testability as
criterion of, 39
Descartes, René, 12, 16, 24n2, 30, 97, 100
Dettmer, Helena R., 109, 110
Dewey, John, 10, 22, 30, 37, 51
Diachrony, 62–63, 64, 149
Diaeresis, 132
Dialects, 148, 149, 150
Diallage, 121, 126
Dialogue, Socratic, 24–25
Diasyrmus, 121, 127
Digestion, 121
Discourse. *See* Conversation
Discovery, 8; context of, 43, 96
Disputation, 120–21
Domar, Evsey, 85
Duhem, Pierre, 12, 13, 97
Durbin-Watson statistic, 172
Durkheim, Émile, 27

Econometrics, 7, 44, 61, 74, 138, 182; prior
beliefs in, 140; rhetoric in, 139–40; as
simulation, 14; tests in, 158
Economics: Austrian, 7, 25, 65, 90, 174;
criticisms of, 6, 174–75, 182–83; as
diachronic, 64, 149; disputes in, 183–84;
economic actor in, 88–91; figures of
speech in, xvii, 69–86; history of, 64,

113, 120, 123, 183; hypotheses in,
138–39; institutionalist, 7; jokes in,
30–32; Keynesian, 17–18, 172; legal
reasoning in, 72–73; linguistics as
model for, 62–64; as literary, 57–62, 69;
and literature, 65–66; Marxist, 7, 25,
174; mathematics in, 3–4 (*see also*
Quantification); methodology in, 8, 9,
11, 21 (*see also* Modernism; Positivism);
as modernist, 5–11, 35; monetarist, 18;
neoclassical, 7, 25, 63, 172, 174; new
welfare, 43–44; objectivity of, 36; and
other disciplines, 58–59, 76, 179–81;
persuasion in, 44; philosophical, 8, 73;
positivist, 12–13, 39; prediction in,
15–16, 90; rhetoric in, 30, 36–53, 72–74;
rules of, 12; as science, 5, 55, 56–68,
123; significance in, 156, 158–59; as
synchronic, 63, 64, 149; rhetoric in
teaching of, 178–79; as theory of value,
63; writing style in, 175, 176–78
Edgerton, H. A. 165
Edgeworth, Francis Y., 71
Einstein, Albert, 17, 20
Ellipsis, 127
Elton, G. R. 125
Empiricism, 22
Engerman, Stanley, 120
Entry principle, 80–90, 100
Equilibrium, 78, 96
Epistemology, 13, 21–22, 23, 26, 47, 62,
99, 110
Euler, Leonhard, 107–8, 109
Evolution, theory of, 15
Ex adversio, 135
Expectations, rational, 89–90, 91, 92, 93,
94, 100–101, 103, 108–9, 113

Fallacies, 48, 49, 50
Falsifiability/falsification, 13–15, 43, 56
Fama, Eugene F., 169
Farley, John, 17
Feferman, Solomon, 33
Feyerabend, Paul, 6, 17, 23, 29, 34, 36, 37
Finley, M. I., 145
Fischer, David H., 48, 49
Fish, Stanley, 151–52
Fisher, R. A., 164, 165
Fishlow, Albert, 114, 116, 117, 119, 123,
135

Flory, Marleen B., 31
Fogel, Robert W.: analogies of, 125;
    arguments of, 119, 126, 132; audience
    of, 116, 117, 122–23, 124, 126, 127,
    131–32, 134–35; on canals, 115, 116,
    123, 131, 132; as cliometrician, 114–15;
    compared to Fishlow, 114, 116, 117,
    119; conversation of, 137; ethical
    appeal of, 121–22, 124, 126, 130; figures
    of speech used by, 126–30; on
    historical method, 125; implied reader
    of, 134–35; on markets, 135; railroad
    study of, 113–37; reasoning of, 129;
    rhetoric of, 116–26; simulation by,
    123–24, 128; speaks to economists,
    130–33; thesis of, 114; topics of, 128–29,
    130–33
Forensics, 121
Foucault, J. B. L., 51
Frankfurt School, 24, 28, 103
Fraser, A. C., 51
Freedman, David, 167
Frenkel, Jacob, 157
Freud, Sigmund, 51
Friedman, Benjamin, 100
Friedman, Milton, 8, 11, 12, 15, 18, 67n5,
    70, 140, 184; on modernism, 9–10; and
    positivism, 10; style of, 175
Frye, Northrop, 67, 98, 182
Functionalism, 6
Gable, Dan, 119
Galbraith, J. K., 75, 184
Galileo Galilei, 17
Gallman, Robert, 114
Gardner, John, 75, 136
Geertz, Clifford, 40, 51
Geison, Gerald, 17
Genberg-Zecher criterion, 145, 156, 159
Gibson, Walker, 133, 134
Goodman, Nelson, 6, 44n4, 46, 48, 57, 100
Gordon, Robert, 100
Gould, Stephen Jay, 17, 106–7
Graff, Gerald, 40n1
Graybill, F. A., 158, 166
Griliches, Zvi, 175

Habermas, Jürgen, 24, 28, 51, 122
Halmos, Paul R., 121n6
Harberger, A. C., 74, 116, 178
Harsanyi, John C., 68

Hausman, Daniel, 80
Hawke, Guy, 116n2
Hayek, F. A., 65
Hegel, G. W. F., 50
Heidegger, Martin, 51
Heinzelmann, Kurt, 66n4
Hempel, C. G., 12
Henderson, Willie, 75
Henkel, Ramon E., 166, 167, 168
Hersh, Reuben, 33, 34
Hexter, J. H., 113
Hicks, J. R. 3, 70, 71
Hilbert, David, 32, 34, 134
Hirsch, Abraham, 10
Hirsch, E. D., 40
Hirschman, Albert, 66, 75
History: appeal to, 123, 127; comparative,
    147n2; economic, 64, 113, 120, 123, 183;
    method in, 125
Hogben, Lancelot, 165
Hooke, Robert, 143
Horace, 109, 110
Horsburgh, H. J. N., 76
Housman, A. E., 111
Houthakker, Hendrick, 58, 155
Huffman, Wallace E., 169
Hughes, J. R. T., 114
Hume, David, 8, 12, 16, 30
Hutchison, Terence, 8, 12, 35, 39, 48
Hypotheses: discovered, 8, 43, 96;
    economic, 138–39; justified, 8, 43, 96;
    null, 157, 168, 170; suggested, 10;
    tested, 10, 13–15, 43–44, 154, 155
Hypothetico-deductive model, 97, 102,
    182
Indignatio, 121
Inductionism, 97
Introspection, 7, 8, 41, 44–45, 53, 59, 61,
    83, 181
Irony, 84, 85–86
Irrationality/irrationalism, 6, 36–37. *See
    also* Rationality/rationalism
Isocolon, 127
Isoglosses, 149–50

Jacox, Ada, 7
James, William, 29, 58
Jevons, W. S., 63
Jonung, Lars, 169
Justification, 8, 43, 96

206

Index

Kant, Immanuel, 30
Kelvin's dictum, 7, 16, 54
Kendall, M. G., 165
Kepler, Johann, 42
Keynes, J. M., xviii, 17–18, 71, 172
Klamer, Arjo, 179
Kline, Morris, 32, 33
Knight, Frank, 46, 48, 65, 71
Knowledge, 5; economic, 36; modernism
  on, 16; as social, 99–100; tacit, 64, 178
Koestler, Arthur, 51
Kravis, Irving, 155–56
Krugman, Paul, 157
Kruskal, William, 164, 171
Kuhn, Thomas, 14, 30, 31, 34, 37, 43, 51,
  97, 101, 136; on measurement, 19
Kurtz, A. K., 165
Kuznets, Simon, 114, 133

Lakatos, Imre, 30, 34, 37, 108, 176
Langland, William, 45
Laplace, Pierre de, 165
Latin literature, 106, 109–11
Leamer, Edward, 139, 140, 162, 171
Leijonhufvud, Axel, 39, 183
Lepienes, Wolf, 27
LeRoy, S. F., 140
Leser, C. E. V., 71
Levi, Edward, 72
Lewis, C. S., 80–81
Linguistics: comparative, 147–50, 151;
  diachronic, 62–63, 149; and economic
  science, 62–64; synchronic, 62–63, 149
Lipsey, Robert, 155–56
Locke, John, 30
Logic, 13; pursuit of, 48–49
Loss function, 158, 166
Lucas, Robert, 87, 90, 96

McClelland, Peter, 116
McCloskey, D. N., 159
McCrea, W. H., 101
McDowell, John M., 169
Mach, Ernst, 12
Machlup, Fritz, 12, 61, 132
Macrobius, 111
Macroeconomics, 90–91
Malthus, Thomas, 15
Manier, Edward, 97
Marchi, Neil de, 10

Markets, compared, 148, 149, 150;
  integrated, 143–47, 154, 159
Marshall, Alfred, 32
Marx, Karl, 27, 121; economic theory of,
  7, 25, 174
Masica, Colin, 150
Mathematics, 64, 70, 105, 107–8; in
  economics, 3–4 (*see also*
  Quantification); and metaphor, 79–83;
  proof in, 32–34; rhetoric of, 33, 34;
  symmetry in, 109, 110
Meaning, 80–81
Mechling, Elizabeth and Jay, 104
Medawar, Peter, 176
Mendel, Gregor, 17
Menger, Karl, 63, 166
Merton, Robert, 51
Metaphor, 72, 74–75, 79–83, 84, 86;
  Becker uses, 76, 77–79; Black on, 82, 83;
  conversation as, 136; in mathematics,
  79–83; and politics, 82; productin
  function as, 79, 80; Richards on, 20, 77
Metaphysics, 12
Method, 24, 25, 26; historical, 125
Methodism, 22, 111
Methodology, 8, 9, 11, 24–27, 178–79;
  anti-, 51; competing, 27; for
  demarcation, 8, 26; function of, 21;
  persuasiveness of, 23–24, 26, 27, 35;
  plural, 26; political arguments for,
  39–41; as prescience, 53; as reasonable,
  52; rule-bound, 20–24; in social
  sciences, 23–24. *See also* Modernism;
  Positivism
Metonymy, 84–85
Mill, James, 98
Millis, Harris, A., 3
Modernism, 3–19, 35, 50, 52, 60–61, 87,
  128, 174, 175, 182; alternative to, 41;
  Booth on, 5, 99; in classroom, 178–79;
  commandments of, 7–8, 22–23; and
  context of discovery, 43; and evidence,
  17–18; fact-value split in, 140, 184;
  flaws in, 11–19, 20; on interpenetration,
  56; intolerance of, 23; on knowledge,
  16; on meaning, 80; as methodology,
  11, 16; Muth's, 96, 99, 103; persuasion
  in, 12, 17, 97; post-, 9; quantification
  and, 19; reaction to, 6–7; as rule-bound,
  20–24; and science, 111; and style, 97.

See also Antimodernism
Moebius, 33
Moffitt, Robert, 170
Monetarism, 18, 71
Mood, A. F., 158, 166
Morgenstern, Oskar, 129
Morris, Charles, 100
Morrison, Denton E., 166, 167, 168
Muth, John, 87–112, 122; analogy used
   by, 108; argument of, 90–91, 96;
   cobweb theorem of, 94–95, 107;
   credence of, 96–97, 100; influence of,
   87, 91, 92; as modernist, 96, 99, 103; as
   persuasive, 98, 100, 101, 104; as
   positivist, 100, 103; on rational
   expectations, 89–90, 91, 92, 93, 94,
   100–101, 103, 108–9, 113; rhetoric of,
   104, 105–12, 128; simulation by, 101,
   102; style of, 87, 88, 97–98; symmetry
   of, 103; on testing, 103–4

Nelson, John, 163
Newman, John Henry Cardinal, 22,
   33–34, 50
Newton, Isaac, 42
Neyman, Jerzy, 165, 166
Nihilism, 40, 41
North, Douglass, 114
Novick, Peter, 41
Nunnally, J., 170

Oakeshott, Michael, 27
Objectivity, 7, 22–23, 36, 41, 152, 180, 181
Observation, 7, 181
Occam's razor, 128, 135
Olbrechts-Tyteca, L., 82–83, 122, 124
Olson, Mancur, 56
Operationalism, 75
Ortony, Andrew, 75
Ostwald, Wilhelm, 12

Paine, Tom, 99
Paleontology, 105, 106
Palmer, L. R., 148–49, 150
Paramologia, 126–27, 129
Parker, William, 114
Passmore, John, 73
Pasteur, Louis, 17
Pearson, E. S., 165, 166
Pearson, Karl, 164

Peek, Joe, 169
Perelman, Chaim, 6, 82–83, 122, 124
Perlman, Mark, 35
Persuasiveness/persuasion, 70, 121;
   arguments for, 38–39, 44–45, 47, 57–58;
   of audience, 124; of law of demand,
   58–62; of methodology, 23–24, 26, 27,
   35; of modernism, 12, 17, 97; of Muth,
   98, 100, 101, 104; v. pursuit of truth,
   46–47, 48; and quantification, 141,
   142–43; of rhetoric, 37–38, 120;
   standards of, 27–28; and statistics, 38;
   and style, 135–36; of thought
   experiments, 59
Peter, L. J., xix
Philosophy: analytic, 51–52; and
   economics, 8, 73; German speculative,
   39; v. rhetoric, 37
Physics, 34–35
Piaget, J., 51
Pisani, Robert, 167
Plato, 27, 37, 47
Pleonasm, 127
Polanyi, Karl, 145, 146
Polanyi, Michael, 6, 14, 28, 37, 51, 97; on
   economic knowledge, 36; on
   modernism, 16; on tacit knowledge, 64,
   178; on teaching, 178
Polya, George, 107
Popper, Karl, 10, 12, 21, 23, 30, 34, 101;
   on falsifiability, 56; on logical
   positivism, 12n6
Positivism, 5, 7, 10, 12–13, 75, 96, 97, 166,
   181–82; and demarcation, 42;
   Hutchison's, 48; logical, 12, 39, 41;
   Muth's, 100, 103
Pragmatism, 10, 21, 22, 29, 50
Prediction, 7, 9, 15–16, 88, 89–90
Preferences, 66, 67
Prescience, 53
Probability, 140
Procatalepsis, 132
Production function, 79, 80, 83–86
Proof, three-line, 116, 117, 132, 135
Psychology, 175
Purchasing power parity, 154, 155,
   156–57, 158, 159
Purves, Roger, 167

Quantification: and conversation, 150–53;

Index

Quantification *(continued)*
and modernism, 19; as persuasive, 141,
142–43; and rhetoric, 138–53, 164;
standards for, 143–47
Questionnaires, 7, 9–10, 83, 181
Quine, Willard, 6, 12, 47
Quintilian, Marcus, 29, 37

Railroads, 114, 115, 116, 132, 133
Ramus, Peter, 30
Rationality/rationalism, 6, 36–37, 39, 48,
89. *See also* modernism
Reason *(logos)*, 122
Reasoning, 21, 22, 23, 129; legal, 72–73
Reductio ad absurdum, 47, 127
Regression analysis, 4, 44, 45, 163, 169,
170
Relativism, 37, 41, 141
Rhetoric: of analytic philosophy, 51–52;
as antimethodology, 51; and audience,
133–37; defined, xviii, 29; and
econometrics, 139–40; of economic
history, 113; of economics, 30, 36–53,
72–74; examines conversation, 28, 29;
good of, 175–85; of mathematics, 33,
34; misused, 38; Muth's, 104, 105–12,
128; new, 30, 32; objections to, 46–50;
persuades, 37–38, 120; v. philosophy,
47; of physics, 34–35; power of, 38; and
quantification, 138–53, 159, 164 *(see also*
Statistics); and sciences, 28–30, 32–35;
as self-conscious, 118–20; and teaching,
178–79; topics in, 128–29
Ricardo, David, 15, 71
Richards, I. A., 30, 67, 68; on metaphor,
20, 77; on pleasure theory, 66–67
Richardson, J. D., 156–57
Robinson, Joan, 24, 85
Robinson, William, 136
Roll, Richard, 10, 11
Root-Bernstein, Robert, 17n8
Rorty, Amelie O., 28, 97, 135–36
Rorty, Richard, 6, 11, 23, 26, 30, 37, 40,
51, 75
Rosen, Stanley, 26, 51–52
Rosenberg, Alexander, 13
Rosenblatt, Louise, 133
Rosenzweig, Mark R., 169
Ross, Stephen, 10, 11
Rostow, W. W., 114, 115

Russell, Bertrand, 12, 30

St. Paul, 121
Sampling, 159–60; error, 167, 171
Samuelson, Paul, 10, 12, 62, 67, 69–70; on
mathematics, 70; on money, 71;
persuasiveness of, 70; uses literary
devices, 70, 72
Sargent, Thomas, 87, 96
Sarkar, Husain, 27
Saussure, Ferdinand de, 62, 63, 64, 92,
150
Schelling, Thomas, 56
Schultz, T. Paul, 169
Schultz, Theodore, 77, 85
Schuster, J. A., 24n2
Schwartz, Anna J., 18
Science, 176; appeal to, 122–23, 127; and
art, 55–56; as disciplined inquiry,
54–55; economics as, 5, 55, 56–68, 123;
as humanism, 57; literary criticism as,
55, 56; meaning of, 54–55; and
modernism, 111; and rhetoric, 28–30,
32–35
Scientism, 8, 50, 121, 182
Scott, Elizabeth, 165
Scott, Robert, 113, 124
Searle, John, 57
Sen, Amartya, 68
Sharpe, William, 11
Significance, 151; economic, 156, 157,
158–59, 163, 164; statistical test of, 139,
141–42, 154, 156, 157, 159–64, 165–66,
167, 171–72; substantive, 171–72
Sign test, 170–71
Simile, 78
Sims, Christopher, 139
Simulation, 4, 74, 92, 106; as affirmation,
14; in econometrics, 14; Fogel's, 123–24,
128; Muth's, 101, 102; role of, 101
Smith, Adam, 15, 27
Socrates, 27
Solow, Robert, 83–86, 87, 101, 180–81; on
production function, 83–86; uses irony,
85; uses metaphor, 84; uses metonymy,
84–85; uses synecdoche, 85
Sophists, 37, 50
Speaker, 121–22, 124
Speech: act, 57, 150–53; speaker and,
121–22. *See also* Conversation

Spooner, Frank, 143
Sprachethik, 24, 25, 26, 27, 28
Standards, 148, 150; for arguments,
    155–59; for conversation, 29; of
    economic significance, 158–59; of
    persuasion, 27–28; of quantification,
    143–47; as social, 152–53
Stanley, Steven, 106–7
Statistics, 41, 138; as deceitful, 38; errors
    in, 159–60, 161, 162, 163, 166; persuade,
    38; significance in, 139, 141–42, 154,
    156, 157, 159–64, 165–66, 167, 171–72;
    specification error in, 162. *See also*
    Quantification
Stebbing, L. Susan, 49
Steiner, Mark, 107, 108
Stigler, George, 8, 31–32, 86
Stone, Lawrence, 48
Stuart, A., 165
Style, 87, 88, 97–98, 135–36
Supple, Barry, 114
Survey research, 181. *See also*
    Observation; Questionnaires
Syme, Ronald, 110
Symmetry, 60, 73, 85, 103, 109, 110, 130
Synchrony, 62–63, 64, 149
Synecdoche, 84, 85

Tautologia, 127, 128
Taylor, Lance, 58
Testability, 96–97, 103–4; and
    demarcation, 39; of hypotheses, 10,
    13–15, 43–44, 154, 155
Thaumasmus, 128
Theil, Hans, 58
Thomas, Brinley, 114
Thought experiments, 59

Tobin, James, 100
Topics, 126; common, 128–29, 130;
    special, 128, 130–33
Toulmin, Stephen, 6, 11, 27, 36, 46, 51
Tropes, 84. *See also* Irony; Metaphor;
    Metonymy; Synecdoche
Truth, 27, 28; as criterion, 96; pursuit of,
    46–47, 48; solipsistic theory of, 99
Tufte, Edward, 38
Turnovsky, Stephen, 90

Urn model, 167, 168

Value theory, 63
Venn, John, 165
Vienna School, 39
von Mises, Ludwig, 15, 65
Wald, Abraham, 30, 158, 166
Walras, Leon, 62
Ward, Benjamin, 72
Ward, W. G., 55
Warren, Ronald S., 170
Weber, Max, 27
Webster, Glenn, 7
Weinberg, Steven, 23, 55
Wenzel, Joseph, 122
Whately, Richard, 81
White, Hayden, 85–86, 135
Williams, Gordon, 69
Williamson, Jeffrey, 74, 133
Wittgenstein, Ludwig, 30
Wordsworth, William, 114

Zecher, J. Richard, 159. *See also*
    Genberg-Zecher criterion
Zellner, Arnold, 87